Miftāḥ al-Falāḥ wa Miṣbāḥ al-Arwāḥ

IBN ʿAṬĀʾ ALLĀH AL-ISKANDARĪ

Miftāḥ al-Falāḥ wa Miṣbāḥ al-Arwāḥ

(The Key to Salvation & the Lamp of Souls)

TRANSLATED FROM THE ARABIC

WITH AN INTRODUCTION AND NOTES BY

Mary Ann Koury Danner

THE ISLAMIC TEXTS SOCIETY

GOLDEN PALM SERIES

This edition published 1996 by The Islamic Texts Society
22a Brooklands Ave, Cambridge, CB2 2DQ, UK.

ISBN 0 946621 27 6 *paper*
ISBN 0 946621 26 8 *cloth*

British Library Cataloguing in Publication Data
A catalogue record of this book is available from
The British Library

Typeset by Goodfellow & Egan, Cambridge
Printed at St Edmundsbury Press

IN MEMORIAM

In memory of my parents Philip A. and Martha H. Koury, who always stressed the importance of education, and the late Shaykh Muzaffer Ozak of the Jerrahi Order, who brought to life the meaning of the spiritual path.

It has been several years since I finished and dedicated this work. Now I have the sad task of adding yet another name. I would especially like to dedicate this book to the memory of my beloved husband Victor Danner who passed away on October 28, 1990. His outstanding scholarship and integrity, fairness and wit endeared him to his students as well as friends and colleagues. It is a great loss to his academic field and to all who knew him.

Mary Ann K. Danner
Bloomington, Indiana

CONTENTS

CONCLUSION OF THE BOOK

It Includes What Has Been Mentioned
in the Way of Remembrance in All Situations and Times
During the Day and the Night 175

ACKNOWLEDGEMENTS

This translation could not have been possible without the help and support of various individuals whom I would like to thank publicly.

To the late Professor Victor Danner of the Department of Near Eastern Languages and Cultures and the Department of Religious Studies at Indiana University, I owe more than words could adequately express for having introduced the field of Islam and Sufism to me, for his guidance and assistance, and particularly for his patience and sense of humour in seeing me through much of the translating of the *Miftāḥ al-Falāḥ*.

I would also like to offer my sincere appreciation to Dr. Wadie Jwaideh, Professor Emeritus of the Department of Near Eastern Languages and Cultures at Indiana University, for his guidance and supervision. His tremendous scholarship in Arabic literature and Islamic history, among a host of other fields, provided many invaluable suggestions, comments, and clarification on obscure points and references.

Likewise, a word of thanks is due to The Islamic Texts Society for having shown considerable patience throughout the inevitable delays that a work of translation produces, and to Ms. Carol Dobson who so patiently typed the entire text in spite of numerous corrections and changes and, no doubt, illegible writing at times.

Needless to say, responsibility for whatever mistakes or errors may occur in the work rests with me.

SYSTEM OF TRANSLITERATION

The transliteration system used throughout the book to represent Arabic sounds is as follows:

(' = *hamzah*), b, t, th, j, ḥ, kh, d, dh, r, z, s, sh, ṣ, ḍ, ṭ, ẓ, ᶜ, gh, f, q, k, l, m, n, h, w, y

The short vowels are a, i, u; the long vowels are ā, ī, ū.

In the construct state, the *tā' marbūṭah* is changed from *-ah* to *-at*.

Diphthongs are written *ay* and *aw*, as in *bayt* and *yawm*.

The definite article *al-* and *'l* is assimilated to the anteropalatals, which results in *ash-shams* rather than *al-shams*.

Long vowels before *hamzat al-waṣl* are written as short: e.g., Abu 'l-Ḥasan rather than Abū 'l-Ḥasan.

QUR'ĀNIC CITATIONS

In translating Qur'ānic verses the English translation of Mohammed Marmaduke Pickthall's *The Meaning of the Glorious Koran* has been our guide except where the context in Ibn ᶜAṭā' Allah's work calls for a different nuance or wording of a Qur'ānic text.

TRANSLATOR'S INTRODUCTION

IT is unfortunate but understandable that Islam has remained something of a mystery to most westerners, since it is viewed as a religion completely beyond the pale of the Judeo-Christian ethos. However, what is astonishing and somewhat ironic is that Sufism is likewise a mystery to many Muslims who see it as some kind of innovation or even deviation bordering on heresy. Comments to the effect that Sufis do not believe in the necessity of saying the five daily prayers or following the *Sharīʿah* attest to the misinformed view of the average believer.

This is due in part to the perceived dichotomy between esoteric and exoteric Islam, the interior life of prayer versus the exterior ritual prayers, the content versus the form. Even Shaykh Ibn ʿAṭā' Allāh, the author of the *Miftāḥ al-Falāḥ wa Miṣbāḥ al-Arwāḥ*, was not totally immune from a certain measure of prejudice in this respect, as will be seen. His ultimate change of heart led him, when discussing *taṣawwuf*, to take great pains to indicate the firm foundation for the esoteric dimension within the traditional framework of Islam, to show its complementarity with exoteric Islam, and its unique ability to provide a deeper and richer spiritual life for believers.

The magnitude of Ibn ʿAṭā' Allāh's contribution to elucidating the principles and practices of Sufism, especially those of the Shādhilī order is incalculable, as is the number of lives he touched and transformed by his own life and through his writings down to the present. Not only was he a realized spiritual master but also an expert in Mālikī *fiqh*. In fact, he was learned in the *Sharīʿah* well before the *ṭarīqah*. His books reveal a keen intellect, at once logical, analytical, perceptive, intuitive, and compassionate. He is a credit to both dimensions of Islam, the formal and the mystical. No doubt, were more Muslims aware of his works and ideas, they would see Sufism for what it really is—the spiritual and contemplative dimension of Islam that observes not just the Law but the spirit of the Law.

Biographical Sketch

Tāj ad-Dīn Abu'l-Faḍl Aḥmad b. Muḥammad b. ʿAbd al-Karīm b. ʿAṭā' Allāh al-Iskandarī al-Judhāmī ash-Shādhilī,[1] known simply as Ibn ʿAṭā' Allāh, was born in Alexandria, Egypt, as his *nisbah* indicates, about the middle of the seventh/thirteenth century. His family were renowned Mālikī scholars from the Banū Judhām tribe, originally from Arabia. His grandfather, ʿAbd al-Karīm (d. 612 AH/1216 AD) had distinguished himself as an expert in *fiqh*, *uṣūl* (principles of jurisprudence), and Arabic, having studied under the famous Abu'l-Ḥasan al-Abyārī. He had written several books, among which were *al-Bayān wa't-Taqrīb fī Sharḥ at-Tahdhīb*, *Mukhtaṣar at-Tahdhīb*, and *Mukhtaṣar al-Mufaṣṣal*, and had been very hostile to Sufism.[2]

On the other hand, Ibn ʿAṭā' Allāh's father Muḥammad (death date unknown) seems to have been of a different mind and although a *faqīh*, he was also the disciple of the great Sufi shaykh Abu'l-Ḥasan ash-Shādhilī (593–656 AH/1197–1258 AD), the founder of the Shādhilī order.[3]

As a youth, Ibn ʿAṭā' Allāh received a traditonal Islamic education in such disciplines as Qur'ānic recitation, *ḥadīth*, *tafsīr* (Qurʿānic commentary), grammar, *uṣūl*, philosophy, belles-lettres, and of course *fiqh*[4] under some of the best and most illustrious teachers of Alexandria, in addition no doubt, to the instruction given him by his own family. While not all of his teachers are known, the most important ones include the following: for the study of *ḥadīth*, Abu'l-Maᶜālī Aḥmad al-Abarqūhī (615–701 AH/ 1219–1301 AD),[5] a Shāfiᶜī traditionist and a disciple of the Suhrawardī order[6] originally from Persia, and Sharaf ad-Dīn ad-Dimyāṭī (613–705 AH/1217–1305 AD),[7] one of the outstanding Shāfiᶜī *muḥaddiths* and *ḥuffāẓ* of his day and a disciple of Shaykh Abu 'l-Ḥasan ash-Shādhilī; for the study of Arabic grammar, *fiqh*, and *adab* (Arabic literature), Muḥyi'd-Dīn al-Mārūnī (d. 693 AH/1294 AD),[8] considered to be the grammarian *par excellence* of Alexandria; for the study of *tafsīr*, Nāṣir ad-Dīn b. al-Munayyir (620–83 AH/1222–85 AD),[9] a great Mālikī *faqīh* who established his reputation in *tafsīr*, *fiqh*, *uṣūl*, philosophical speculation, Arabic, rhetoric, and genealogy and was also a disciple of Shaykh Abu'l-Ḥasan ash-Shādhilī; for Qur'ānic recitation, *fiqh*, and related subjects, Makīn ad-Dīn al-Asmar (c. 612–92 AH/ 1215–93 AD), 'the shaykh of the Qur'ān reciters in Alexandria',[10] who was likewise the disciple of both Shaykh Abu'l-Ḥasan ash-Shādhilī and his successor Shaykh Abu'l–ᶜAbbās al-Mursī (616–86 AH/1220–88 AD); and for the study of *kalām* (Islamic theology), *uṣūl al-fiqh* (principles of jurisprudence) Ashᶜarism, logic, disputation and rhetoric, Shams ad-Dīn al-Iṣfahānī (616–88 AH/1220–90 AD),[11] a brilliant Shāfiᶜī jurist who taught at the Mashhad of al-Ḥusayn and then at the Mashhad of Imām ash-Shāfiᶜī in Cairo. He only accepted students who were already well versed in the *Sharīᶜah*.

There were probably many other teachers who shaped Ibn ᶜAṭā' Allāh's intellectual formation,[12] but the above list is sufficiently indicative of the fact that he received the best possible education of his day. That, together with his love of learning,[13] resulted in his achieving quite a reputation for Mālikī scholarship by the time he was a young man in his twenties.

Ironically, in spite of his father's attachment to the Shādhilī master Abu'l-Ḥasan, Ibn ᶜAṭā' Allāh was initially rather hostile to Sufism much like his grandfather, as he himself admits in his book

Laṭā'if al-Minan,[14] but not for any definite reason. In fact, what precipitated his meeting with Shaykh Abu'l-ᶜAbbās al-Mursī, the successor of Shaykh Abu'l-Ḥasan[15] was an argument with one of al-Mursī's disciples. Consequently, Ibn ᶜAṭā' Allāh decided to see for himself who this man was because after all, 'a man of Truth has certain signs that cannot be hidden'.[16] He found him holding forth on such lofty spiritual matters that he was dazzled. Ibn ᶜAṭā' Allāh states that at that moment God removed whatever objections he had previously had. Something had obviously touched his heart and mind, so he went home to be alone and reflect.

That was apparently the turning point for him, for shortly thereafter Ibn ᶜAṭā' Allāh returned to visit Shaykh Abu'l-ᶜAbbās al-Mursī who received him so warmly that he was embarrassed and humbled. Ibn ᶜAṭā' Allāh states, 'The first thing that I said to him was "O Master, by God, I love you". Then he answered, "May God love you as you love me".'[17] Then Ibn ᶜAṭā' Allāh told him of various worries and sadnesses he had, so the shaykh told him:

> There are four states of the servant, not five: blessings, trials, obedience, and disobedience. If you are blessed, then what God requires of you is thankfulness. If you are tried, then what God requires of you is patience. If you are obedient, then what God requires of you is the witnessing of His blessings upon you. If you are disobedient, then what God requires of you is asking forgiveness.[18]

After leaving Shaykh al-Mursī, he mentions that he felt that his worries and his sadness were like a garment that had been removed. From that time in 674 AH/1276 AD when Ibn ᶜAṭā' Allāh was initiated into the Shādhilī order until the death of Shaykh al-Mursī twelve years later, he became his devoted disciple and says that in all those years he never heard his shaykh say anything that contradicted the *Sharīᶜah*.[19]

Although the *barakah* of Shaykh Abu'l-ᶜAbbās' presence was

such that Ibn ʿAṭā' Allāh's attitude was virtually transformed overnight, nevertheless, he had certain misgivings. When he heard some students say that those who keep company with Sufi shaykhs do not do well in their studies,[20] it grieved him to think of foregoing his schooling or foregoing his shaykh's company. Later he went to see Shaykh al-Mursī, without saying a word to him about it, yet the shaykh told him,

> If a merchant associates with us, we do not say to him, 'Leave your trade and come'; or to an artisan, we do not say to him, 'Leave your craft and come'; or to a student, we do not say to him, 'Leave your studies and come'. Rather, we take everyone as he is, where God has placed him, and what is decreed for him through our hands will be given to him.[21]

At another point in time, Ibn ʿAṭā' Allāh entertained thoughts of quitting his position in order to devote himself fully to the Path. He was already a Mālikī *faqīh* of note by the time he met Shaykh al-Mursī. Again without saying a word to his spiritual master, the shaykh told him that once when one of his disciples asked him if he should quit his job, he told him that it was not necessary, that he should stay wherein God had placed him since 'what is decreed to you by our hands will be conferred upon you'.[22] Consequently, any previous thoughts of leaving his position left Ibn ʿAṭā' Allāh, and he was satisfied with his lot.

Shaykh Abu'l-ʿAbbās even predicted that Ibn ʿAṭā' Allāh would become an authority in both the *Sharīʿah* and the *ṭarīqah*. According to an account told to Ibn ʿAṭā' Allāh by Jamāl ad-Dīn, the son of his spiritual master, he said to his father, 'They want to establish Ibn ʿAṭā' Allāh in *fiqh*'. So the Shaykh told his son, 'They will establish him in *fiqh*, and I will establish him in *taṣawwuf*'.[23] Afterwards when Ibn ʿAṭā' Allāh visited Shaykh al-Mursī, the latter told him, 'When the *faqīh* Nāṣir ad-Dīn[24] regains his health, he will seat you in the place of your grandfather. He will sit on one side and I on the other. You will speak, if God wills, concerning both areas of knowledge.' Then Ibn ʿAṭā' Allāh simply adds, 'So it was as he had said'.[25]

Again, on another occasion, the shaykh said to him, 'Persevere, for by God, if you persevere, verily you will be a *muftī* in both domains'. As Ibn ʿAṭā' Allāh explains, 'He meant the domain of the *Sharīʿah*, of exoteric knowledge, and the domain of the Truth, of esoteric knowledge'.[26]

One might justifiably wonder what sort of man Shaykh Abu'l-ʿAbbās al-Mursī could be who could change a man's long-held view virtually overnight. Yet if one delves into his background, one realizes that he, like his predecessor Shaykh Abu'l-Ḥasan ash-Shādhilī, was no ordinary man.[27] Rather, he was a spiritually enlightened master who obviously had a clear, intuitive perception of things – as witness his foretelling of the future of Ibn ʿAṭā' Allāh as a great teacher in both the Law and the Path or his foretelling of the death of one of his disciples in a year's time.[28] Moreover, Shaykh Abu'l-Ḥasan, the great founder of the Shādhilī order, acknowledged his disciples's immense spirituality.[29] The sheer presence of Shaykh al-Mursī and his inspired words evidently went straight to the heart of Ibn ʿAṭā' Allāh, striking a chord within that recognized the truth of what he heard instinctively.

Shaykh Abu'l-ʿAbbās whose full name is Shihāb ad-Dīn Abu'l-ʿAbbās Aḥmad b. ʿUmar al-Anṣārī al-Mursī al-Mālikī[30] was the foremost disciple of Shaykh Abu'l-Ḥasan ash-Shādhilī,[31] the *quṭb*[32] of his day and one of the greatest Sufi masters in the history of Islam. After Shaykh Abu'l-Ḥasan's death in 656 AH/1258 AD, Shaykh Abu'l-ʿAbbās, who was already a teacher of the path in his shaykh's lifetime,[33] became his direct successor and head of the order.

Due to his own lofty spiritual station, Shaykh al-Mursī likewise became the *quṭb* of his day and was so recognized by many disciples and followers.[34] In fact, one of the Shādhilī disciples had a dream in which he saw a group of people standing looking toward the sky. Then he saw Shaykh Abu'l-Ḥasan dressed in white descending. At this point Shaykh Abu'l-ʿAbbās firmly planted his feet on the ground, and Shaykh Abu'l-Ḥasan entered into him from his head and disappeared. This was generally interpreted to mean that Shaykh Abu'l-ʿAbbās' teaching and methods were an unbroken continuation of his master's, without any divergence.[35] Of course, each was different in personality but their teachings on the path were identical.

As Shaykh Abu'l-ʿAbbās used to speak of his master with respect and deference, so too did Ibn ʿAṭā' Allāh. Referring to his teacher, he states,

> You would only hear him speak about the Great Intellect, the Greatest Name[of God], Its four aspects, the Names,[36] letters, the circles of saints, the spiritual stations of the pious, the angels near to the Throne, the science of the esoteric mysteries (*ʿulūm al-asrār*), supports of invocation (*amdād al-adhkār*), the Day of Judgment . . . and so on.[37]

Moreover, Ibn ʿAṭā' Allāh affirms that 'the basis of his order, (may God be pleased with him), is concentration on God, non-dispersal (*ʿadam at-tafriqah*), perseverance in spiritual retreat, and invocation',[38] which refers as much to the way of Shaykh Abu'l-Ḥasan ash-Shādhilī.

That Shaykh Ibn ʿAṭā' Allāh must have practiced the above-mentioned methods is obvious. He repeatedly emphasizes their importance in the text of the *Miftāḥ al-Falāḥ*, as will be seen. What spiritual fruits he must have received cannot be known, but his development into a Sufi master capable of guiding and teaching others took place within the lifetime of his shaykh, i.e., well within the twelve-year period before 686 AH/1288 AD.[39] His discipline and progress in the path coupled with his great learning made him renowned as a religious authority.[40]

Ibn ʿAṭā' Allāh's virtue, majestic presence, eloquence, and spiritual insights were such that he had many followers.[41] He even performed miracles, some of which have been recorded, such as speaking from his grave to one Kamāl ad-Dīn b. al-Ḥamām who had gone to the shaykh's tomb to recite *Sūrat Hūd*.[42] As a result, Ibn al-Ḥamām was counseled to be buried there. Another miracle attributed to Shaykh Ibn ʿAṭā' Allāh is his having been seen in Mecca at three different places by one of his disciples who had gone on Pilgrimage. When the latter returned, he asked if the shaykh had left the country in his absence and was told no. Then he went to see him and Ibn ʿAṭā' Allāh asked him, 'Whom did you see on this trip of yours?' 'The disciple anwered, 'O Master, I saw you'. So he smiled and said, 'The realized sage fills the universe. If he summoned the *quṭb*, verily he would answer.'[43]

Still another miracle recorded is the story of three men on their way to attend Shaykh Ibn ʿAṭā' Allāh's public lecture or *majlis*.[44] One said, 'If I were free from the family, I would become an ascetic'; the second one said, 'I pray and fast but I do not see a speck of benefit'; and the third said, 'Indeed, my prayers do not please me so how can they please my Lord?' After arriving, they heard Ibn ʿAṭā' Allāh discourse and in their presence he said, 'There are among people those who say . . .' and he repeated their words exactly.

Ibn ʿAṭā' Allāh taught at both the Azhar Mosque and the Manṣūriyyah Madrasah in Cairo as well as privately to his disciples. However, it is not known where his *zāwiyah* was located. His stature and authority were so great in both the esoteric and exoteric domains that when he had a confrontation in 707 AH/1307 AD with Taqi'd-Dīn b. Taymiyyah (d.728 AH/1328 AD), the Ḥanbalī *faqīh*, hundreds attended. He was in the forefront of those who accused Ibn Taymiyyah of attacks against the Shaykh al-Akbar Muḥyi'd-Dīn b. al-ʿArabī and other Sufi practices, such as the repetition of the Name of God in the ritual of *dhikr*, which Ibn Taymiyyah denounced as *bidʿa*.[45] This was as much an attack against Ibn ʿAṭā' Allāh as other mystics, since he stressed its importance for the initiate's spiritual advancement in several of his works, most particularly *al-Qaṣd al-Mujarrad fī Maʿrifat al-Ism al-Mufrad*. However, Ibn Taymiyyah was not charged.

Shaykh Ibn ʿAṭā' Allāh died within two years of this public trial at around sixty years of age in the middle of Jumāda II 709 AH/November 1309 AD[46]. As befitting an eminent and learned teacher, he died in the Manṣūriyyah Madrasah. His funeral procession was witnessed by hundreds of people and he was buried in the Qarāfah Cemetery in Cairo[47] in what is today called the City of the Dead, at the foot of Jabal al-Muqaṭṭam. His tomb became famous as the site of homage, visitation, prayer, and miraculous occurrences.[48] To this day this is still the case.

This pious and extraordinary contemplative figure left behind a spiritual legacy no less impressive than those of his own beloved shaykh, and the august founder Shaykh Abu'l-Ḥasan ash-Shādhilī. All the biographers refer to Ibn ʿAṭā' Allāh with illustrious titles and reverence[49] and mention how marvellously he spoke and how uplifting his words were.[50] In spite of the fact that he followed the Mālikī *madhhab*, the Shāfiʿīs laid claim to him, most probably because some of his earlier teachers had been Shāfiʿī scholars, not to mention some of his students.[51]

Hence, his disciples could only be all the more devoted in their attachment to and love for him. Of the untold numbers of followers that Shaykh Ibn ʿAṭā' Allāh had, both in Cairo, Alexandria, and elsewhere, only very few names are known. That is, doubtless, due to the fact that the Shādhilīs did not advocate withdrawing from the world or wearing special clothing to distinguish themselves. They were 'in the world but not of the world', so to speak. Ibn Ḥajar al-ʿAsqalānī quotes adh-Dhahabī who recounts, 'I saw Shaykh Tāj ad-Dīn al-Fāriqī when he returned from Egypt, extolling his [Ibn ʿAṭā' Allāh's] sermons and spiritual signs'.[52]

Tāj ad-Dīn as-Subkī comments that, 'He was the teacher of my father [Taqi'd-Dīn as-Subkī] in Sufism', which is corroborated by as-Suyūṭī and Ibn Ḥajar.[53] Taqi'd-Dīn as-Subkī was one of the most famous *ʿulamā'* in his day, eminent in *fiqh*, *tafsīr*, *aḥādīth*, theology, and juridical formulation. Ironically he was praised by no less an *ʿālim* than Ibn Taymiyyah!

Several names are mentioned in the *Laṭā'if al-Minan*, Ibn ʿAṭā Allāh's biography of both his shaykh al-Mursī and Shaykh ash-Shādhilī (which also reveals glimpses of his own life), but it is difficult to ascertain in many instances whether they are companions in the *ṭarīqah*, spiritual mentors, shaykhs in the general sense of learned doctors of the *Sharīʿah*, or his followers. One of the more frequently quoted names is that of Shaykh Makīn ad-Dīn al-Asmar, a pious teacher and disciple of Shaykh Abu'l-ʿAbbās.[54] However, it is known that Ibn ʿAṭā' Allāh counseled many people from all levels of society including the Sultan al-Malik al-Manṣūr Ḥusām ad-Dīn Lājīn (r. 696–98 AH/1296–98 AD).[55]

According to certain sources, one of the disciples of Shaykh Ibn ʿAṭā' Allāh to succeed him was Shaykh Dā'ūd al-Bākhilī (d. 733 AH/1332 AD), [56] the fourth Sufi master in the Shādhilī *silsilah*. He was learned in many disciplines and the author of *al-Laṭīfah al-Marḍiyyah bi-Sharḥ Ḥizb ash-Shādhiliyyah*. Concurrently, Shaykh Shihāb ad-Dīn b. al-Maylaq (d. 739 AH/1349 AD), a man of deep spiritual insights is also mentioned as another successor,[57] whose public sermons touched the heart.

Through them and most assuredly others such as Shaykh Abu'l-Ḥasan ʿAlī al-Qarāfī, the Shādhilī *ṭarīqah* branched out to form different *silāsil*, all going back to its namesake. As Ibn ʿAṭā' Allāh was one of several disciples of Shaykh Abu'l-ʿAbbās who became teachers and spiritual guides in their own right, so too did many of Shaykh Ibn ʿAṭā' Allāh's disciples, thus continuing the spiritual tradition and legacy of their founder down to the present. Where Ibn ʿAṭā' Allāh differs from his two predecessors is in his writings, to which we now turn.

Literary Works

Neither the founder of the Shādhilī order nor his successor, Shaykh al-Mursī, composed any books or treatises on *taṣawwuf*. When each was asked why he did not write on such mysteries,

Shaykh Abu'l-Ḥasan said, 'My books are my companions',[58] while Shaykh Abu'l-ᶜAbbās replied, 'The sciences of this way are the sciences of realization and the minds of people cannot bear them'.[59]

However, the list of books used by both shaykhs is quite impressive and indicative of the high calibre of their religious instruction. Some of the works mentioned include the following:[60]

Iḥyā' ᶜUlūm ad-Dīn by Abū Ḥamīd al-Ghazālī[61] – on beliefs and practices
Khatm al-Awliyā' by Muḥammad al-Ḥakīm at-Tirmidhī[62] – on the lives of saints; for novices
Kitāb al-Mawāqif by an-Niffarī – on gnostic illuminations
Kitāb al-Irshād by Imām al-Ḥaramayn al-Juwaynī – on *uṣūl ad-dīn*
Kitāb Maṣābīḥ as-Sunnah by Abū Muḥammad al-Ḥusayn al-Baghawī – on *aḥādīth*
Kitāb ash-Shifā' by al-Qāḍī ᶜIyāḍ[63] – on the life of the Prophet
Qūt al-Qulūb by Abū Ṭālib al-Makkī[64] – on esoteric and exoteric beliefs

Although neither spiritual master felt the need to write, both composed spiritual litanies called *aḥzāb*. Those of Shaykh Abu'l-Ḥasan 'were considered by him to be of an inspired nature, coming from the Prophet'.[65] Some were given titles like '*Ḥizb al-Baḥr*' and '*Ḥizb an-Nūr*' and are still recited for their special *barakah*, while the *aḥzāb* of Shaykh Abu'l-ᶜAbbās are 'sometimes modifications of those issuing from Abu'l-Ḥasan and sometimes they are of his own inspiration [but] not as numerous as those of his master, nor as famous'.[66] These *aḥzāb* contain various phrases, Divine Names, and verses from the Qur'ān in a particular order intended to bestow blessings on those reciting them. 'Their powerful influence and vast dissemination throughout the Muslim world and at all levels of society, in the course of centuries down to the present may suggest that, in this respect alone the *Laṭā'if* is a work of major importance in the history of Islamic devotion.'[67]

Thanks to Shaykh Ibn ʿAṭā' Allāh these *aḥzab*, as well as personal prayers (*duʿā*, pl. *adʿiyah*), conversations, and many comments of both predecessors have been preserved in *Laṭā'if al-Minan*, a unique book on the pious and extraordinary lives of the first two Shādhilī *quṭbs* and their spiritual views.[68] Although it is one of the last works that Ibn ʿAṭā' Allāh wrote – if not the last one[69] – it is, no doubt, the most valuable for the information it provides on the teachings of the Shādhilī *ṭarīqah*.

> This book is the most precious document that we possess for following and understanding the development of the new order and for seeing the two great persons, the founders of the order and esoteric poles of their time evolve in the middle of a society in full transformation in its political and also religious constitution under both the doctrinal and ceremonial aspect.[70]

Certainly it is the earliest. Written to honour his shaykh and the Shādhilī founder and extol their virtues, esoteric knowledge, and miraculous abilities, and because no one else had undertaken to do so,[71] the *Laṭā'if* reveals a wealth of background on Sufi tradition including important autobiographical details of its author.[72]

The book is basically divided into an introduction, ten chapters, and a conclusion. Within these sections such topics as the meaning of prophecy, the superiority of saints to religious scholars, quotations from the Qur'ān and *Ḥadīth*, the question of miracles, sanctity, *adab*, spiritual stations, and explanations of mystical phrases by gnostics, and other doctrinal matters are discussed. Various people are also mentioned, some the contemporaries of Shaykh Abu'l-ʿAbbās and Ibn ʿAṭā Allāh and others, the contemporaries of Shaykh Abū'l-Ḥasan ash-Shādhilī. In his conclusion, Ibn ʿAṭā' Allāh gives his *silsilah*, affirming that Shaykh Abu'l-ʿAbbās al-Mursī was indeed his only spiritual master and adds a letter of counsel to his disciples in Alexandria dated 694 AH/1294 AD,[73] and a poem, ending as he had begun, in praise of the Prophet of Islam.

In spite of the fact that Shaykh Ibn ʿAṭā' Allāh sets forth what each chapter deals with, it must be said that there is nothing very organised about the book in terms of providing any chronological order–contrary to Taftazānī's views.[74] It is as if the author selected topics to discuss and then interjected anecdotes or comments about his life or the lives of others, *vis-à-vis* Shaykh Abu'l-ʿAbbās to show his shaykh's spiritual discernment and rank. Yet when all is said and done, the *Laṭā'if* remains highly interesting, informative and easy to read.

Not only did it ensure the memory and reputation of his two predecessors but it also provided a written legacy to succeeding generations of followers. As a result, Ibn ʿAṭā' Allāh had the added distinction of becoming the source to whom subsequent biographers of the Shādhilī order turned,[75] a fitting honour for his life's work.

Of all his works that have come down to us,[76] namely, *Laṭā'if al-Minan*, *Kitāb al-Ḥikam*, *at-Tanwīr fī Isqāṭ at-Tadbīr*, *al-Qaṣd al-Mujarrad fī Maʿrifat al-Ism al-Mufrad*, *Miftāḥ al-Falāḥ wa Miṣbāḥ al-Arwāḥ*, *Tāj al-ʿArūs al-Ḥāwī li-Tahdhīb an-Nufūs*, and *ʿUnwān at-Tawfīq*, by far the most popular and the most well known is the *Kitāb al-Ḥikam*. Composed in the lifetime of his master Shaykh Abu'l-ʿAbbās (i.e. before 686 AH/1288 AD) who praised it highly,[77] the *Ḥikam* is no doubt Ibn ʿAṭā' Allāh's earliest work, for references to it are found in his other books such as the *Laṭā'if*, *Kitāb at-Tanwīr*, and *Tāj al-ʿArūs*.[78]

Considered to be the 'fruit of his spiritual realization or as an expression of it in a literary vehicle',[79] the *Ḥikam* is a collection of aphorisms, treatises or epistles (*rasā'il*), and supplications (*munājāt*) having to do with many aspects of the spiritual path such as belief in the oneness and unity of God (*tawḥīd*), gnosis (*maʿrifah*), spiritual states and stations (*aḥwāl* and *maqāmāt*), struggle against one's self (*mujāhadat an-nafs*) one's *adab vis-à-vis* God, and advice to the *murīd*. Written in a beautiful and often rhyming prose, its ellipitical observations belie its depth and intensity of meaning. The work assumes a great deal of knowledge of Sufi terminology and doctrine on the part of the reader.

Although ostensibly the text is one flowing composition nonetheless there is a measure of disjointedness as the author goes from one idea to the next. Western translations have attempted to divide the original according to content,[80] but there is no logical progression between the passages. However, this is hardly seen as a shortcoming. In other words:

> The aphorisms of the *Ḥikam* are strung together like a necklace of precious jewels of different sorts, each jewel reflecting the diverse aspects of the contemplative life of Islam. But it is illuminative knowledge, or gnosis (*maᶜrifah*), that constitutes the inner thread which holds them all in place and gives an underlying unity to the whole.[81]

In fact, the *Ḥikam* is considered a kind of Sufi manual and Ibn ᶜAṭā' Allāh became known thereafter in Sufi circles as '*Ṣāḥib al-Ḥikam*.'

If the number of commentaries on the text is an indication of anything at all, they are a testament to the outstanding success of the *Ḥikam*.[82] The Shādhilī Shaykh Aḥmad Zarrūq (d. 899 AH/1494 AD) wrote about thirty himself, but the most well-known belong to Ibn ᶜAbbād ar-Rundī (733–92 AH/1332–89 AD).[83] The Moroccan Shādhilī Shaykh Ibn ᶜAjībah (1160–1224 AH/1747–1809 AD) in his *sharḥ* of the *Ḥikam* quotes the Shaykh Mawlay al-ᶜArabī, the shaykh of his own master Sīdī Muḥammad al-Buzīdī al-Ḥasanī, who said, 'I heard the *faqīh* al-Bannānī say, "The *Ḥikam* of Ibn ᶜAṭā' Allāh is almost a revelation [*waḥy*]. If it were permitted to recite the *ṣalāt* without the Qur'ān, verily, the words of the *Ḥikam* would be allowed".'[84] That is quite a compliment, especially coming from a *faqīh*, but that is part of the appeal of the *Ḥikam*:

there is nothing therein that contradicts the *Sharīʿah*. If it did, Taqi'd-Dīn as-Subkī would not have regarded it as lawful.[85]

Not only did *fuqarā'* and *fuqahā'* of the past appreciate the *Ḥikam* but also those of recent times. Many great scholars in the early part of this century taught it at the Azhar. The late Shaykh Muḥammad Bakhīt who was the *muftī* of ad-Diyār al-Miṣriyyah used it to instruct people at the mosque of al-Ḥusayn after the *ʿasr* prayer during Ramaḍān.[86] 'The Muslim University of Tunis, Jāmiʿ al-Zaytūnah, maintains deep respect for this book and indicates it as an obligatory text for the advanced teaching of mysticism.'[87]

The fact that the *Ḥikam* is still being published today is evidence of its undiminished popularity. Moreover, recent translations of it into French and English attest to the extraordinary power, style, and appeal of its message and by extension to the authority of its author.[88]

The *Kitāb at-Tanwīr fī Isqāṭ at-Tadbīr* was written, according to Shaykh Ibn ʿAṭā' Allāh, to clarify the way to union with God through abandoning self-direction and struggling with the decrees of fate. In other words, he emphasizes the importance for the believer of relying on God's choices and accepting His Will. To support his arguments, as in all his works, the Shaykh refers to the Qur'ān and *aḥādīth* of the Prophet. Naturally he also stresses the spiritual virtues and states that there are nine stations of certitude (*maqāmāt al-yaqīn*): repentance (*tawbah*), asceticism (*zuhd*), patience (*ṣabr*), gratitude (*shukr*), fear (*khawf*), contentment (*riḍā'*), hope (*rajā'*), trust (*tawakkul*), and love (*maḥabbah*) with the *sine qua non* that not one of these stations is valid unless accompanied by the elimination of self-direction *vis-à-vis* God.[89]

The work is written in a didactic style with citations throughout from his shaykh Abu'l-ʿAbbās and Shaykhs Abu'l-Ḥasan ash-Shādhilī and Abū Madyan. References from the *Kitāb al-Ḥikam* are found and explained,[90] making the *Tanwīr* a kind commentary. It is divided into various sections with verses of poetry. In addition, anecdotes relating to Ibn ʿAṭā' Allāh, his shaykh, and founder are mentioned, which likewise appear in the *Laṭā'if al-Minan*.[91] The book concludes with a series of *munājāt* but unlike the *Ḥikam*, these proceed from God to the servant, and the book ends with a supplication (*duʿā'*). Whether the *Laṭā'if* or the *Tanwīr* was composed first is difficult to establish. A reference to Shaykh Abū Muḥammad al-Marjānī with the formual *raḥimahu'llāh* (may God have mercy upon him) after his name indicates that the *Tanwīr* must have been written after 699 AH/1299 AD.[92] However, Brockelmann provides a different but more precise date by stating that the book was begun in Makkah and completed in Damascus in 695 AH/1296 AD.[93]

In terms of its importance in general and in relation to Ibn ʿAṭā' Allāh's other works, the *Tanwīr* was obviously very popular due to its numerous copies and printings.[94] When asked by a Sufi aspirant about which books to read on *taṣawwuf*, Shaykh Ibn ʿAbbād ar-Rundī (733–92 AH/1332–90 AD) wrote back that 'the book which you have by Ibn ʿAṭā' Allāh, the *Kitāb at-Tanwīr*, comprises all that the books on Sufism, whether detailed or condensed, contain including both detailed explanations and concise expressions'.[95] This is quite an endorsement of its value and comprehensiveness. 'An indispensable companion-piece to the *Ḥikam*', the *Tanwīr* is a kind of *tafsīr* of the *Ḥikam*[96] and as such is extremely valuable not only for expounding on the spiritual content of the *Ḥikam* but also for elaborating on the relationship of the virtues to the *dhikru'llāh*. The true meaning of *tawakkul* is carried to its logical conclusion and the necessity for eliminating one's ego-centered will with respect to the Divine Will is constantly emphasized. The result is the amazing variety of Ibn ʿAṭā' Allāh's arguments and the scope of his knowledge and skill.

While *al-Qaṣd al-Mujarrad fī Maʿrifat al-Ism al-Mufrad*[97] deals with the remembrance of God in a general fashion, its focus is more specifically on the significance and uniqueness of the Divine Name *Allāh*, which the Shaykh defines as that of the

> Supreme Essence (*adh-Dhāt al-ʿAliyyah*), described by the attribute of Divinity (*al-Ulūhiyyah*), known by the quality of Lordship (*ar-Rubūbiyyah*), characterized by the attribute of Oneness (*al-Aḥadiyyah*), unique by the unity of His solitude (*waḥdat al-waḥdāniyyah*), qualified by everlasting eternity (*ṣamadāniyyat aṣ-ṣamadiyyah*), transcending all manner of species and types of comparisons. He is sanctified beyond any point where human intelligence could comprehend the innermost depths of His knowledge (*maʿrifah*).[98]

As the Name of Supreme Essence, *Allāh* is the greatest Name because It is the synthesis of all the Divine Attributes and Intelligible Realities. As such, the Shaykh envisages this Name as 'the concrete embodiment of ultimate metaphysical reality'.[99] After stating that some authorities refute the notion that the Name is etymologically derived,[100] he presents the other side and offers several possibilities.[101] Ibn ʿAṭā' Allāh not only cites the sacred sources, namely, the Qur'ān and tradition, but also other eminent spiritual authorities and verses of poetry.

He constantly lays emphasis on the importance of the Name *Allāh* as the Absolute Necessary Being (*al-Wājib al-Wujūd al-Muṭlaq)* and the only True Reality (*al-Ḥaqqiyyu'l-Ḥaqq*). Whereas certain of the Attributes of the Ninety-Nine Beautiful Names (*al-Asmā'l-Ḥusnā*) can apply to man and creation, albeit as imperfect reflections of their Divine prototypes, this Name of Divinity cannot be used to describe anyone but God. The former is for *takhalluq* (appropriation) while the latter is for *taʿalluq* (attachment).[102] Hence, for example, a person can be kind or generous or strong, reflecting the qualities of *al-Ḥalīm* or *al-Karīm* or *al-Qawī*, but one cannot reflect the quality of Ultimate Being.

Moreover, Shaykh Ibn ʿAṭā' Allāh explains that the Name *Allāh* is a perfect Name in form as well as essence, because if the *alif* or *hamza* is deleted, the Name becomes *li'llāh*, to or for God. If the first *lām* is deleted, it becomes *lahu*, to Him and if the second *lām* is deleted, it becomes *Hū*, the Name of Pure Essence.[103] He expounds on the symbolism of each letter, the numerical value of each, the mystery connected with the Divine Name, and the categories of the Ninety-Nine Names.[104]

The Divine Name *Allāh* takes precedence over all the other names and attributes. 'All other names describe Him or are an attribute or are attached to Him . . . It is said that they are among the Names of Allah and not among the names of *aṣ-Ṣabūr* or *al-Ghafūr* or *al-Jabbār*.[105] All the names contain mysteries but the greatest Name contains mysteries not found in the other Names. Also, unlike the other Names, the Divine Name *Allāh* cannot be enumerated. This Name is like 'pure light, [it] contains all colours within itself when refracted, and these "colours" are the rest of the names of God, or the even more numerous Qualities'.[106]

Part Two deals with the role and significance of *dhikr* in achieving spiritual realization. Ibn ʿAṭā' Allāh mentions the various kinds of remembrance and the supremacy of invoking the Divine Name. He cites Qur'ānic verses much as in the *Miftāḥ al-Falāḥ*, which will be discussed later. Once again, the shaykh presupposes a good deal of background on the part of the reader, both doctrinal and otherwise. 'The author presents his subject without developing certain aspects relating to precise definitions, difficult doctrinal points, [and] analysis of details which may have the disadvantage of making the exposition abstract.'[107] His style is clear, direct, and didactic which is normal, considering that his position, and his knowledge of the doctrine of Divine metaphysical and spiritual realities is extraordinary. Ibn ʿAṭā' Allāh's 'philosophical and theological education emerge as does his use of philosophical and scholastic terminology on the Eternal and Contingent'.[108]

Some repetition from his other works can be seen, but to a certain extent that is to be expected given that each work is basically a variation on the same theme of *tawḥīd*. The date of the work is unknown. However, one passage is a paraphrase of the same idea in *Laṭā'if al-Minan* on the states of the novice,[109] and others include the same *aḥādīth* and stories found in the *Miftāḥ al-Falāḥ*.[110] One can only conclude, therefore, that it was probably written some time near the end of his life for his disciples, perhaps as a help in meditational practices on the Divine Name.

All in all, the *Qaṣd* is a highly interesting, inspired, and thought-provoking work which still continues to fascinate even students of today. A recent translation into French with commentary is an eloquent testimony to its timeless message and universal appeal.[111]

One of Shaykh Ibn ʿAṭā' Allāh's lesser known compositions which have come down to us is *Tāj al-ʿArūs al-Ḥāwī li-Tahdhīb an-Nufūs*.[112] A short work, perhaps less than fifty pages, it is printed on the margin of *Kitāb at-Tanwīr fī Isqāṭ at-Tadbīr*.[113] The *Tāj* begins with an opening salutation on the Prophet, his family and Companions by the editor or compiler, then plunges immediately into the text, giving one the impression that it might have been put together by one or more of Ibn ʿAṭā' Allāh's disciples rather than by the shaykh himself. It does not flow as smoothly as do most of his other works, revealing a certain disjointedness as it moves from one topic to the next and back again.

The book seems to be a series of basic lectures – perhaps public lectures – that Ibn ʿAṭā' Allāh might have given at some point and which were later written down. By basic is meant that the subject matter deals with the importance and necessity of repentance and obedience to God, of renouncing one's bad or immoral behaviour, of associating with pious individuals, and of following the *Sharīʿah*. The work contains scores of analogies, the requisite references to the Qur'ān and *aḥādīth*, stories of saints and even quotations from Shaykhs Abu'l-Ḥasan ash-Shādhilī, Abu'l-ʿAbbās-al-Mursī, and Makīn ad-Dīn al-Asmar, a leading disciple of al-Mursī. But it is a far cry from the lofty and sophisticated mystical and metaphysical expositions found in his other books.

Passages from the *Laṭā'if*, such as the story about the founder Shaykh Abu'l-Ḥasan's being given food by Christians following a three-day retreat and fast[114] or *munājāt* from the *Kitāb al-Ḥikam*,[115] can be found here. This might lead one to conclude that the *Tāj al-ʿArūs* was one of the Shaykh's later compositions. Actually Ibn ʿAjībah states that it was compiled from the *Kitāb at-Tanwīr* and the *Laṭā'if*.[116] It is hortatory in tone and the emphasis on the basic virtues and *adab* makes it clear that '. . . it was intended for the general public, not the élite'.[117] 'In all likelihood, the *Tāj al-ʿArūs* was put together by his disciples as an *aide-mémoire*, a handy little manual of extracts from his other works . . .'[118]

Whether or not Shaykh Ibn ʿAṭā' Allāh or his disciples compiled the book, the content is obviously that of Shaykh Ibn ʿAṭā Allāh's thoughts and views. There can be no question but that it filled a definite need and function: the common man needed guidance as much as the spiritual élite, and *Tāj al-ʿArūs* was the answer.

Another little known work is *ʿUnwān at-Tawfīq fī Ādāb aṭ-Ṭarīq*, which is actually a commentary (*sharḥ*) on a poem (*qaṣīdah*) by the Sufi Shaykh Abū Madyan Shuʿayb al-Maghribī (d. 594 AH/ 1197 AD).[119] The *qaṣīdah*, composed of twenty-two verses, deals with the relationship of the novice to his shaykh and to the *fuqarā'*, i.e., the other disciples. Shaykh Ibn ʿAṭā' Allāh takes this one step further with his *sharḥ* and expounds on each verse. In a clear and concise fashion, he discusses the mystical concepts of companionship and states that a true shaykh is harder to find than red sulphur or the phoenix.[120] With regard to the novice to whom the *qaṣīdah* is addressed, Ibn ʿAṭā' Allāh stresses the importance of repentance, humility, being careful about one's behaviour (*adab*), and especially of associating with the *fuqarā'*—much like the previous work. He quotes the great spiritual masters ʿAbd al-Qādir al-Jilānī (d. 561 AH/1166 AD) and Ibn al-ʿArabī (560–638 AH/ 1165–1240 AD)[121] to support his point of view and even refers to his *Ḥikam*.[122]

The *ʿUnwān* is a short piece evidently written sometime after the *Kitāb al-Ḥikam* when Ibn ʿAṭā' Allāh was already a spiritual master. It is in keeping with his other books on the importance and necessity of a spiritual guide and reveals his 'knowledge of the sparse writings of the great Maghribī saint'[123] Abū Madyan as well as poetry, grammar, logic, Qur'ān, Prophetic tradition, and of course, the degree of his spiritual awareness.

As for Ibn ᶜAṭā' Allāh's unpublished or unknown works, some are to be found in Brockelmann[124] or are mentioned by Arab biographers.[125] However, as noted by Danner, 'Some of these treatises have been given generic titles, as if they are independent works; others are imbedded in still larger collections containing compositions by other authors; [or are] simple extractions from one of Ibn ᶜAṭā' Allāh's better known books.'[126] Even the poetry that he wrote has only survived as a few lines scattered here and there in various works or quoted by other biographers.[127]

While the greater part of Ibn ᶜAṭā' Allāh's works have remained unpublished and therefore largely unknown, others have been completely lost with only titles as reminders. Nevertheless, on the basis of his published books and extant manuscripts, we may conclude that these, too, would likewise have attested to his prolific powers, the variety of his expertise, the degree of his perspicacity and spiritual discernment, the esteem in which he was held, and the respect accorded his writings by both his contemporaries and succeeding generations.

Miftāḥ al-Falāḥ wa Miṣbāḥ al-Arwāḥ

Of all Ibn ᶜAṭā' Allāh's writings, one of his most informative and most crucial for our knowledge of Shādhilī mystical practices and methods is the *Miftāḥ al-Falāḥ wa Miṣbāḥ al-Arwāḥ*.[128] Like the *Qaṣd al-Mujarrad* previously discussed, it is a work on the *dhikru'llāh*. Yet unlike the *Qaṣd*, whose focus is on the remembrance of the Divine Name of *Allāh*, the *Miftāḥ al-Falāḥ* deals with the Shādhilī principles and all possible manner and ways of invoking, the variety of techniques used, and the benefits derived from so doing.

The translation which follows is based on a master copy made from the collation of the photocopies of two manuscripts from Dār al-Kutub al-Miṣriyyah, No. 44262, dated 1050 AH (1640–41) and No. 52746, dated 1273 AH (1856–57) and from the 1381/1961 Cairo edition first published by Maṭbaᶜat Muṣṭafā al-Bābī al-Ḥalabī. This Cairo edition of 141 pages is obviously based on yet another manuscript dated 861 AH (1456–57), because at times all three have variant readings. The aim of collating was to obtain an intelligible rendering of the three texts. Consequently, it is not to be regarded as an exhaustive critical recension.

The older manuscript, No. 44262, seems closest to the published text and is in good condition overall. The first fifty-seven pages are written in a very compact Naskhī script. Then the handwriting switches to a Maghribī script, which takes some re-adjusting to become accustomed to, as if an apprentice with a less fine hand might have taken over. Then it reverts to the original handwriting from pages 102–11. Perhaps the master copier had returned to guarantee and seal his work. At any rate, both scripts are difficult to read in places, and there are the inevitable blurred words and faded areas due to the passage of time. Like the Cairo edition, this manuscript ends with a section from Muḥyi'd-Dīn b. al-ᶜArabī's *al-Futūḥāt al-Makkiyyah*.[129]

As to the state of the other manuscript No. 52746, it is 187 pages in length and in excellent condition – much clearer than the first one – and written in a fine uniform Naskhī hand. However, there are grammatical errors to be found as in the other two texts, but unlike them, it does not end with the section from Ibn al-ᶜArabī's *Futūḥāt*.

In collating the three texts, normally two out of three usually agreed, if not all three, which facilitated reading a difficult or hastily written word or choosing the best word. Yet in spite of having such controls, there were a few instances when each text had a different verb, all synonyms of each other, or a different noun, each a species of insect! At such moments one could only make a decision based upon which manuscript tended to be the most consistently correct, since grammatical or spelling mistakes as well as variant readings of prepositions are to be seen in all the texts.

The structure of the *Miftāḥ* is, as stated by Shaykh Ibn ʿAṭā' Allāh, 'arranged . . . into two parts: Part One has an introduction, sections (*fuṣūl*), chapters (*abwāb*) and foundations (*uṣūl*); Part Two has sections and chapters'.[130] However, on closer examination, one finds that many of the divisions seem rather haphazardly made and perhaps are no more than stopping and starting points for his thoughts. For example, Part One is not actually delineated except as mentioned in the above quote contained in the book's Preface. Within this first part are three sections with no apparent separation of ideas that would warrant such subdivisions. Section three, which is so numbered for the convenience of the reader, is seen to be further subdivided into two foundations, the second of which is still further broken down into sections with titles for the first two but not the third. All this is before coming to chapter one – again numbered for the benefit of the reader but not done in the original text.

The first chapter contains two sections with titles before coming to another subsection which the author calls the 'third foundation', rather than the first. In other words, Ibn ʿAṭā' Allāh considers it to be a continuation of the two foundations in Part One instead of the first foundation in chapter one. Yet in terms of content, it is totally unrelated. The first two foundations deal with proofs from the Qur'ān and *Sunnah* regarding the merit of invoking while the third deals with sincerity of belief. The latter heading is also divided into categories called *al-qism al-awwal* and *al-qism ath-thānī*[131] which have titles. Section three ends this chapter. Here the three main sections (*fuṣūl*) appear as separate and appropriate subthemes of the main heading.

Chapter two, however, is quite short and without any subdivisions. Chapter three is divided into two sections but this subdivision seems to be pointless since the entire chapter deals with the spiritual benefits attached to each particular Divine Attribute. Again like chapter two, chapter four has no subsections. Chapter five contains one untitled section and chapter six, none. Chapter seven is very short also with one untitled section. It seems that the above-mentioned sections of both chapters five and seven are rather arbitrarily arranged and more indicative of what would normally amount to a change of paragraph.

Chapter eight contains four sections, only the first of which is titled. However, in this case, sections two and three appear as separate categories insofar as they focus on different facets of *tawḥīd*, while section four shifts its emphasis to the dangers of travelling on the spiritual path. Chapter nine is not subdivided.

Part Two noticeably changes its format in that it is one long text composed of nine sections, followed by a conclusion and then chapter ten. Sections one, two, and seven each have headings and are of such lengths that they could very easily have been separate chapters. The first *faṣl* contains nine numbered discussions – each called a *baḥth* – on the sacred formula *Lā ilāha illa' llāh*, whereas the second one goes into a lengthy exposition on the Oneness of God, listing eighteen proofs. As to the seventh section, it deals with the names and meanings of *Lā ilāha illa'llāh*.

The eighth, though untitled, focuses on the etymology of the word *ilāh*, similar to the discussion found in *al-Qaṣd al-Mujarrad*.[132] The remaining sections three to six and nine are much shorter and only the fifth one has any headings.

The conclusion is primarily a collection of those traditions that deal with the subject of *dhikr*, but it is also subdivided into a section without a heading, which is merely a continuation of the previous *aḥādīth*. Hence, such divisions seem superfluous. This is followed by a rubric about asking for forgiveness on Fridays, but it is not called a *faṣl*.

Chapter ten, oddly enough, follows the conclusion and it, too, is essentially more of the same traditions of the Prophet. The first section is the longest, with more *aḥādīth* about invoking; the second one deals with what to say when travelling. Although the third section has no heading, its subject matter is the *aḥādīth* to be recited in times of illness and affliction.

If the structure of the *Miftāḥ al-Falāḥ* seems at times uneven, not so the content. For here Shaykh Ibn ʿAṭā' Allāh's mastery of the Qur'ān, Traditions, and sayings of the Companions, saints, and mystics combine with his expertise in Arabic grammar, poetry, logic, law, Mālikī *fiqh* and *uṣūl* to produce a unique work of simple but moving prose on the doctrine of *tawḥīd*, its importance, necessity, and benefits for the individual, and the method of spiritual realization, *viz.*, the *dhikru'llāh*.

In the shaykh's own words, he acknowledges that he wrote the book for two reasons: (1) because he had never seen 'an adequate and complete book or . . . a clear and comprehensive treatise' on the subject and (2) because he was asked to do so 'by a pious brother'.[133] As a result, his stated purpose is to 'facilitate understanding of the remembrance of God', elucidate any obscurities, 'steer the seeker away from difficulties', and make 'the book accessible to those desirous of spiritual gifts . . .'[134] In other words, Ibn ʿAṭā' Allāh took it upon himself to set down in writing for posterity spiritual directions which would serve as lights to guide the seeker out of the darkness of spiritual ignorance and death. Clearly he was a very learned and well-read scholar, so the obvious conclusion one must draw is that this work represents the first of its kind devoted exlusively to the doctrine and method of the *dhikru'llāh*.

The Introduction begins with a general overview of the meaning and nature of the *dhikru'llāh* which Ibn ʿAṭā' Allāh simply defines as 'the repetition of the Name of the Invoked by the heart and the tongue'.[135] He provides examples of invoking which include remembering God or one of His attributes, commandments, deeds or mentioning His Name, or reciting the Qur'ān. He offers types of *dhākirs* such as the theologian, *faqīh*, teacher, *mufti*, and so forth. The shaykh elaborates further by differentiating among degrees of *dhikr*, whether with the tongue, heart, or body, whether in secret or in public, whether restricted by Sacred Law such as the times of prayer or unrestricted, and other nuances. Then Ibn ᶜAṭā' Allāh delves into a more detailed discussion of the definition and scope of *dhikr*. He emphasizes its different aspects like an artist painting a canvas, first concentrating on one thing, then another and returning to add touches until each part combines to create a complete idea or picture.

In the beginning, remembrance is with the tongue with effort and when invoking takes over, the body experiences subtle changes.[136] There are degrees of invoking which culminate in the so-called 'hidden invocation', i.e., when one becomes so absorbed that one is no longer aware of oneself. This is self-extinction or *fanā'*. The lowest level is invoking God aloud, then with the heart, soul, spirit, intellect (*ᶜaql*), and ultimately with one's 'innermost Self' (*sirr*). Ibn ᶜAṭā' Allāh mentions the corresponding panoply of creation which invokes simultaneously with the *dhākir*.

He moves on to describe the three kinds of souls: the soul that incites to evil (*an-nafs al-ammārah bi's-sū'*), the self-blaming soul (*an-nafs al-lawwāmah*), and the recollected soul (*an-nafs al-muṭma'innah*) with all their tendencies. To support his comments, he then furnishes proofs from the Qur'ān and *Sunnah* as well as sayings from the Companions and other recognized spiritual authorities. An example of Ibn ᶜAṭā' Allāh's grammatical expertise comes through in his discussion of the etymology of the word *al-mufarridūn* (pious recluses) in connection with one of the *aḥādīth*. The last section of the Introduction deals with the preferred status of the invoker over others. Again *aḥādīth* are cited.

In chapter one, the shaykh relates several *aḥādīth* on the merits of invoking in a low or loud voice and the importance of invoking constantly. He inserts anecdotes from pious individuals and authorities. Under 'Third Foundation' Ibn ᶜAṭā' Allāh expounds on the meaning of sincerity with regard to conduct and belief—

whether the motive behind a deed is spiritual or egocentric or a combination of the two—and describes each. His knowledge of logic is readily apparent here. He concludes with a discussion of the *adab* associated with invoking, i.e., what the seeker must do to prepare himself: from disciplining himself and withdrawing from the world, to eating lawfully and dressing appropriately, to how he must conduct himself during the ceremony of *dhikr*—how to sit, what to say, and how to behave at its conclusion. This section is one of the most interesting for its insights into the Shādhilī method of invoking, the importance of the *Shahādah*, and the rigorous discipline which a novice was expected to undergo.[137]

Chapter two focuses on the many fruits of invoking, briefly mentioned in the Introduction and enumerates the physical, emotional, and spiritual benefits to the *dhākir* and the importance of the spiritual formulas in leading to redemption and gnosis. 'Of all deeds there is none more redemptive from the chastisement of God, who possesses Majesty, than the invocation . . . The invocation is a tree whose fruit is gnosis.'[138]

In chapter three Ibn ʿAṭā' Allāh develops the subject of the benefits of invoking even further, taking it in another direction, which is unique among his writings and indicative of his spiritual mastery. He presents some of the Ninety-Nine Beautiful Names of God (*al-Asmā' al-Ḥusnā*), indicating the particular spiritual remedy which invoking each Name will produce, and for what type of individual each Name is best suited, whether novice, intermediate, or advanced disciple and at what level. He also warns that each remedy or Divine Name, like a physical prescription, is for a certain illness of the soul and should not be used in connection with another. For example, invoking repeatedly *al-ʿĀlim* (the Knower) brings vigilance.

This discourse was obviously not meant for the novice but rather as a guide to meditational practices. Since Ibn ʿAṭā' Allāh composed this work for his disciples to facilitate the journey, and some of them became shaykhs themselves, it could be reasonably argued that this esoteric information was for the benefit of those rare enlightened individuals who were destined to guide others.

If focusing inwardly on God through constant remembrance is of utmost importance for drawing closer to Him, then choosing the right type of invocation is a profoundly serious matter. Chapter four elaborates on the various possible sacred formulas and expressions which the seeker may use as well as the significance of each. He cites arguments in favour of one or the other but ultimately the question is not one of preference but one of appropriateness. The choice, for example, between invoking *Lā ilāha illa'llāh* or simply *Allāh* or *Hū* depends upon the seeker's spiritual state. 'Each invocation has its own state and time wherein it is better than another type of remembrance.'[139]

But how to determine which is best at a given moment requires an extraordinarily discerning teacher as described in the next chapter. Here in chapter five Ibn ʿAṭā' Allāh explicates the central role of a realized spiritual master or Sufi shaykh in guiding the seeker, the importance of finding and obeying such a person, the necessity of discipline and virtuous conduct, and the diverse types of spiritual paths. This chapter is essentially a recapitulation of what has already been stated. He reiterates the blessings to be had through reciting the prayer upon the Prophet and recommends that the novice begin with that.

The last section concentrates on how to actually begin the process of repentance and turning toward God—in other words, how to prepare oneself in order to take the first step of the spiritual journey. This is similar to the earlier discussion on the *adab* associated with invoking in chapter one. However, the difference here is that the Shaykh's attention is on the manner of dealing with an absolute beginner, i.e., one who asks to enter such a discipline and such an order. Hence, for Ibn ʿAṭā' Allāh, the nature, background, and temperament of the novice must be evaluated before assigning him any spiritual exercises. Whether he is learned or simple, well-balanced or hot-tempered, has led a moral or immoral life are all factors to be taken into consideration when deciding on the type of invocation and the number of its repetitions. 'Fruits [of invoking] vary according to individuals; but they derive from one source.'[140]

Then he moves on to the actual manner of invoking: how to sit, what to say, the necessity of confiding in one's shaykh and reciting a morning and evening litany (*wird*). The significance of constantly invoking the Divine Name inwardly until it becomes second nature, as it were, for the individual is continually emphasized. From this Shādhilī discipline and method, Ibn ʿAṭā' Allāh goes on to describe other more rigorous ways such as that of Shaykh al-Junayd.[141]

A concomitant of the path is the spiritual retreat (*khalwah*). Chapter six defines the retreat and enumerates its salutary benefits to the soul and its purpose. Forgetfulness (*ghaflah*) in the heart is likened to rust on a mirror, a popular imagery in Sufism. Only by polishing it can the mirror shine as it was originally intended. So too with the heart. Invoking, especially in solitude and aided by fasting, removes forgetfulness and worldly attachments and helps the soul to focus on God, as it was meant to do—when man was God's *khalīfah* on earth.

Ibn ʿAṭā' Allāh discusses the preparation and procedure to follow before going into a retreat, since it is not an easy thing to do. This is yet another aspect of the *adab* of invoking previously mentioned, particularly in chapters one and five. From the importance of solitude and right intention, the Shaykh moves on to an actual description of the physical structure and dimensions of the cell used for the initiate's retreat, and the conditions for undertaking it. He even explains how to eat, the proper type of clothing to wear, and personal hygiene. In short, Ibn ʿAṭā' Allāh provides us with further insights into the Shādhilī method of conducting a retreat and the value of each part to the whole.

Once the manner of a retreat has been established, the Shaykh turns his attention suddenly to delineate the difference between angelic and satanic inspirations and the four categories of suggestions that often come over a disciple. Starting from the highest, the divine, to the lowest, the satanic, Ibn ʿAṭāʾ Allāh interprets the accompanying feelings of each. Divine and angelic inspirations produce calm and bliss due to their proximity to God, while psychical (*hājis*) and satanic (*waswās*) suggestions leave the soul agitated due to their being closer to passion and contrary to the Sacred Law.

The central theme of *tawḥīd*, God's Oneness, is the focus of chapter seven. Quoting the great Shaykh al-Ghazālī[142] on the nature of *tawḥīd*, Ibn ʿAṭāʾ Allāh expounds upon it and the varying degrees of people's awareness. He concludes this short chapter with the revelation that 'all creatures affirm the Oneness of God Most High in accordance with the subtleness of their "breaths".'[143] This universality of remembrance is supported by a verse from the Qur'ān and refers to every kind and species including non-living things.

Invoking, whether in the midst of one's daily tasks or in solitude, is the best form of worship because it is meant to be continuous. Gnosis (*maʿrifah*) is its fruit. In chapter eight Ibn ʿAṭāʾ Allāh defines *maʿrifah* as 'the perception of something as it is in its essence and attributes'.[144] It is of two types: general and particular, the latter arising from contemplation and leading to certitude. He adds that what distinguishes one soul from another after death is its degree of knowledge and awareness gained in this life.

> Its discernment in the Hereafter is not greater than its discernment in this world except in terms of unveiling and clarity. Contemplation and vision will be commensurate with one's knowledge of God Most High . . . because gnosis in this world will be transformed in the Hereafter as a contemplative vision . . .[145]

Section one of this chapter, as its title clearly states, deals with the question of whether invoking or reciting the Qur'ān is better. Ibn ᶜAṭā' Allāh again quotes al-Ghazālī who states under which conditions reciting the Qur'ān is preferable. Then Ibn ᶜAṭā' Allāh offers additional support by citing several *aḥādīth*. Yet deftly as he argues in favour of the Qur'ān, the Shaykh just as skillfully returns to al-Ghazālī to cite the opposite view, *viz.*, that 'when the servant is not in need of refining his character and attaining gnostic knowledge . . . then perseverence in the invocation is more suitable'.[146] In other words, Ibn ᶜAṭā' Allāh's spiritual mastery is such that he also argues convincingly in favour of the invocation of various Divine Names and sacred formulas, especially the formula *Lā ilāha illa'llāh*, which he expatiates on in section two.

As for section three, it continues with an explication of the variety of types of invocations and the efficacy of each; however, the *Shahādah* is considered the best. ' . . . it is evident that a certain probability attaches to the claim of the person who holds that saying *Allāh*, *Allāh*, or *Huwa*, *Huwa* is the most special invocation, for it is among the sum of expressions of which *Lā ilāha illa 'llāh* is the best, according to the knowers of God'.[147] An admonition to show compassion and mercy to all creation ends this division.

Section four shifts its focus to the dangers inherent in travelling on the spiritual path – the illusions a novice may have – as well as the signs and blessings of proximity to God. Ibn ᶜAṭā' Allāh enumerates a range of emotional and spiritual states indicative of the servant's standing with God, e.g., 'The signs of devotion to God are three: abandoning choice, rejecting self-determination, and denying self-willing'.[148] It is as if this last part were meant to serve as a gauge for reflection and self-examination and perhaps to help the *murshid* evaluate the progress of the *murīd*.

Chapter nine, the last chapter in Part One, develops yet another aspect of *adab*, *viz.*, the ideal conduct expected of the advanced initiate, which goes beyond the Golden Rule of 'do unto others . . .' Here the emphasis is on dealing with oneself, the spiritual attitudes and practices to adopt, the conditions one must undergo to discipline and purify one's soul of egocentric and worldly attachments.

The Sufi is to be rigorous and abstemious with himself, know and follow the *Sharīʿah*, defer to those higher in rank in the *ṭarīqah*, follow his shaykh's instructions completely, be content with his lot, and share his goods. In his dealings with outsiders he should be compassionate and non-judgmental, offer help when needed, withdraw from distracting company or influences, yet not deem himself better than others. He should lead an examined life, guard his tongue, and strive to remove worldly concerns from his heart. In short, the Sufi must focus inwardly on God, put others before himself, and be in the world but not of the world. Ibn ʿAṭā' Allāh has obviously written a prescription for saintly people, the practice of which can only be for a select spiritual élite.

Part Two, unlike Part One, is divided into major sections that would normally be seen as chapters. The first section contains nine subsections called discussions on the nature of the phrase *Lā ilāha illa'llāh* from different levels of reality and including grammatical and philosophical points of view. The Shaykh's expertise in grammar and logic, not to mention the Qur'ān and *Sunnah*, is here unquestionable as he presents one argument after another, dissecting all the possible nuances of meaning of the formula of *tawḥīd*.

Beginning with the first discussion, he gives a short grammatical analysis of the negative particle *lā*; in the second, the various philosophical and religious ramifications of the phrase *Lā ilāha illa'llāh* with regard to *tawḥīd*. The third returns to a grammatical explanation of the word *Allāh* which is in the nominative case and therefore in apposition to *lā*.

In the fourth discussion, Ibn ʿAṭā' Allāh continues with an analysis of *illā*, explaining that it signifies *ghayr* (other than) in the phrase, rather than exception. The fifth discussion further elucidates this idea through philosophical reasoning to show that the phrase *Lā ilāha illa'llāh* actually means negation of other deities instead of affirmation of God's existence.

As for the sixth discussion, it is an elaboration of the first but concerns the *lā* of absolute negation. According to Ibn ʿAṭāʾ Allāh, it is a more forceful negation, because the noun governed by *lā*, in this case *ilāha*, is in the accusative which is more emphatic than a noun in the nominative case. The seventh discussion opens with a philosophical explanation of how affirmation normally precedes negation. Then Ibn ʿAṭāʾ Allāh points out how its opposite in the phrase *Lā ilāha illa'llāh* indicates emphasis as well as spiritual symbolism.

In the eighth discussion the Shaykh stresses the importance of knowing, for the sake of salvation, that there is only One God. The ninth discussion enumerates the different conditions under which one should recite the invocation of *tawḥīd*. These evolve by degrees from orally declaring the phrase to inwardly doing so and combining therewith arguments and proofs which strengthen belief.

Section two of Part Two sets out to establish that there can only be One God, not two in partnership. Ibn ʿAṭāʾ Allāh furnishes eighteen proofs based on traditional and intellectual arguments, some of which are quite subtle. Once more his expertise in philosophy and logic, in addition to his religious and spiritual formation, come to the fore as he responds to every conceivable or hypothetical question. For the modern reader, the positing of such proofs for the existence of One God as opposed to two might seem rather strange, if not naive, since the problem today would be most likely one of belief in One God versus atheism. Furthermore, while many people may tend to idolize ambition or the pursuit of status, power, or wealth, they do not necessarily regard them as gods. Nevertheless, the Shaykh's reasoning and argumentation are impressive and reveal his immense range of knowledge and spiritual awareness. Naturally the highest appeal to proof in God's Unity is the Qur'ān, and in the eighteenth and final proof Ibn ʿAṭāʾ Allāh enumerates and comments upon several verses.

In section three earlier Sufi authorities are quoted who confirm the significance of *Lā ilāha illa'llāh* and its unique salvational function. Sections four and five continue to develop this theme and emphasize that invoking the spiritual formula is incumbent upon all Muslims. Stories and verses from the Qur'ān, *aḥādīth*, and anecdotes about the Companions and other historical persons constantly support Ibn ʿAṭā' Allāh's beliefs in the necessity and transforming power of invoking the profession of God's Oneness.

In section six the Shaykh provides commentary upon the different meanings of the formula *Lā ilāha illa'llāh* and interprets the symbolism of the number of letters making up the phrase. In section seven he amplifies on yet another dimension in his treatise by focusing on the names describing, or synonymous with, the Testimony of Faith, such as *tawḥīd*, *ikhlāṣ* (sincerity of faith), *iḥsān* (virtue), and *ʿadl* (justice). With each of the nineteen names, Ibn ʿAṭā' Allāh interprets its relationship to the *Shahādah*, thus again affirming the latter's uniqueness among the formulas of remembrance.

The etymology of the word *Allāh* is discussed in section eight in similar fashion to the author's exposition in *al-Qaṣd al-Mujarrad*.[149] The Shaykh begins by defining *al-ilāh* (the deity) and then explains that the word *Allāh*, according to certain scholars, is considered a derivative. He presents their differing arguments: that it originates either from the verbs *aliha* or *waliha* or *lāha*. Then he gives opposing comments by others who say that the word *Allāh* is not a derivative. Ibn ʿAṭā' Allāh agrees with this latter explanation and carries it another step, *viz*., that it is neither a derivative nor a proper noun since nouns describe, and the word *Allāh* is greater than the sum total of all the Ninety-Nine Names. Hence, it is a Name which refers to Essence and not a quality to be described.

Ibn ʿAṭā'Allāh adds that the Name *Allāh* was not used among the Arabs before or after the time of the Prophet Muḥammad for anything other than to indicate this Supreme Essence, i.e., not for any of His Attributes. From this highly interesting discourse, he interjects seven principles that the seeker should observe in order to draw closer to God and concludes with a symbolic interpretation of the letters in the Name *Allāh* without any further explanation.

Section nine introduces a couple of anecdotes whose purpose is to show the importance and effect of reciting *Lā ilāha illa'llāh*. The second one is so indicated through the mention of both the *adhān* and *iqāmah* which contain this formula. Next, Ibn ᶜAṭā' Allāh proceeds to illustrate the symbolism of the entire *Shahādah*, according to the number of its individual letters and words, then the symbolism of the first part only, according to its number of letters. From this he turns to the pronoun *Hū*, which esoterically represents both 'He', meaning God, and His Divine Essence[150] and likewise interprets the mystery of its letters. As a seeming afterthought, the Shaykh ends with an explanation of the meaning of *subḥāna 'llāh wa bi-ḥamdihi*, an invocation of praise to God.

The Conclusion (*khātimah*) of the book appears to have been misplaced because a final chapter succeeds it. At any rate it contains many *aḥādīth* about invoking during times of difficulty or distress. Several of the Companions are mentioned. Section one is more restricted to *aḥādīth* dealing with asking for forgiveness, while the next division is still more so and focuses specifically on *aḥādīth* related to asking for forgiveness on Fridays, obviously considered the most propitious day of the week.

Chapter ten, the last chapter, begins with an obscure incantation against snake bites that seems like an afterthought or digression. Then more *aḥādīth* follow like those previously mentioned in the Conclusion. As if to summarize all that has been said about the importance of invoking God's Name or one of the sacred formulas containing His Name, Ibn ᶜAṭā' Allāh again enumerates many Qur'ānic verses and *aḥādīth* in section one that relate to it, particularly those on remembering God in the morning and evening, often with a prescribed result such as protection for oneself and/or one's family from illness, disaster, or hellfire. As is the norm, the names of Companions and traditionists are included as authorities who either witnessed the Prophet's telling or performing of such an act or who received the information from a reliable source or sources.

Interspersed among these are various traditions – some related to remembering God on Fridays – which would have been more appropriately inserted with those in the Conclusion, or related to invoking at unresticted times, or even those repeated from other chapters in the text. But no matter, for to Ibn ʿAṭā' Allāh they all serve the same purpose, that is, to enable the seeker to realize that the religion, especially through the *Sunnah* of the Prophet, provides the means to protect and guide the sincere servant back to God in the easiest, quickest, and safest manner possible.

In section two the Shaykh sets down the *aḥādīth* to be used in times of travel. To repeat the formulas is to be protected from the dangers of calamity, predatory animals, and criminals associated with journeying. Likewise with health: section three focuses on the conditions of illness and provides *aḥādīth* which instruct the believer in how to conduct himself when visiting the sick, what to say, and how to alleviate one's own illness. It then concludes with a few traditions related more to misfortune than sickness.

The *Miftāḥ* is written in a clear, lucid style as are all the works of Shaykh Ibn ʿAṭā' Allāh. Although well-known, the book does not seem to enjoy the widespread popularity of the *Kitāb al-Ḥikam*, especially in view of all the commentaries on the latter. Yet the *Miftāḥ* is unprecedented for the light it sheds on the central role and scope of the *dhikru'llāh* in the Shādhilī *ṭarīqah*, and the *adab* and practices associated with invoking, such as the retreat (*khalwah*). 'The *Miftāḥ al-Falāḥ* is considered to be among the most important works of Ibn ʿAṭā' Allāh from the standpoint that it contains the principles of the actual Sufi mystical practices such as *dhikr*, seclusion, and retreat.'[151]

The *Miftāḥ* offers a glimpse into the Sufi world of the seventh/thirteenth centuries and allows us to see almost at firsthand how the novice was guided, the central function of the Sufi shaykh, the *adab* expected, the manner of interaction and, above all, the purpose and preparation involved in engaging in the *dhikru'llāh*. Since salvation was taken quite seriously in the traditional world, Ibn ʿAṭā' Allāh sets forth at once to define *dhikr*, to explain its nature and power, to state the results it bestows, and to prove that it is part of the *Sunnah*. Obviously, the fact that he had previously been so anti-Sufi himself plays a large part in this. Consequently, he must have known that many others looked upon *taṣawwuf* as some sort of aberration, if not *bidʿah*. Therefore, the author goes to great lengths to point out the many Qur'ānic verses and *aḥādīth* that refer to remembering God and cites many noted authorities. Perhaps, too, the work was written to counteract the formalistic trend within Islam as well as within Sufism.[152]

Ibn ʿAṭā' Allāh was neither the first to write about the importance of the *dhikr* in Sufism, nor the last. Others before him, such as ʿAbd al-Karīm b. Hawāzin al-Qushayrī (d. 465 AH/1074 AD) in his *Risālah*, al-Ghazālī (d. 505 AH/1111 AD) in his *Iḥyā' ʿUlūm ad-Dīn*, Najm ad-Dīn al-Kubrā (d. 618 AH/1221 AD) in his *Fawā'iḥ al-Jamāl wa Fawātiḥ al-Jalāl*, and Ibn al-ʿArabī (d. 638 AH/1240 AD) in his *al-Futūḥāt al-Makkiyyah* also discuss it. In fact, a few passages in the *Miftāḥ* are taken from al-Kubrā's *Fawā'iḥ al-Jamāl*.[153] However, this should not be construed as plagiarism since what is foremost in the religion is the Truth rather than the person who has spoken it. That is the reason why throughout his work Ibn ʿAṭā' Allāh often says 'It has been said', or 'One of the gnostics has said', rather than stating the name of each person quoted. Moreover, these few passages which amount to perhaps three or four pages are sometimes cited verbatim, and sometimes paraphrased.

In any case, he differs from the above spiritual masters in that he devotes an entire book to the subject instead of a few pages or a chapter, and the Shaykh systematically explains all the nuances of the contemplative prayer. 'Rare are the works in Sufism that deal with the comprehensive aspects of invocation (*dhikr*) more thoroughly or succinctly than the *Miftāḥ* of Ibn ᶜAṭā'Allāh.'[154]

Of all the Sufi writers, he is the first to put down in writing the mysteries connected with an orally transmitted religious tradition. His works as a whole form an integral part of the corpus of Sufi literature, and his contribution is inestimable in the field of Sufi studies. He has provided posterity with historical details on the origins of the Shādhilī *ṭarīqah*, one of the largest Sufi orders of North Africa, including Egypt and parts of the Middle East, and information about its great founder, Shaykh Abu'l-Ḥasan ash-Shādhilī, and his immediate successor Shaykh Abu'l-ᶜAbbās al-Mursī. Without him, no doubt, the Shādhilī order would most probably have been clouded in obscurity and legend and perhaps might have faded into oblivion.

In his lifetime, through personal guidance and teaching, Ibn ᶜAṭā' Allāh influenced hundreds of Sufis and non-Sufis alike. His stature and eminence as a Sufi and scholar were such that even the *fuqahā'* and historians have praised him.

> Most of them [his biographers] were historians and biographers of the *fuqahā'*. There is no doubt that the testimonies of the historians and biographers of the *fuqahā'* are more indicative of his rank than are the testimonies of the Sufis themselves, because the former are usually less likely to be biased and to exaggerate in mentioning his virtues.[155]

By his writings, however, he has influenced untold thousands of Muslims down through the ages who became Shādhilī disciples, spiritual guides, and commentators on his works. They in turn continued the momentum of the teachings of the founder and *quṭb* Shaykh Abu'l-Ḥasan. Non-Muslims have not gone untouched by his life either.[156] Even now his books are still being published in the Arab world and still affecting Muslim and non-Muslim, Arab and non-Arab alike, as witnessed by the various translations and studies made by both Arabs and Westerners.[157]

Although we have no way of gauging their number, there can be no question that the Shādhilī *ṭarīqah*—started in the seventh/thirteenth century—is alive and well, as evidenced by the continued publication of Shādhilī works. It has continued down to the present day in an unbroken chain through its spiritual authorities. One of its last great shaykhs of the twentieth century was Aḥmad al-ʿAlawī of Algeria, who died in 1934. He left behind several works and thousands of disciples,[158] one of whom was Muḥammad al-Hāshimī, author of *Kitāb ash-Shaṭranj*. The latter became a highly respected Sufi teacher in Damascus where he lived and guided many followers until his death in the decade of the seventies.

If one wonders how or why such a religious tradition could endure so long, one need only look to Islam which provides the framework for Sufism. The Qur'ān speaks of God as *aẓ-Ẓāhir* and *al-Bāṭin*. Exoteric Islam suffices for the generality of believers, but esoteric Islam or Sufism obviously addresses itself to some deeper need in the souls of pious Muslims. Islamic mysticism provides them with spiritual nourishment amid the instability of daily life, a continuum with their past heritage, and a more intense form of devotion harking back to the days of the Prophet.

Translation of the

Miftāḥ Al-Falāḥ wa Miṣbāḥ Al-Arwāḥ

PREFACE

In The Name of God, The Compassionate, The Merciful

May God bless our master Muḥammad, his family, and his companions, and grant them peace!

PRAISE be to God who opens sealed hearts through the remembrance of His name, who lifts the veils of defects through His righteousness, who purifies the innermost nature of hearts to confer upon them His own mysterious Self, who reveals wonders from the world of His power, and who increases the signs of abundance for those who are grateful to Him! I praise God for having made me one of those affirming His Oneness, and I thank Him, asking His grace and increased abundance. I also ask God's blessings on our master Muḥammad, the noblest of His servants, and on his family and companions, the possessors of great virtue and honour!

Now then, on to our subject: Verily, the remembrance of God Most High is the key to salvation and the lamp of souls, through the grace of God the Generous, the Victorious. The remembrance of God is the foundation of the Path and the pivotal support of realized sages. Yet I have never seen anyone who has written an adequate and complete book or compiled a clear and comprehensive treatise on it. That, together with the suggestion by a pious brother, who likes to give sincere counsel, prompted me to compose a book wherein I have assembled those things that would facilitate understanding the remembrance of God and elucidate whatever is obscure in it. In so doing, I have steered the seeker away from difficulties and made the book accessible to those desirous of spiritual gifts, hoping for reward, for this effort from God, and praying for the seeker's success in his quest:

> O traveller going toward the Protected Land,*
> Forget me not upon alighting there!

Upon God Most High do I rely, and through Him am I helped: 'There is no power or strength save in God, the Lofty, the Supreme'.

I have arranged this work into two parts: Part One has an introduction, sections, chapters, and principles; Part Two has sections and chapters.

* The reference is to the land of the Holy cities of Makkah and Medina.

PART ONE OF THE BOOK

INTRODUCTION

On the Nature of Remembrance and Its Explanation

REMEMBRANCE OF GOD is liberation from ignorance and forgetfulness through the permanent presence of the heart with the Truth. It has been said that it is the repetition of the Name of the Invoked by the heart and the tongue. It is alike whether it is God who is remembered, or one of His attributes, or one of His commandments, or one of His deeds, or whether one draws a conclusion based on any one of these. Remembering God may take the form of a supplication to Him, or the remembrance of His Messengers, Prophets, saints or of anyone related to Him or close to Him in some way, or because of some deed, such as reciting the Qur'ān, mentioning God's Name, poetry, singing, a conversation, or a story.

Therefore, the theologian is one who remembers God; the Muslim legal jurist is one who remembers God; the teacher is one who remembers God; the *muftī* is one who remembers God; and the preacher is one who remembers God. Anyone who meditates on the greatness and majesty and omnipotence of God Most High and on His signs in the heavens and the earth is one who remembers God. Whosoever observes what God has commanded and abstains from what God has forbidden is one who remembers God.

Remembrance may be with the tongue, the heart, or the members of the body. It may be practised secretly or openly; but whosoever combines all these forms has truly perfected it. Invoking with the tongue is remembrance of the letters of God's Name without presence of mind. It is the 'outward remembrance', but it has great virtue as witnessed by the verses of the Qur'ān, the sayings of the Prophet, and the remarks of others that have been handed down. It may be either restricted by time and place or unrestricted.

That which is restricted is like the remembrance of God during and after the five daily prayers, the pilgrimage to Makkah, before sleep and after waking, before eating, upon riding a mount, in the morning and evening, and so forth.

That which is unrestricted is not confined by time or place or moment or spiritual state. To this latter type of remembrance belongs the glorification of God, as in each of the following formulas: 'Glory be to God!' (*subḥāna'llāh*);[1] 'Praise be to God!' (*al-ḥamdu li'llāh*);[2] 'There is no divinity but God' (*Lā ilāha il-la'llāh*);[3] 'God is Most Great!' (*Allāh Akbar*);[4] and 'There is no power or strength save in God, the Lofty, the Supreme' (*Lā ḥawla wa-lā quwwata illā bi'llāh al-ʿAlī al-ʿAẓīm*).[5]

Then there is the remembrance which includes a supplication such as 'Our Lord, condemn us not if we forget or err',[6] or a personal entreaty, as well as the expression 'O God, bless our master Muḥammad'.[7] This has a greater effect on the heart of the novice than a remembrance that does not include an entreaty, because he who supplicates feels his heart close to the One whom he implores: remembrance touches his heart and envelops it with awe.

Other unrestricted forms of remembering God include being vigilant as well as requests dealing with this world or the Hereafter. Vigilance is exemplified in such remarks of yours as 'God is with me', 'God is looking at me', 'God sees me'; for there is within them a vigilant regard for the well-being of the heart. Truly, remembrance is used to strengthen one's presence with God Most High, to maintain the proper conduct toward Him, to guard against heedlessness, as a refuge from the accursed devil, and to help foster the attentiveness of the heart during acts of worship.

Section [One]

There is no form of remembrance which does not have a result specifically associated with it; and any form practiced will bestow upon you whatever particular power it has. Invoking with receptivity and vigilance leads to illumination, but only in accordance with the invocation.

The Imām al-Ghazālī* has said

> Invocation is an inner reality in which the Invoked takes possession of the heart while the invoker is effaced and vanishes. But it has three coverings, one closer to the kernel than the others. The kernel as such is beyond the three coverings, yet the virtue of the coverings lies in their being the way to the kernel.

The uppermost covering is remembrance with the tongue only. The invoker unceasingly invokes with his tongue, striving for the presence of the heart simultaneously, since the heart must consent to be present in the invocation. If it were left to its own nature, it would certainly wander through the valleys of thought until it joined the tongue; and then the light of the heart would burn away passions and evil spirits. Its own invocation would take hold and that of the tongue would become weaker; the body and soul would become filled with light; and the heart would be purified of other-than-God. At this stage temptations cease and there is no abode for the devil. The heart becomes a receptacle for inspirations and a polished mirror able to reflect divine revelations and gnostic perceptions. When remembrance permeates the heart and

*Persons mentioned in the text are identified in the Appendix, pp. 226 ff.

diffuses throughout the body, then every member of the body invokes God commensurate with its spiritual state.

Al-Jurayrī said, 'One of our friends used to say '*Allāh*, *Allāh*' frequently. One day a tree trunk fell on his head and fractured his skull. The blood spilled on the ground spelling *Allāh*, *Allāh*.'

Section [Two]

Remembrance is like a fire that neither stays nor spreads. When it enters a house, it says, 'It is I; there is no one else but Me,' which is one of the meanings, of 'There is no divinity but God'. If it finds kindling inside, it consumes it and becomes fire. If it finds darkness therein, it becomes light, thus illuminating the house. If there is already a light in the house, then it becomes 'light upon light'.[8]

Likewise with the body: invoking removes from it impure substances which are due to intemperance in eating or result from consuming forbidden foods. As for what is obtained from lawful food, it does not affect it. When the injurious parts are burned away and the sound parts remain, every part will be heard invoking as if the trumpet had been blown.[9]

At first, remembrance occurs in the area of the head, so it is here that you will experience the sound of cymbals and horns. Invoking is powerful: when it descends into a place, it does so with its horns and cymbals, because the invocation is against everything except the Truth. When it settles in some place, it actively seeks to expel its opposite, as we find in the combination of water and fire. After these sounds, you hear various others, such as the rippling of water, the wind blowing, fire blazing, the sound of the windmill, horses galloping, and leaves rustling in the wind.

The reason for this is due to the fact that man is composed of every substance, both noble and base, from soil and water, fire and air, and heaven and earth; these sounds are between these pairs. Every element and basic nature belongs to these substances. Whosoever has heard something of these sounds glorifies God and declares Him holy with his whole tongue. That is the result of invoking with the tongue with the force of total absorption. Perhaps the servant will reach the stage where, if he should stop invoking orally, his heart will stir in his breast seeking remembrance, like the movements of an unborn child in the womb of his mother.

Some have said that the heart is like Jesus, son of Mary عليه السلام and the remembrance his breast milk. When the heart grows and becomes strong, there arises in it a longing for the Truth as well as sighs and compulsive pangs of yearning for the invocation and the Invoked. The invocation of the heart is similar to the buzzing of a bee, neither a loud, disturbing sound, nor hidden and mysterious. When the Invoked takes possession of the heart and the invocation is effaced and disappears, the invoker should not pay attention to the remembrance or to the heart. If he should do so, then they would become a distracting veil.

This is self-extinction: that a man be extinguished from himself. Therefore, he does not feel anything in his limbs or anything exterior to himself nor any inner phenomena. Rather he is oblivious to all that, and all that vanishes from him as he goes first to his Lord, then comes back again to himself. Should it occur to the invoker during that time that he is completely extinguished from himself, then that would be a flaw and an opaqueness. For perfection is to be effaced from oneself and from the state of extinction. Hence, extinction from the state of extinction is the goal of extinction. Extinction is the beginning of the path: it is travelling to God Most High. Guidance comes afterwards. What I mean by guidance is the guidance of God, as described by the Friend of God, Abraham: 'Lo! I am going unto my Lord Who will guide me'.[10]

This total absorption rarely remains or lasts. If the invoker perseveres, it will become a deeply-rooted habit and a permanent state by which he may ascend to the highest domains. In this state of absorption, he may look upon pure, real Being and be imprinted with the nature of the invisible Realm (*al-Malakūt*) and have the holiness of the Divinity (*al-Lāhūt*) revealed to him. The first thing that is manifested to the invoker in that domain is the essence of the angels and the spirits of the Prophets and saints, and this, in beautiful forms through which certain realities overflow upon him. That is the beginning, until his degree of realization is higher than the prototypal forms and he encounters the self-evidence of the Truth in everything.

This is the fruit of the essence of invoking. Its beginning is only with the tongue; then comes invocation with the heart with effort; then comes invocation with the heart naturally; then comes possession of the heart by the Invoked and the effacement of the invoker. This is the secret of the *ḥadīth* of the Prophet ﷺ 'Whosoever wishes to feast in the gardens of Paradise, then let him remember God frequently',[11] as well as the *ḥadīth*: 'Hidden remembrance is seventy-fold better than the remembrance which the guardian angels hear'.

The sign of the invocation's reaching the innermost Self is the absence of the invoker from both the invocation and the Invoked. The invocation of the Self (*dhikru's-sirr*) is ecstasy and drowning in it. Amongst its signs is that when you quit the invocation, it does not quit you. That is the exaltation of the invocation in you that rouses you from absence of mind to presence of mind. Another of its signs is the feeling that your head and limbs are bound as if you were shackled with chains. Still another sign is that its fires never abate nor do its spiritual lights disappear. Rather, you will always see lights ascending and others descending, while the fires are around you, pure, blazing, and burning. When the invocation reaches the innermost centre of consciousness at the moment the invoker becomes silent, the invocation becomes like a needle piercing his tongue or as if his whole face were a tongue invoking through a profuse light.

Subtle point: Know that every remembrance that your heart is conscious of is heard by the guardian angels. Their awareness unites with your awareness. Herein lies a mystery: when your invocation is absent from your consciousness by your total absorption in the Invoked, your remembrance is also absent from the consciousness of the guardian angels.

Note: Invoking the letters of God's Name without presence of mind is invocation of the tongue; invoking with presence of mind is invocation of the heart; and invoking with an absence of self-awareness because of absorption in the Invoked is the invocation of the Self – this is the hidden invocation!

Section [Three]

Sustenance of the outer man comes from the movements of the body; sustenance of the inner man comes from the movements of the heart; spiritual sustenance of one's most interior being is through tranquility; and sustenance of the intellect is through extinction of one's consciousness of tranquility, so that the servant is tranquil for God and with God. There is no nourishment in food for the spirit, for it sustains physical forms. But the sustenance of the spirit and the heart is the remembrance of God, the Knower of the Invisible. God Most High has said, 'Those who believe and whose hearts have rest in the remembrance of God: verily in the remembrance of God do hearts find rest!'[12]

When you invoke God Most High, all who hear you invoke with you, because you invoke with your tongue, then with your heart, then with your soul, then with your spirit, then with your intellect, then with your innermost Self. All of that is one invocation. When you invoke God Most High with your tongue, all inanimate things invoke with the invocation of your tongue. When you invoke with your heart, the universe and all of God's worlds therein invoke with your heart. When you invoke with your soul, the heavens and all therein invoke with you. When you invoke with your spirit, the Pedestal of God and all of its worlds invoke with you. When you invoke with your intellect, the bearers of the Throne, the angels, archangels, and the spirits drawn near to God, all of whom circumambulate the Throne, invoke with you. When you invoke with your innermost Self, the Throne, with all of its worlds, invokes with you until the invocation is united with the Essence.

Addendum: The breath (*nafas*) is the subtle, ethereal substance which carries the life force, sensory perception, and volitional movement. Al-Ḥakīm called it 'the animal spirit'; it is the intermediate between the heart, which is the rational soul, and the body. It is said that the soul is referred to in the venerable Qur'ān as the olive tree that is described as being blessed . . .'neither of the East nor of the West . . .' [13] because the soul confers a greater rank on man and because it effects his purification, for it is neither from the East of the world of pure spirits, nor from the West of the world of material bodies. It is of three types: the one that incites to evil; the self-blaming one; and the recollected one.

The soul that incites to evil (*an-nafs al-ammārah bi's-sū'*) is that which inclines to physical nature and commands one to engage in sensual pleasures and carnal appetities. It draws the heart toward the lowest region and is the abode of iniquity and the source of blameworthy morals and evil deeds. It is the soul of the masses. It is tenebrous; and for it, the invocation is like a lamp lit in a dark house.

The self-blaming soul (*an-nafs al-lawwāmah*) is that which is illuminated by the light of the heart to an extent commensurate with its degree of wakefulness from the slumber of forgetfulness. It is vigilant and begins by correcting its state, which wavers between the Divinity and creatures. Every time something bad issues forth from the self-blaming soul by virtue of its dark nature and character, the light of divine admonition suddenly comes upon it, and it starts blaming itself. The soul repents of its errors, asking God's pardon and returns to the door of the Forgiving, the Merciful. For this reason God has extolled it by mentioning it in His words (exalted be He!): 'Nay, I swear by the Day of Resurrection; nay, I swear by the self-blaming soul.'[14]

It is as if it saw itself in a house full of objectionable things, such as filth, dogs, pigs, panthers, tigers, or elephants, and it worked diligently to eliminate them, after having been soiled by the different impurities and injured by the various types of predatory animals. So the self-blaming soul perseveres in invoking and turning to God in repentance until the power of the invocation triumphs over all those things and expels them. Then the soul approaches peacefulness and does not cease to gather furnishings for the house until the house is adorned with all kinds of praiseworthy things and is thereby made lustrous. The house is then suitable for the descent of the Sovereign Lord into it. When the Sovereign Lord descends into the soul and the Truth is revealed, the soul becomes recollected.

The recollected soul (*an-nafs al-muṭma'innah*) is the one whose enlightenment is brought about by the light of the heart until it is stripped of blameworthy attributes and takes on praiseworthy virtues. Then it turns in the direction of the heart completely, following it in its ascent to the regions of the world of Holiness (*ᶜālam al-quds*) far above the world of impurity, diligent in acts of obedience and tranquil in the presence of the 'Exalter of ranks'[15] until its Lord addresses it by His words: 'But ah! thou soul at peace! Return unto thy Lord, content in His good pleasure! Enter thou among My servants! Enter thou My Garden!'[16]

First Foundation: Proofs from the Qur'ān

God Most High said, 'O ye who believe! Remember God often with much remembrance. And glorify Him morning and evening.'[17]

He Most High also said, 'Such as remember God, standing, sitting, and reclining . . .'.[18]

'. . . and men who remember God much and women who remember—God hath prepared for them forgiveness and a vast reward.'[19]

'Therefore remember Me, I will remember you.'[20]

'Those who believe and whose hearts have rest in the remembrance of God: verily in the remembrance of God do hearts find rest!'[21]

'Remember thy Lord much, and praise Him in the evening and in the morning.'[22]

'Remember the name of thy Lord at morning and evening.'[23]

Second Foundation: Proofs from the Sunnah

Section [1]: On What Has Been Transmitted and Agreed Upon Concerning the Merit of the Invocation.

It was reported that Abū Saʿīd al-Khudrī (may God be pleased with him!) said 'Muʿāwiyah came upon a circle of people in the mosque, so he said, 'Why have you assembled?'

They said, 'We have gathered to remember God Most High.'

He said, 'By God, you have not gathered except for that?'

They said 'By God, nothing else has brought us together.'

He said, 'Verily, I have not made you swear out of suspicion of you. Amongst those who were with the Prophet ﷺ I had the lowest rank, nor was there anyone who told fewer *ḥadīths* than I. Nevertheless, the Messenger of God ﷺ came upon a circle of his companions and said:

'Why have you assembled?'

They said, 'We are sitting invoking God Most High and we praise Him for having guided us to Islam and for having blessed us.'

The Prophet said, 'By God, you have not gathered except for that?'

They said, 'By God, only that has brought us together.'

He said, 'Verily, I have not made you swear out of suspicion of you, but rather because Gabriel came to me and informed me that God Most High boasts of you to the angels.'

Muslim and at-Tirmidhī transmitted this *ḥadīth*, whereas an-Nasā'ī transmitted the chain of authority only.[24] Razīn added by saying, 'Then the Prophet related to us the following':

> Never do a people gather together in any house of God Most High, reciting God's Book, studying it amongst themselves, and invoking God, without peace descending upon them, mercy enveloping them, the angels surrounding them, and God remembering them amongst those with Him.[25]

It is related through Muslim and at-Tirmidhī that Abū Muslim al-Agharr said, 'I testify that Abū Hurayrah and Abū Saʿīd witnessed that the Messenger of God ﷺ said, 'A people do not sit invoking God without the angels surrounding them, mercy enveloping them, peace descending upon them, and God remembering them amongst those with Him.''[26]

Peace (*as-sakīnah*) comes from tranquillity and repose. The Qāḍī ʿIyāḍ reported the following words of the Prophet ﷺ 'This peace descends due to the reading of the Qur'ān'.[27] It is a mercifulness, it is also said to be repose or dignity or that by which man becomes calm (using Form I of the verb *sakana*); and this is well known. (It is said that some linguists construe this as Form II of the verb *sakkana*, which intensifies it so that it means 'that which makes man be or become calm'; this on the authority of al-Farrā' and al-Kisā'ī.) It is very likely that that which descended due to the reading of the Qur'ān is the peace which God Most High mentioned in His Book: '. . .wherein is peace of reassurance from your Lord'.[28]

It is said that peace is a mystery like the wind, or was created with a face like that of a human being, or that it is a spirit from God which speaks to men and guides them when they differ on a matter, and so on. From what we have already mentioned, peace is probably something similar to that which descends on whoever recites the Qur'ān or gathers to invoke, because it belongs to the Spirit and the angels. God knows best!

Abū Hurayrah (may God be pleased with him!) related that 'The Messenger ﷺ was walking along the road to Mecca over a mountain called Jumdān and he said, "Walk on, this is Jumdān. The pious recluses have gone before!" Those with him said, "Who are the pious recluses, O Messenger of God?" He said, "Those who remember God often." This account is from Muslim.[29] However, at-Tirmidhi's version states, 'They said, "O Messenger of God, who are the pious recluses?" He said, "Those who are greatly devoted *(al-mustahtarūn)* to the remembrance of God, which rids them of their burdens so that they arrive on the Day of Judgment unburdened."'[30]

In Arabic the pious recluses are called *al-mufarridūn*; it is also said to be written as *al-mufridūn*. One says, 'The man was alone *(farada)* in his opinion.' Form I *(farada)*, Form II *(farrada)*, Form IV *(afrada)*, and Form X *(istafrada)* of the verb all have the same meaning, that is, to be independent and alone in one's planning. What is meant by this is that the *mufarridūn* are those who invoke God alone. The word is also defined as 'the ones whose contemporaries have died and the times in which they lived have passed, leaving them behind so they remember God Most High.' He who is utterly devoted to something *(al-mustahtar)* is enamoured of it and assiduously applies himself to it out of love and desire for it.

The Qāḍī ʿIyāḍ states in his book *al-Mashāriq* that Ibn al-ʿArabī said that Form II of the verb *(farrada)* is used when what is meant is that a person devotes himself to the acquisition of religious knowledge and secludes himself from people and is by himself for the sake of observing religious commandments and prescriptions.

Al-Azharī has said of the *mufaridūn*, 'They are the ones who withdraw to invoke God and do not associate anything else with Him'. It is said that the meaning of *uhtirū* is 'They were afflicted with confusion.' The meaning of *mufaridūn* is said to be 'Those who affirm the Oneness of God and remember naught but God Most High and worship Him faithfully and sincerely.' It has the same meaning as in the sentence: 'So-and-so was totally absorbed in obedience to God', that is, he did not cease to persevere in prayer and remembrance until he passed away due to decrepitude and loss of strength and vigour. Some grammarians have said that *uhtirū* means 'to be very devoted to something'.

Al-Bukhārī transmitted the following tradition from Abū Hurayrah, (may God be pleased with him!): 'The Messenger of God ﷺ said, "Indeed, God has angels who circle over the public ways, seeking those who invoke. When they find people invoking God, they call out, 'Tell us your needs'. Then they surround them with their wings from the earth to the lowest heaven. Their Lord, Who is more knowing than they, asks the angels, 'What do my servants say?'"'

'They say they praise Thee and exalt Thee and extol Thee.'

'Then God says, "Have they seen Me?"'

'No, by God, they have not seen Thee.'

'He asks, "How would they have been if they had seen Me?"'

'The angels reply, "If they had seen Thee, they would have been far more adoring servants of Thine and more praising of Thee".'

'God says, "What do they ask?"'

'The angels respond, "They ask Thee for Paradise".

'Have they seen it?'

'No, by God, they have not seen it, our Lord.'

'Then how would they have been if they had seen it?'

'The angels say, "If they had seen Paradise, they would have been more eager for it, more beseeching of it, and much more desirous".'

'God asks, "From what do they seek protection?"'

'They seek protection from hellfire.'

'Have they seen it?'

'The angels say, "If they had seen it, they would have fled from it more intensely and feared it much more".'

'God says, "I call upon you as witnesses that I have pardoned them".'

'One of the angels says, "There is So-and-So among the

invokers who is not one of them but has only come out of a need".'

'They are all participants; their companion will not suffer.'[31]

At-Tirmidhi transmitted from Anas (may God be pleased with him!) that the Messenger of God ﷺ said, 'When you pass by the gardens of Paradise, graze therein.' Those with the Prophet asked, 'What are the gardens of Paradise?' He answered, 'Circles of people invoking'.[32]

The Imām Aḥmad transmitted the following *ḥadīth* of the Prophet from Ibn Masʿūd: 'Verily the devil moved amongst a people gathered to remember God but could not divide them. Then he came upon a circle of people conversing about this temporal world, so he lured them until they fell to fighting with each other. Those invoking God arose and restrained the latter and they dispersed.'

Section [2]: On the Merit of the Invoker with Respect to Others.

At-Tirmidhī reported that Abū Hurayrah (may God be pleased with him!) witnessed that the Messenger of God ﷺ said, 'No servant ever said "There is no divinity but God" sincerely from the heart but that the gates of Heaven were opened to him so that he could reach the Throne of God, as long as he avoided mortal sins.'[33]

Mālik said, 'It has reached me that the Messenger of God ﷺ used to say, "One who remembers God among the forgetful is like one who fights while others flee, or one who remembers God among the forgetful is like a green twig on a dry tree".'[34] Another account reads that he is

> like a green tree in the midst of a dry forest; and one who remembers God among the forgetful is like a lamp in a dark house; God shows the one who remembers Him among the forgetful his place in Paradise while he is alive. The one who remembers God in the midst of the forgetful is forgiven sins equal to the number of articulate and inarticulate beings.[35]

The 'articulate beings' are mankind; the 'inarticulate beings' are animals. (The Imām Mālik transmitted it thus.)

In his book *al-Muwaṭṭa'*, Mālik transmitted the following: Muʿādh ibn Jabal related that 'The servant cannot perform a better deed which will save him from God's punishment than the remembrance of God.'[36]

Through at-Tirmidhī, Abū Saʿīd al-Khudrī (may God be pleased with him!) related that the Messenger of God ﷺ was asked, 'Which servants are the most virtuous and the most highly esteemed by God on the Day of Judgment?' He said, 'Those who remember God often.' Someone asked, 'O Messenger of God, and who among the warriors for the cause of God and Islam?' He answered, 'If one struck with his sword until it was broken and became red with blood, verily, even so, the one who invokes God is higher than he in rank.'[37]

Razīn reported the following account: 'The Messenger of God ﷺ was asked, "What type of worship is best and most highly esteemed by God on the Day of Judgment?" He said, "Invoking God Most High".'

Abū Mūsā al-Ashʿarī (may God be pleased with him!) related that the Prophet ﷺ said, 'The difference between a house wherein God is remembered and a house wherein He is not is like the difference between the living and the dead.' This is thus reported in Muslim's *Ṣaḥīḥ*.[38] According to al-Bukhārī, the account reads: 'The difference between someone who remembers His Lord and someone who does not is like the difference between the living and the dead.'[39]

Abū Hurayrah (may God be pleased with him!) reported that the Messenger of God ﷺ said, 'God Most High says, "I am of the same thinking as my servant is toward Me, and I am with him when he remembers Me. For if he remembers Me in himself, I remember him in Myself; if he remembers Me in a gathering, I remember him in an assembly better than his; if he approaches Me a span, I approach him a cubit; if he approaches Me a cubit, I approach him a fathom; and if he comes to Me walking, I come to him running".' (Al-Bukhārī, Muslim, and at-Tirmidhī transmitted it.)[40]

Abū Umāmah said, 'I heard the Messenger of God ﷺ say, "For him who goes to bed in a state of purity and invokes God until sleep overcomes him, not a night will pass when he asks of God of the good things of this world and the next but that God will give them to him".' (At-Tirmidhī transmitted it.)[41]

ʿUmar (may God be pleased with him!), related 'that the Prophet ﷺ sent an expedition toward Najd. They took a great amount of spoils and hastened to return. A man among those who did not go said, "We have never seen an expedition as quick to return or with better spoils than this one". Then the Prophet ﷺ said, "Shall I not show you a people who have greater spoils and are faster in returning? They are a people who witness the dawn prayer than sit to invoke God Most High until the sun rises. Those are the quickest to return to God and have the best spoils".' (At-Tirmidhī transmitted it.)[42]

Section [Three]

ʿAbd Allāh ibn Bishr [or Busr] reported that a man said, 'O Messenger of God, indeed the ways of doing good are many but I cannot perform them all, so tell me something which I can follow, but do not make it too long for me, lest I forget'.

Another version of the above reads, 'Verily the religious laws of Islam are numerous and I have become old, so tell me something which I can follow, but do not make it too long for me, lest I forget'. The Prophet said, 'Your tongue should not cease to be moist with the remembrance of God.' (At-Tirmidhī transmitted it.)[43]

ʿĀ'ishah (may God be pleased with her!) said, 'The Messenger of God ﷺ used to remember God at all times.' (Muslim, Abū Dā'ūd, and at-Tirmidhī transmitted it.)[44]

CHAPTER [ONE]

Invoking Aloud

AT-TIRMIDHĪ relates that ʿUmar (may God be pleased with him!) reported that the Messenger of God (may God bless him and grant him peace!) said,

> Whoever enters the marketplace and utters, 'There is no divinity but God, the One; He has no partner; to Him belong the Kingdom and praise; He gives life and takes life; He is alive and never dies; in His hand is all that is good; and He has power over everything', God records one million good deeds for him and erases one million bad ones for him, and elevates him one million degrees.[1]

In another account, the last line reads instead, '. . . and builds a house for him in Paradise'.[2]

Yet another version states that the Messenger of God ﷺ said, 'He who enters the market place and calls out at the top of his voice'—and the rest of the above *ḥadīth* is cited up to 'everything', followed by: 'God records for him a hundred thousand good deeds'.[3]

In al-Bukhārī's account, Abū Saʿīd, the client of Ibn ʿAbbās, reports that Ibn ʿAbbās informed him that raising the voice in invocation when people had departed from the prescribed prayer was a practice in the time of the Messenger of God ﷺ. Ibn ʿAbbās said, 'I would know when they left by that'.

The Prophet ﷺ has said from God, 'He who remembers Me in an assembly, I remember him in an assembly greater than his.'[4]

It is related that Abū Bakr (may God be pleased with him!) used to lower his voice in prayer at night and not raise his voice in reading the Qur'ān, whereas ʿUmar used to raise his voice in prayer. So the Messenger of God ﷺ asked Abū Bakr about is way and the latter answered, 'He to whom I speak intimately hears my voice'. Then he questioned ʿUmar, who responded, 'I stir the somnolent and drive out the devil and please the Merciful'. Then the Messenger of God ﷺ instructed Abū Bakr to raise his voice a little and ʿUmar to lower his a little. Do you not see that he ﷺ instructed Abū Bakr to raise his voice aloud and did not instruct ʿUmar to whisper, but rather to lower his voice, which is not whispering? If this is so with respect to Qur'ānic recitation—which is the best of all forms of remembrance—then other invocations should be done likewise, and it is even more appropriate that they should be done that way.

It is incumbent upon the invoker, when he is alone, if he is of the advanced, to lower his voice in invocation, but if he is of the generality of believers, to invoke aloud. If the invokers are gathered in an assembly, then it is more fitting that they raise their voices in unison while invoking in a rhythmically balanced manner. Some have said,

> the likeness between the invocation of one person alone and that of a group is as the likeness between one muezzin and a group of muezzins. Just as the voices of a group of muezzins cut through a mass of air more than one voice does, so too does the invocation of a group of people of one heart make a deeper impression and have a stronger impact in lifting the veils from the heart than does the invocation of one invoker by himself. Moreover, in such a case, everyone obtains the reward of both invoking by himself and hearing others invoke.

God compares hardened hearts to stone in His words (exalted be He!): 'Then, after that, your hearts were hardened and became as stone, or worse than stone for hardness . . .'.[5] Stone does not break except by force. Likewise the hardness of the heart does not vanish except by a powerful invocation.

Section [1]: *On Warning Against Abandoning the Invocation.*
God Most High has said, 'And he whose sight is dim to the remembrance of the Beneficent. We assign unto him a devil who becometh his comrade; and lo! they surely turn them from the way of God, and yet they deem that they are rightly guided.'[6]

According to Abū Dā'ūd, Abū Hurayrah (may God be pleased with him!) reported that the Messenger of God ﷺ said, 'Whosoever sits down in a place and does not remember God therein is subject to God's retribution, and whosoever lies down on a bed and does not remember God therein is subject to God's retribution.'[7]

In at-Tirmidhī's version, the Messenger said, 'Never have a people sat together without remembering God therein or praying upon their Prophet but that they were subject to God's retribution. If He wished, He could either chastise them or pardon them'.[8] Concerning this, Abū Hurayrah reported that the Messenger of God ﷺ said, 'There is not a people who depart from a gathering without having remembered God therein but that they depart with a smell more offensive than that of a donkey's cadaver, and affliction befalls them.' (Abū Dā'ūd transmitted it.)[9]

The etymology of the word *tirah* (retribution) has to do with 'shortcoming'; but here it means 'consequence'. One says: 'I inflicted harm on the man' (*watartu' r-rajula tirah*), which is of the same grammatical pattern as 'I made him a promise' (*wa ͨadtuhu ͨidah*).

Muͨādh ibn Jabal reported that the Messenger of God ﷺ said, 'The inhabitants of Paradise are not distressed except when an hour passes in which they do not remember God'. (Ibn as-Sunnī transmitted it.)[10] It is related that 'Every soul will leave this world thirsty except the invoker of God Most High.'

Sahl said, 'I do not know of a viler disobedience than abandoning the remembrance of this Lord.' An-Nawawī said, 'Everything has a punishment, and the punishment of the gnostic is his severance from the invocation.'

Section [2]: *On the Invocation According to Traditions of the Pious Ancestors.*

Anas ibn Mālik (may God be pleased with him!) said, 'The invocation of God is a sign of faith, a liberation from hypocrisy, a protection from the devil, and a refuge from hellfire.'

Mālik ibn Dinār said, 'Whosoever does not prefer the intimacy of discourse with God to that of mankind diminishes in knowledge, becomes blind of heart, and wastes his life away.' In this regard al-Ḥasan has said,

> Seek for sweetness in three things: in ritual prayer, in the invocation, and in reciting the Qur'ān. If you have found it, well and good. If not, then know that the door is closed, because every heart which does not know God has no intimacy with the invocation of God and relies not on Him.

God Most High has said, 'And when God alone is mentioned, the hearts of those who do not believe in the Hereafter are repelled and when those whom they worship beside Him are mentioned, behold! they are glad.'[11]

One of the gnostics said:

> Sustenance of the outer man comes from the movements of the body; sustenance of the inner man comes from the movements of the heart; sustenance of one's most interior being is through tranquillity; and sustenance of the intellect is through extinction of one's consciousness of tranquillity, so that the servant is tranquil for the sake of God, through God, and with God.

And this has been said: 'Whoever, for the sake of God, carries out the inner reality of the invocation, of the praise of God, and of gratitude, He subjects unto him the universe and all creatures therein.'

Mutarrif ibn Abī Bakr said, 'The lover never tires of conversing with his Beloved.' And this has been said: 'Whoever does not experience the loneliness of heedlessness will not savour the taste of the intimacy of remembrance.' ʿAṭā said, 'Lightning will not strike the invoker of God Most High.'

Al-Ḥāmid al-Aswad said,

> I was with Ibrāhīm al-Khawāṣṣ on a journey, and we came to a place where there were many snakes. He unsaddled his mount and sat down, so I did likewise. When the night began to cool and the air to chill, the snakes came out. I cried out to the Shaykh, but he said, 'Remember God!' So I did, and the snakes left. Then they returned, and I called out to him but he said the same thing. I did not cease being in that state till morning. When we arose in the morning, the Shaykh got up and walked, and I walked with him. Suddenly a huge snake, which had been coiled around him, fell from the inner folds of his garment. I said to him, 'Did you not feel it?' He answered, 'No, it has been a long time since I have seen a night more pleasant than last night.'

This has been said:

> The remembrance of God in the heart is the sword of the novices with which they combat their enemies and repel the afflictions that befall them. Indeed, when tribulation leads the servant astray, if he occupies his heart with God, all that he dislikes leaves him immediately.

And this has been said:

> When the invocation takes possession of the heart, if the devil draws near, he is made prostrate the way a man would

> be felled. As a result, the devils gather about the heart and ask, 'What happened to it?' Some of them respond, 'Intimacy with God has smitten it!'

This has been said: 'Verily, the angel of death consults with the invoker when the time comes to take his soul.' In the Gospel there is this: 'Remember Me when you are angry and I will remember you when I am angry. Be content with My help to you, for My help to you is better than your own help is to yourself.' Dhu'n-Nūn al-Miṣrī said, 'Whoever truly remembers God forgets everything alongside of the invocation, while God takes care of everything for him, and is for him a compensation for everything.'

Third Foundation: Sincerity

Know that everything is to be thought of as being mixed with something else. When its mixture is purified, it is called 'pure' (*khāliṣ*); a purified deed is called 'sincerity' (*ikhlāṣ*). Everyone who performs a voluntary act purely necessarily has a certain personal interest in that deed; so, when there is but one fault in the deed, that deed is called 'sincerity', except that custom dictates specifically that sincerity of devotion is the stripping of all faults from one's intention to draw near to God, just as heresy is 'deviation', but custom specifies that it is 'deviation from the Truth'. When you have learned that, then we maintain that the motive for a deed is either spiritual only—and this is sincerity—or it is diabolical only—and this is hypocrisy; or it is composed of both. If it is the last-named, either the first two are equal, or the spiritual is stronger, or the psychical is stronger.

First Category: When the Motive Is Spiritual Only

This is not to be conceived of except as coming from the lover of God Most High, who is drowned in preoccupation with Him to such an extent that no place remains in his heart for the love of this world. At that moment all his actions and movements reveal this quality. He does not fulfil a need nor does he sleep, or like to eat or drink, for example, unless this be done in order to carry out a necessity or to strengthen obedience. The likes of such a one, were he to eat or drink or fulfil a need, would be pure of deed in all his movements and repose.

Second Category: When the Motive Is Psychical Only
This is not to be conceived of except as coming from the lover of 'self' and of this world, who is drowned in preoccupation with them to such an extent that no place remains in his soul for the love of God. Then all his actions take on this characteristic and none of his religious observances are free of it.

As for the remaining third category in which the two motives are equal, the Imām Fakhr ad-Dīn ar-Rāzī said, 'It appears that both are in opposition to one another and will gradually become imbalanced'. Then a deed will be neither for nor against a person. Whenever one of the two tendencies dominates in a person, then that which could have equalized the other tendency in him is lost. The excess cannot but then be the cause for its corresponding effect. That is what is meant by His words (exalted be He!): 'Whosoever doeth an atom's weight of good will see it and whoso doeth ill an atom's weight will see it.'[12]

To be perfectly exact in this matter, actions produce effects on the heart. If the influence is free of opposition, the effect is free of weakness. If the influence is combined with its opposite, then, if they are equal to one another, they gradually cancel each other out. When one of the two motives gains ascendancy, then it is inevitable that excess should occur in proportion to the diminishment of the other. Hence, an equibalance between both motives can take place or an imbalance; in the latter case, the excess amount would remain devoid of its opposite, so that it would most certainly have some effect.

Just as the effect of an atom's weight of food or drink or medicine is not lost on the body, so too the effect of an atom's weight of goodness or evil is not lost either in drawing near to God's door or in estrangement from Him. When a person combines something that will draw him closer to God by a span with something that takes him back by a span, then he returns to a previous condition which was neither for nor against him. If one of two deeds brings him closer by two spans while the other sets him back by one span, he has most assuredly gained a span.

He who claims that there is no reward for the action of mixed motives advances two arguments. The first one is based on what Abū Hurayrah related that the Prophet ﷺ said to him about the person who had associated partners with God in his deed: 'Take your recompense from the one for whom you have worked.' The second is also based on his authority ﷺ when he said, 'Verily, God Most High says, "I am of all partners the least in need of association; whoever performs a deed in which he makes a partner of someone other than Me, I leave My share therein to My partner".'[13]

I reply that the word 'partner' (*sharīk*) is to be related to an equality between two motivating causes. We have already shown that when there are two equal things, each cancels out the other.

Know that a diabolic suggestion might be present in the forms of devotional acts, in the various types of good deeds, and in the love of charismatic phenomena. The devil does not cease being with man until man is purified. When he becomes sincere, the devil leaves him; man then no longer covets and exerts himself in thankfulness. The good does not come to man in just any way but only through the door of sincerity. So be sincere! If you were to be in a state of sincerity, you would not think of yourself as being in a state of sincerity!

Section [3]: *On the Rules of Conduct for the Invocation.*

The invocation has rules of conduct preceding it, subsequent to it, and associated with it. Some of them are outward and some are inward. As for the rules of conduct which precede, we say that after repentance and self-discipline, the seeker must engage in spiritual exercises, refine his inner nature, and prepare himself for the decrees of the Divine Presence by withdrawing from creatures, lessening outside contacts, removing obstacles, acquiring knowledge of this world and the next—which is enjoined upon all men—and by consecrating himself to God. These rules are the inner life of the seeker's spiritual stations, for they are based on religious law, not on custom. The seeker must choose an invocation which is appropriate to his state; then he must devote himself to it and persevere.

Among the rules of conduct are the wearing of proper, clean, sweet-smelling clothes and maintaining purity of the stomach by eating lawful food. Although the invocation expels the parts arising from unlawful food, nevertheless, when the stomach is empty of unlawful food or whatever is doubtful, the benefit of the invocation is in a greater or more lasting illumination of the heart. When there is unlawful food in the stomach, the invocation washes it out and purifies the stomach. Consequently, at such times its benefit in illuminating the heart is weaker. Do you not see that if you wash soiled things in water, it removes the dirt, but they are not very clean? For that reason, it is preferable to wash them a second or a third time. However, if an area to be washed is already free of dirt, it increases in beauty and radiance from the first laundering. When the invocation descends into the heart, if there is darkness within, it illuminates it; and if there is already light, the invocation increases the light and intensifies it.

The rules of conduct associated with the invocation[14] are sincerity, perfuming the place of invoking with a sweet fragrance for the sake of the angels and jinn, sitting cross-legged facing the direction of prayer, if one is alone, and if one is in a group, then one sits wheresoever one winds up in the gathering. One should put the palms of one's hands on the thighs, close one's eyes and face straight ahead. Some say that if one is under the direction of a shaykh, one should imagine him in front of oneself, because the shaykh is one's companion and guide along the path. At the beginning of the invocation, the novice should ask with his heart for the help of his shaykh's inspiration (*himmah*), believing that asking help of him is the same as asking help of the Prophet ﷺ for the shaykh is his representative.

The novice should invoke with perfect force and respectful veneration. 'There is no divinity but God' (*Lā ilāha illa'llāh*) should rise from above his navel. By the phrase 'There is no divinity' (*lā ilāha*), he should intend excluding from the heart what is other-than-God. By the phrase 'but God' (*illa'llāh*), he should intend uniting the formula with the cone-shaped physical heart so as to fix *illa'llāh* firmly in the heart and let it flow throughout all the members of the body, causing the meaning of the invocation to be present in his heart at every instant.

One of the sages said that it is not proper to invoke repetitively time after time except with a meaning which differs from the first one. He said, 'The lowest level of the invocation is the one wherein every time one says, "There is no divinity but God", one expels from the heart whatever is other-than-God. But if one pays attention to it, then one has as much as ascribed to it the position of deity.' The Most High has said: 'Hast thou seen him who chooseth for his god his own passion?'[15] 'Set not up with God any other god . . ..'[16] 'Did I not charge you, O ye sons of Adam, that ye worship not the devil? . . ..'[17]

In a *ḥadīth* of the Prophet ﷺ he says, 'Perish the servant of the *dinār*, perish the servant of the *dirham*!' Even if the *dinār* and the *dirham* are not worshipped through actual bowing and prostration, nevertheless they are worshipped by turning one's heart to them. So, the invoker's 'There is no divinity but God' is not valid except by negating whatever is in one's soul and heart that is other-than-God Most High. Whoever fills his heart with the forms of sensorial things, then, even if he were to utter the phrase a thousand times, rarely would he realize its meaning in his heart. But if he emptied his heart of all that is other-than-God and said

Allāh one time, he would find such bliss that the tongue could not describe. Shaykh ʿAbd ar-Raḥīm al-Qināʾī [or Qunnāʾī] said, 'I said *Lā ilāha illa 'llāh* one time, then it did not happen to me again'.

A black slave was with the tribe of Isrāʾīl when it was wandering in the desert. Whenever he said *Lā ilāha illa'llāh*, he became white from head to feet. The realization of *Lā ilāha illa'llāh* by the slave is one of the states of the heart that can be neither expressed by the tongue nor thought out by the mind. While *Lā ilāha illā'llāh* is the very essence of the ways of approaching God, it is also the key to the inner realities of the heart and to the seeker's ascension to the invisible worlds.

There are those who choose to invoke constantly in such a manner that the two phrases are like one without any outside or mental interruption occurring between them, so that the devil cannot intrude himself therein. For, in the likes of such a situation, the devil lies in wait because he knows the weakness of the traveller in treading through these valleys that he is not used to, especially if he is a beginner in the path. Some authorities have said, 'This uninterrupted invocation is the quickest way to the illumination of the heart and to approaching God.'

One of the authorities has said,

> The lengthening of the vowel *ā* in *Lā ilāha* (There is no divinity) is considered good and recommended because, during the time of the elongation, the invoker can visualize in his mind all opposites and contraries and expel them. That is followed by the *illa'llāh* (but God), and that is closer to sincerity because it is the acknowledgement of the Divinity. Although he negates His essence with *Lā ilāha*, he nevertheless affirms His Being with *illa'llāh*. Indeed, *illa* (except) is a light placed in the heart, illuminating it.

Another authority has said, 'Omitting the vowel elongation is more appropriate because perhaps one might die in the interval of pronouncing *Lā ilāha* before reaching *illa'llāh*.' Still another authority has said, 'If the change from disbelief to belief is intended, then omitting the elongation is more suitable in hastening the transition to belief. But if one is already a believer, then the vowel elongation is better' due to what has been previously said.

With regard to the rules of conduct subsequent to the invocation: when one becomes silent by choice, he is 'present' with his heart as one who is receptive to the inspiration of the invocation. Those rules have to do with the 'absence' (*al-ghaybah*) that takes place following the invocation, which is also called 'a sleep'. Just as God Most High made it customary to send winds as an announcement preceding the mercifulness of His cascading rain, so too did He make it customary to send the winds of the invocation as an announcement preceding His lofty mercifulness. Perhaps the invoker's heart will be filled in an instant by an inspiration that all the efforts and ascetic exercises of thirty years could not achieve. These rules of conduct are binding upon the invoker who is consciously free to choose.

As for the one who has no free choice, he is subject to whatever comes over him in the way of invocations and whatever he himself comes across among the sum total of divine mysteries. Hence there might flow from his tongue *Allāh*, *Allāh*, *Allāh* or *Hū*, *Hū*, *Hū* or *lā lā lā lā lā*, or *ā ā ā ā ā*, or *āh āh āh āh*, or a sound without any letter or noise. His behaviour, therefore, is to submit to the inspiration. After the passing of the inspiration, he should be very quiet. These are the rules of conduct for the one who needs to invoke with the tongue. As for the one who invokes with the heart, he is in no need of these rules.

CHAPTER [TWO]

Benefits of the Invocation in General

LET WHOSOEVER desires the benefits of invoking follow the established texts, inasmuch as its benefits are not insignificant nor can they be exhausted. The invocation of the traditional authorities has numerous advantages, so let us mention what comes to mind. We say: invoking repels, subdues, and tames Satan, but pleases the Compassionate (*ar-Raḥmān*). It angers Satan, removes worry and grief from the heart, attracts joy and happiness, and eliminates sadness and evils.

Invoking strengthens the heart and the body, puts inner and outer affairs in order, gladdens the heart and face, making the latter radiant. Moreover, it procures sustenance and facilitates obtaining it. It clothes the invoker in dignity; it inspires correct behaviour in every affair. Its permanence is one of the means of obtaining the love of God; it is one of the greatest of the gateways leading to that love.

Invoking causes the vigilance that leads to the station of spiritual virtue (*iḥsān*), wherein the servant adores God as if he saw Him with his very own eyes. It causes one to turn to God often; for whoever turns to God by remembering Him frequently will eventually turn to Him in all his affairs. Invoking brings closeness to the Lord and opens the door of gnosis within the heart. It bestows on the servant the veneration and reverential fear (*haybah*) of his Lord, while for the forgetful man the veil of reverential fear over his heart is very thin.

Invoking causes God's remembrance of the servant, which is the greatest honour and loftiest distinction. Through the invocation, the heart of man lives just as the seed lives through the downpour of rain. The invocation is the nourishment of the soul just as food is the nourishment of the body. Invoking polishes the heart of its rust, which is forgetfulness (*ghaflah*) and the pursuit of its passions. It is to meditation like a lamp that guides one in the dark towards an open road. It thwarts sinful actions: '. . .Verily, good deeds annul bad deeds . . .'.[1] Invoking puts an end to the estrangement that occurs between the Lord and the forgetful servant.

Whatever the formula used by the servant to remember God with, such as: 'Glory be to God!' (*subḥāna'llāh*) or 'God is Most Great' (*Allāhu Akbar*) or 'There is no divinity but God' (*Lā ilāha illa'llāh*) or any formula or praise, it calls the attention of God on the Glorious Throne to the servant. All acts of worship withdraw from the servant on the Day of Resurrection except the remembrance of God, the belief in His Oneness (*tawḥīd*), and praise of Him. Whoever gets to know God in times of prosperity through his invoking, gets to know Him in times of adversity through his piety.

A tradition states,

> Indeed, when misfortune befalls the obedient servant who frequently remembers God Most High, or when he asks of God a need, the angels say, 'My Lord, there is a familiar voice from a familiar servant'. When the forgetful person who shuns God calls upon Him or asks something of Him, the angels say, 'My Lord, there is an unknown voice from an unknown servant'.

Of all deeds there is none more redemptive from the chastisement of God, Who possesses Majesty, than the invocation. For the servant it is the cause for the descent of peace (*sakīnah*) upon him, for the encircling of angels around him, for their alighting by him, and for his being enveloped by Mercifulness. How sublime is such a grace! The invocation is for a tongue undistracted by slander, lying, and every falsehood!

The companion who sits with the invoker is not troubled by him; the invoker's close friend is happy with him. On the Day of Judgment, the invoker's encounters with others will not be a source of sorrow for him or of harm or remorse.

Invoking with tears and lamentation is a cause for obtaining the shelter of the umbral Throne on the great Day of Requital, when mankind stands for a period awaiting judgment. Whoever is diverted by the remembrance of God from making a request will be given the best of what is given to the one who does ask; and things will be made easy for the servant most of the time and in most situations.

The movement of invoking with the tongue is the easiest movement for a person. The plants of the gardens of Paradise are the invocation. Paradise is a good earth and sweet water; it is composed, indeed, of plains, and the plants therein are 'Glory be to God' (*subḥāna' llāh*), 'Praise be to God' (*al-ḥamdu li'llāh*), 'There is no divinity but God' (*Lā ilāha illa'llāh*), and 'God is Most Great' (*Allāhu Akbar*), as are found in the sound *ḥadīths*. These formulas are a means of liberating oneself from the fires of Hell and are a protection from forgetfulness in this world, the world of ignominy. The textual proof of this, as found in the Qur'ān, is: 'Therefore remember Me, I will remember you'.[3] Forgetfulness of God is what makes servants forget their souls and that is the extreme of corruption.

Invoking is a light for the servant in this world, his grave, his resurrection, and his assembling with others on the Day of Judgment. It is the fundamental principle and the door to spiritual union; it is the sign of authority whereby it assails the ego and passional desires. When the invocation is firmly rooted in the heart and drops down in it and the tongue becomes subordinate to it, the invoker is in need of nothing; so he progresses and ascends. As for the forgetful man, even if he be wealthy, he is in reality poor, and if he be powerful, he is actually base.

For the one who remembers God, invoking unites his dispersed heart and pervades his will and his broken resolve. It scatters his sadness, his sin, and the forces of Satan and his followers. Invoking brings the heart closer to the Hereafter and keeps the world away from the heart, even though the world is around it. Invoking warns the heedless heart to abandon its pleasures and deceptions. It redresses what has passed and prepares itself for what is to come.

The invocation is a tree whose fruit is gnosis; it is the treasure of every gnostic: God is with the invoker through His nearness, authority, love, bestowal of success and protection. The invocation puts in proper perspective the emancipation of slaves, the holy war and its hardships, fighting in the way of God, injury, and the expenditure of money and gold. The invocation is the summit, source, and basis of gratitude of God. He whose tongue does not cease being moist with the remembrance of God and who fears God in His prohibitions and commands is granted entrance into the Paradise of the beloved ones and nearness to the Lord of Lords. '. . . Lo! the noblest of you, in the sight of God, is the best in conduct . . ..'[4]

The invoker enters Paradise laughing and smiling and is at home therein, living in ease. Invoking removes hardness from the heart and engenders tenderness and mildness. Forgetfulness of the heart is a disease and an ailment, while remembrance is a cure for the invoker from every malady and symptom, as was said by a poet:

إذا مَرِضْنا تداوَينا بذكْرِكُمْ ونترك الذِّكْرَ أحْياناً فَنَنْتَكِسُ

When we became ill, by Your remembrance we were cured,
And when at times we abandon it, a relapse do we suffer.

Remembrance is the source and foundation of God's friendship; forgetfulness is the origin and summit of His enmity. When forgetfulness takes possession of the servant, it drives him back to God's enmity in the ugliest way. Invoking removes misfortunes, pushing them to one side, and draws unto itself blessings and every beneficial thing. It is a cause for the blessings of God and the noble angels upon him, so that he emerges out of the darkness into the light and enters the abode of peace. The gatherings to invoke are gardens of Paradise, and indulging therein pleases the Compassionate. God Most High boasts of those who remember Him to the angels of heaven, for its place among the acts of worship is the highest and most sublime.

The most excellent of those who perform good deeds are those who most often remember God in all situations. Remembrance takes the place of all deeds, it being alike whether they are connected with wealth or with something else. Invoking strengthens the limbs and facilitates pious work. It eases difficult matters, opens locked doors, mitigates hardships, and lessens toil. It is a security for the fearful and deliverance from desert wastelands. Among the participants in the race track for the winning trophy, the invoker is triumphant. Soon you will see, when the dust settles: was it a horse you rode – or a donkey?

Invoking is a cause for God's approval of His servant, because the invocation has made him aware of His Majesty and Beauty and praise. Through the invocation the dwellings of Paradise are built; but for the forgetful, no dwelling in Paradise is built. Invocations are a barrier between the servant and hellfire. If the remembrance is continuous and permanent, then the barrier is good and solid; if not, it is fragile and torn.

Remembrance is a fire that neither stays nor spreads. When it enters a house, it leaves no substance or trace therein. It eliminates the portions of food remaining which exceed one's bodily need or are forbidden to consume. Invoking removes darkness and brings forth radiant lights. Angels ask forgiveness for the servant when he perseveres in the remembrance and praise of God. Lands and mountains are proud of the one who, amongst men, remembers God while on them.

Remembrance is the sign of the thankful believer, whereas the hypocrite is rarely found to be invoking. He whose wealth or children distract him from remembering God is lost; but the one who remembers God experiences delights sweeter than the pleasure of food and drink. In this world the invoker's face and heart are covered with beauty and happiness; in the Hereafter his face is whiter and more luminous than the moon. The earth witnesses on his behalf just as it does for every person who obeys or disobeys God. Invoking elevates the participant to the most exalted of ranks and conveys him to the highest of stations.

The invoker is alive even if he be dead; while the forgetful man, even though he is alive, is actually to be counted among the dead. The invoker has his thirst quenched at death and is safe from the apprehensions of the perils associated with death. Among the forgetful, the one who remembers God is like a lamp in a dark house, while the forgetful are themselves like a dark night with no morning to follow.

If something occupies the invoker and distracts him from the remembrance of God, then he risks chastisement. If he is unmindful of this point, then it is like someone sitting with a king without the proper conduct: that will expose him to being punished. Concentrating on the remembrance of God for a while is being careful not to mix sins with pious deeds. 'Being careful', if only for a short while, has tremendous benefit.

CHAPTER [THREE]

On the Benefits of the Invocations Used by the Novice Travelling the Path

KNOW THAT the Most Beautiful Names (*al-Asmā' al-Ḥusnā*) of God Most High are a medicine for the maladies of the heart and the sicknesses of those travelling to the presence of the Divine Knower of the Invisible World. A remedy is not to be used except for illnesses which that particular Name benefits. For example, where the name 'the Giver' (*al-Muʿṭī*) is beneficial for a particular illness of the heart, a Name which is not salutary for that situation is not prescribed, and so forth.

The rule is that whosoever uses an invocation, and that invocation has an intelligible meaning, the influence of that meaning attaches itself to his heart, followed by the corollary significations of the meaning, until the invoker is characterized by those qualities. This is so unless the Name be one of the Names of vengeance in which case fear clings to the heart of the invoker; and if inspiration comes to him, it is from the world of Majesty (*al-Jalāl*).

His Name (exalted be He!) 'the Truthful' (*aṣ-Ṣādiq*): Its invocation bestows on the one who is veiled truthfulness (*ṣidq*) of tongue; on the Sufi adherent, truthfulness of heart; and on the gnostic, realization.

His Name (exalted be He!) 'the Guide' (*al-Hādī*): It is salutary during spiritual retreat (*khalwah*). It is beneficial against the state of dispersion and distraction, and eliminates them. Whosoever seeks the help of God but does not see the visible signs of assistance forthcoming, then let him know that his continually asking for God's help is what is sought from him.

His Name (exalted be He!) 'the Resurrector' (*al-Bāʿith*): Those who are forgetful invoke it; but those who are possessed of extinction (*fanā'*) do not invoke it.

His Name (exalted be He!) 'the Pardoner' (*al-ʿAfuw*): It is appropriate for common people to invoke it, because it improves them; but its invocation is not the concern of travellers on the path to God, because the remembrance of sin is implicit therein. The invocation of the initiates (*al-qawm*) does not contain the remembrance of sin, nor for that matter, the remembrance of good deeds. However, when the common people invoke the Name, it ameliorates their spiritual state.

His Name (exalted be He!) 'the Protector' (*al-Mawlā*): He is the Victor and the Master. Only servants having a special affinity with this Name invoke it. If others who are spiritually above them invoke the Name, it has a different significance.

His Name (exalted be He!) 'the Virtuous' (*al-Muḥsin*): It is appropriate for the generality of believers when attainment of the station of trust in God is desired for them. Invoking this Name necessitates intimacy with God and hastens spiritual insight. With it the novice is treated against the awesome fear of the world of Majesty (*Jalāl*).

His Name (exalted be He!) 'the All-Knowing' (*al-ʿAllām*): Its invocation arouses one from forgetfulness and makes the heart be present with the Lord. It teaches proper conduct accompanied with vigilance. Amongst the devotees of Beauty (*al-Jamāl*), the Name confers upon the heart intimacy (*uns*) with God; and amongst the devotees of the world of Majesty (*Jalāl*), the Name renews fear and awe in the heart.

His Name (exalted be He!) 'the Forgiving' (*al-Ghāfir*): It is assigned for the generality of disciples who fear punishment of sin. As for those who are worthy of the Divine Presence, remembrance of the forgiveness of sins causes alienation in them. Likewise the remembrance of good deeds causes thoughtlessness, generating in the soul a notion somewhat as if it had done God a favour in serving Him through acts of obedience or in remembering the harm of evil deeds.

His Name (exalted be He!) 'the Firm' (*al-Matīn*): It means hard. This name is harmful to those in seclusion (*khalwah*); but it is beneficial to those who mock religion and returns them, throughout the duration of their remembrance of it, to submissiveness and obedience.

His Name (exalted be He!) 'the Rich' (*al-Ghanī*): Invoking it is beneficial to those who seek disengagement from worldly things but are unable to do so alone.

His Name (exalted be He!) 'the Reckoner' (*al-Ḥasīb*): If the invoker of it is infatuated with the activities of gaining a livelihood, he emerges from them toward disengagement because of contentment with the Reckoner, that is, the Sufficient (*al-Kāfī*).

His Name (exalted be He!) 'the Nourisher' (*al-Muqīt*): Invoking it helps in disengaging oneself from the cares of gaining a living and bestows trust in God.

His Name (exalted be He!) 'the Possessor of Majesty' (*Dhu'l-Jalāl*): It is good during retreat for those who are forgetful.

His Name (exalted be He!) 'the Creator' (*al-Khāliq*): It is among the Names invoked by the people who have the station of religious devotion (*ʿibādah*) by virtue of conjoining beneficial knowledge with pious deeds. It is not suitable to be taught to those with a unique receptivity, for it estranges them from gnosis and draws them toward mental reckoning.

His Name (exalted be He!) 'the Fashioner' (*al-Muṣawwir*): It is among the invocations of pious servants.

His Name (exalted be He!) 'the Knower' (*al-ʿĀlim*): It is among the invocations of pious servants. It is good for the beginners among those travelling the path, for there is a reminder of vigilance in it; and through it fear and hope are obtained.

His Name (exalted be He!) 'the Counter' (*al-Muḥṣī*): It is among the invocations of pious servants.

His Name (exalted be He!) 'the Watcher' (*ar-Raqīb*): When those who are forgetful invoke it, they awaken from their slumber. When the wakeful invoke it, they remain in a wakeful state. If pious worshippers invoke it, they are freed of hypocrisy. Neither those who are in control of their actions nor the gnostics need to invoke it; nor does it have any relationship with those who are utterly extinguished in the Goal, because they have gone beyond the Names.

One of the shaykhs used to teach his disciples the following: 'God is with me, God is watching me, and God sees me'. He would instruct them to repeat that always with their tongues and hearts. His intention in all that was to treat the illness of the heart, stemming from the malady of forgetfulness. He would draw their attention to the invocation of *ar-Raqīb* in conformity with its meaning. The result was that they reached the state of 'presence' with God Most High through proper comportment; and this is the state of those who perform pious devotion with the heart. The most perfect of them are those who control their breaths, i.e., those who do not inhale a breath without their hearts being present with God Most High, nor exhale a breath without their being in the presence of God Most High. It is a very difficult spiritual station for those veiled from God. It is burdensome on them, because in observing it, not a share remains to human habits but that it falls by the wayside.

Section [One]

His Name (exalted be He!) 'the Trustworthy' (*al-Wafī*): It is the invocation of the intermediates on the path. Invoking it during retreat confers acceptance to the ultimate content of one's receptivity.

His Name (exalted be He!) 'the Thankful' (*ash-Shākir*): That is, the One Who is grateful to His pious servant for his deed, namely, He commends him for it. It bestows on the adepts of the invocation the station of love if they are Sufis, the station of extinction if they are gnostics, and the station of centrality (*quṭbiyyah*) and eminence if they are of those who have reached the end. It is a holy presence surrounded by intimacy with God, and in retreat has far-reaching effects.

His Name (exalted be He!) 'the Glorious' (*al-Majīd*): It is not used in retreat by novices, whereas it is incumbent upon intermediates to invoke it when the Truth manifests itself to them by descending to the level of 'the presence of limitations' (*taqyīd*). Verily, invoking *al-Majīd* removes all forms.

His Name (exalted be He!) 'the Loving' (*al-Wadūd*): He is Loving towards all Creation. When adepts invoke it, they achieve intimacy and love.

His Name (exalted be He!) 'the Benefactor' (*al-Mannān*): Its invocation in retreat is very beneficial to those who have quit the pleasures of the ego, but it is harmful to those whose desires of the self remain.

His Name (exalted be He!) 'the Affectionate' (*al-Hannān*): Its invocation in retreat strengthens intimacy until it takes its practitioner to love.

His Name (exalted be He!) 'the Benign' (*al-Barr*): It bestows intimacy and hastens partial insight, but not union.

His Name (exalted be He!) 'the Outward' (*aẓ-Ẓāhir*): Invoking it is beneficial during a very difficult journey.

His Name (exalted be He!) 'the Cleaver' (*al-Fāliq*): Its invocation during a retreat profoundly benefits the renouncer and hastens the coming of illumination upon him when accompanied by the name 'the Self-Subsistent' (*al-Qayyūm*) or 'the Living' (*al-Ḥayy*); but it slows down illumination if 'There is no divinity but God' (*Lā ilāha illa'llāh*) is invoked with it.

His Name (exalted be He!) 'the Gracious' (*al-Laṭīf*): It carries with it the all-encompassing meaning of mercifulness. Invoking it during retreat benefits those who are opaque in nature and makes them more refined. It benefits the contemplatives: it strengthens the contemplation of those who were previously weak.

His Name (exalted be He!) 'the Light' (*an-Nūr*): It is quick to bestow light and insight on those in retreat, because it does so by degrees. Rarely does it give total illumination.

His Name (exalted be He!) 'the Inheritor' (*al-Wārith*): It is appropriate for gnostics and attracts them towards absolute extinction in God: it is the station that ends the path.

His Name (exalted be He!) 'the Giver' (*al-Muʿṭī*): Of all the Names invoked in retreat, it is the one most likely to bring about illumination, albeit a weak one.

His Name (exalted be He!) 'the Superior' (*al-Fā'iq*): The gnostics invoke it, but not the novices.

His Name (exalted be He!) 'the Grateful' (*ash-Shakūr*): Its invocation is a characteristic of the élite who have achieved union.

His Name (exalted be He!) 'the Almighty' (*Dhu'ṭ-Ṭawl*): Among God's graces to us are submission (*islām*), then faith (*imān*) then virtue (*iḥsān*), then peace, then uprightness, then the freedom of conduct, then gnosis, then comprehension, then realization by degrees, and then the function of viceregent (*khilāfah*). This invocation hastens illumination. Likewise His Names 'the Opener' (*al-Faṭṭāḥ*) and 'the First' (*al-Awwal*) hasten illumination.

His Name (exalted be He!) 'the Dominating' (*al-Jabbār*): It is conferred in retreat upon whosoever is overcome by a state and it is feared that the expansion (*basṭ*) which initiates find radiating from the Name 'the Expander' (*al-Bāsiṭ*) will overwhelm him. When someone whose substance is mixed with expansion invokes it, contraction (*qabḍ*) comes upon him, and thus he becomes equilibriated in treading the path.

His Name (exalted be He!) 'the Proud' (*al-Mutakabbir*): It is invoked in retreat and elsewhere to bring reverential fear back to the one who has been overcome by expansion.

His Name (exalted be He!) 'the Able' (*al-Qādir*): The fruit of its invocation is that it benefits those who consider miracles (*kharq al-ᶜawā'id*) as far-fetched. So when one of them invokes the Name in his retreat, his inner being is given the grace to see their validity to a certain extent.

His Name (exalted be He!) 'the Judge' (*al-Qāḍī*): That is, He whose judgment is obeyed. Whosoever has hestiated in matters out of ignorance and invokes this Name, God decrees for him the contemplation of Truth in his inner being.

His Name (exalted be He!) 'the Strong' (*al-Qawī*): Its invocation benefits those who become sick during retreat or forget or become too weak to invoke or become dispersed. Truly, it unites: its virtue lies in its belonging by right to the path of kings and great men inasmuch as when they invoke it, the Name unites them in comformity with the Truth.

His Name (exalted be He!) 'the Guardian' (*al-Ḥafīẓ*): Its characteristic is the preservation of a state. Whoever fears deception invokes it.

His Name (exalted be He!) 'the Honoured' (*al-Mukarram*): The shaykh should order the novice to use it when the latter has a low opinion of himself and his intimacy with God is non-existent because of his asking for forgiveness.

His Name (exalted be He!) 'the Planner' (*al-Mudabbir*): Invoking it is not good for the traveller on the path except when the shaykh fears that the process of unification (*tawḥīd*) will overcome him.

His Name (exalted be He!) 'the Great' (*al-Kabīr*): The shaykh should instruct the disciple to invoke it when the manifestation of nearness to God overcomes him and when the shaykh fears that the disciple will be distraught by it.

His Name (exalted be He!) 'The Exalted' (*al-Mutaᶜālī*): Like the name 'the Great' (*al-Kabir*), it benefits whoever is overcome by nearness to God and is beside himself. When he invokes the Name, he returns to his senses.

SECTION [TWO]

His Name (exalted be He!) 'the Potent' (*al-Muqtadir*): Its meaning is 'the Able' (*al-Qādir*). He whom the shaykh wishes to manifest charismatic phenomena (*karamāt*) without union invokes this Name.

His Name (exalted be He!) 'the Efficacious' (*al-Faʿʿāl*): Its invocation benefits whoever desires to produce effects and charismatic phenomena.

His Name (exalted be He!) 'the Reliable' (*al-Wāthiq*): The shaykh should give it as an invocation to whosoever he fears will be unreceptive, which would veil illumination from him.

His Name (exalted be He!) 'the Restorer' (*al-Muʿīd*): The shaykh should assign it to whosoever he wishes to veil whenever the shaykh fears for him that illumination will make him unbalanced.

His Name (exalted be He!) 'the Advancer' (*al-Muqaddim*): The shaykh should assign it to those who turn away from the wisdom of the Wise; hence, it brings them back to Him.

His Name (exalted be He!) 'the Inward' (*al-Bāṭin*): It is invoked by whoever is overcome by 'outward illumination', and mental confusion is feared for him. The shaykh should give it to whoever is overcome by a feeling of nearness to God to the point where he might almost become unbalanced.

His Name (exalted be He!) 'the Most Holy' (*al-Quddūs*): The shaykh should order that it be invoked by those who are subjected in retreat to the doubts of the anthropomorphists and those who compare things with God, or those who have a similar creed. So let them avail themselves of this Name by invoking it much! But the shaykh should not order that it be invoked by any others, especially by those whose creed is Ashʿarī, since it would make illumination impossible for them. Instead the shaykh should give them in exchange for this Name the Names 'the Near' (*al-Qarīb*), 'the Watcher' (*al-Raqīb*), 'the Loving' (*al-Wadūd*), and the likes of these Names.

His Name (exalted be He!) 'the Examiner' (*al-Mumtaḥin*): The shaykhs use its signification: it makes their disciples fit for guidance, so that the shaykhs can test thereby their disciples predispositions in order to find out which way they should proceed with their disciples toward God Most High. But they should not assign this Name in retreat except to someone who has suffered a misfortune, so that it reminds him of his Lord.

CHAPTER [FOUR]

On Choosing the Type of Remembrance

NOTE THAT there are those who choose *Lā ilāha illa'llāh Muḥammadun rasūlu'llāh* (There is no divinity but God, Muhammad is the Messenger of God) at the beginning and at the end, and there are others who choose *Lā ilāha illa'llāh* in the beginning, and in the end confine themselves to *Allāh*. These latter are the majority. Then there are those who choose *Allāh*, *Allāh* and others who choose *Huwa* (He). He who affirms the first view advances as his proof that faith is not sound nor acceptable unless the Testimony of Messengerhood is connected with the Testimony of the Unity of God. They maintain:

> If you say, 'That is so only at the beginning of faith, but that if one's faith is established and becomes stable, then the two formulas can be separated', the answer is that if separation is not permitted in the beginning, then it is all the more fitting that it not be permitted in the end.

Do you not see that the call to prayer, which is one of the rituals of Islam, is not valid except on condition that the two Testimonies be always together? Just as the call to prayer never varies from the condition prescribing that the two Testimonies be joined together, so similarly the believer cannot change the condition that makes his faith acceptable through his uttering the two

Testimonies. Hence, there is no way one can separate the two Testimonies. God Most High has said, '. . . He misleadeth many thereby, and He guideth many thereby,'[1] up to His word (exalted be He!), '. . . and they sever that which God ordered to be joined . . .'.[2]

One of the commentators has said, 'God has commanded that the mention of the Prophet be connected with the mention of Himself; so whosoever separates them separates what God has decreed should be joined; and whosoever separates what God has commanded should be joined is called "lost".'

God Most High has said, 'We have exalted thy fame' (*dhikrak*).[3] Another of the commentators has said, 'The verse means: "I am not to be mentioned unless you are mentioned with Me".' It is maintained that if a claimant alleges that he is in the station of extinction (*maqām al-fanā'*) and says 'I see naught but God, and I contemplate naught but Him; therefore, I do not remember anyone but Him,' the response is that, when Abū Bakr aṣ-Ṣiddīq, (may God be pleased with him!) brought all his wealth to the Prophet ﷺ the latter said to Abū Bakr, 'What have you left for your family?' He replied, 'I left God and His Messenger for them'. He did not confine himself to saying *Allāh*, but rather he combined the two remembrances. Similarly, in the circumambulation of the Kaʿbah, sand is prescribed for a reason; but when the reason vanishes, the sand remains.

As for the second invocation,[4] it is *Lā ilāha illa'llāh* (There is no divinity but God), and its textual proof is in the words of God (exalted be He!): 'Know that there is no divinity but God . . .;[5] and in the words of the Prophet ﷺ 'The best thing that I and the Prophets before me have said is "There is no divinity but God".'[6]

In this Testimony there is the negation (*nafy*) of any divinity apart from God and the affirmation (*ithbāt*) of the divinity of God Most High. No worship exists without there being implicit in it the meaning of 'There is no divinity but God'. Thus, ritual purity implies the negation of uncleanness and the affirmation of ritual purity. In almsgiving, there is negation of the love of money and affirmation of the love of God; there is the manifestation of being in no need of the world, of being in need of God Most High, and of being satisfied with Him.

Also, for the heart filled with that which is other-than-God (*ghayru'llāh*), there must be a formula of negation to negate the alterities (*al-aghyār*).[7] When the heart becomes empty, the *mimbar* of the Divine Oneness is placed therein and the sultan of gnosis sits upon it. In general, only the best of things, the most universally beneficial, and the most significant are placed therein, because they are the prototypes against which the heart measures their opposites. Enough power must exist in that locus of the heart to permit it to confront every opposite. For that reason the Prophet ﷺ said, 'The best thing that I and the Prophets before me have said is "There is no divinity but God".[8]

Thus, it is apparent that a certain preponderance must be given to the statement of anyone who maintains that the invocation *Allāh, Allāh* is special. For the knowers of God, it is one of the total number of invocations amongst which 'There is no divinity but God' is the best of all.

You must find the most appropriate and generally constant invocation, for that is the most powerful one; it has the most radiant light and loftiest rank. No one has the good fortune of sharing in all that except him who perseveres in it and acts in accordance with it until he masters it. For verily, God has not established mercifulness except as something all-embracing that helps one reach the desired goal. So whosoever negates his nature by 'There is no divinity' (*Lā ilāha*) affirms His Being by 'but God' (*illa'llah*).

The third invocation is the one that rejects all comparability (*tanzīh*) between creature and God. It is found in the phrases 'Glory be to God' (*subḥāna'llāh*) and 'Praise be to God' (*al-ḥamdu li'llāh*). When that is manifest to the seeker, it is the fruit of the invocation of negation and of affirmation, as will be explained later, God willing.

The fourth invocation is *Allāh*. It is called the single invocation, because the invoker contemplates the Majesty and Sublimity of God, while being extinguished from himself. God Most High has said, '. . . Say: *Allāh*. Then leave them to disport themselves with their idle talk.'[9]

It is related that ash-Shiblī was asked by a man, 'Why do you say *Allāh* and not *Lā ilāha illa'llāh*?' So ash-Shiblī answered,

> Because Abū Bakr gave all his wealth to the point where not a thing remained with him. Then he took off a garment in front of the Prophet ﷺ. So the Messenger of God ﷺ said, 'What did you leave for your family?' He answered, '*Allāh*'. Likewise I say *Allāh*.

Then the questioner said, 'I want a higher explanation than this'. So ash-Shiblī said, 'I am embarrassed to mention an expression of negation in His presence, while everything is His light'. Then the man said, 'I want a higher explanation than this'. Ash-Shibli answered, 'I am afraid that I will die during the negation of the phrase before reaching the affirmation.' The questioner again said, 'I want a higher explanation than this.' So ash-Shiblī said, 'God Most High said to His Prophet ". . . Say *Allāh*. Then leave them to disport themselves with their idle talk".'[10]

Then the young man got up and let out a shriek. Ash-Shiblī said *Allāh*. He screamed again; and ash-Shiblī said *Allāh* then he screamed a third time and died, may God Most High have mercy upon him! The relatives of the young man gathered together and grabbed ash-Shiblī, charging him with murder. They took him to the caliph and were given permission to enter, and they accused him of murder. The caliph said to ash-Shiblī, 'What is your response?' He answered, 'A soul yearned, then wailed and aspired, then screamed, then was summoned, then heard, then learned, then answered. So what is my crime?' The caliph shouted, 'Let him go!'

The reason for this teaching on the simple invocation is because God is the goal and the most worthy of being invoked; because the invoker of 'There is no divinity but God' (*Lā ilāha illa'llāh*) might die between the negation and the affirmation; because saying *Allāh* only is easier on the tongue and closer to the heart's grasp; because the negation of imperfection in One for Whom imperfection is impossible is an imperfection; because being occupied with this formula conveys to one the grandeur of the Truth through the negation of alterities, since the negation of alterities actually derives from the heart's preoccupation with those very alterities. That is impossible for the person who is absorbed in the Light of Divine Unity.

Whoever says, 'There is no divinity but God' (*Lā ilāha illa'llāh*) is indeed occupied with what is other than the Truth; whereas whoever says *Allāh* is indeed occupied with the Truth. Hence, what a difference between the two positions! Likewise, negating the existence of something is needed only when that thing comes to mind; but it does not come to mind save through the imperfection of one's state.

As for those who are perfect, for whom the existence of a partner alongside God would never occur to them, it is impossible that they be put under the obligation of negating the partner. Rather, for these people, only the remembrance of God comes to their minds or enters their imagination. So it suffices them to say *Allāh*. Also, God has said, ' . . . Say: *Allāh*. Then leave them to disport themselves with their idle talk.'[11] Thus, he has enjoined upon the Prophet the remembrance of God (*dhikru'llāh*) and has forbidden him idle discussion with them in their vanities and diversions. Holding to associationism (*shirk*) is idle talk and constitutes rushing headlong into that state of affairs.

It is more appropriate to be content with saying *Allāh*. The response of the one who upholds negation and affirmation with respect to the meaning of this Name is that the negation is for purification and the affirmation is for illumination. If you wished, you could say that the negation is for emptying oneself and the affirmation is for adorning oneself. If a tablet is not wiped clean of its figures, nothing can be written upon it. A single heart cannot serve as the place for two things, let alone for several things. If the heart is filled with the forms of sensory perceptions, it is rare that it would perceive the meaning of *Allāh*, even if one were to say *Allāh* a thousand times. When the heart is empty of all that is other-than-God, if one uttered *Allāh* only once, one would find such bliss that the tongue could not describe.

The fifth invocation is *Huwa* (He).[12] Know that *Huwa* is a personal pronoun, having an indicative function. Among the exoterists, a sentence is not complete without its predicate, as in the case for 'standing' (*qā'im*) or 'sitting' (*qāʿid*); so you say, 'He is standing' (*huwa qā'im*)' or 'He is sitting' (*huwa qā'id*). But among the esoterists, *Huwa* indicates the ultimate goal of realization, and they are content with it and need no further explanation. They recite it to extinguish themselves in the realities of nearness to God and in order to have the invocation of the Truth take possession of their innermost being. Therefore, what is other-than-He is nothing at all that one should refer to it.

One of the mentally confused was asked, 'What is your name?' He said, '*Huwa*'.

'Where are you from?' He said, '*Huwa*'.

'Where did you come from?' He said, '*Huwa*'. Whatever he was asked, he would only reply '*Huwa*'. So someone said, 'Perhaps you desire God'. Then he screamed loudly and died.

If you say, 'You have mentioned proofs for every invocation to the point where the observer thinks that each invocation is the best, which causes confusion when choosing a remembrance,' I respond: Each invocation has its own state and time wherein it is better than another type of remembrance. For every station there is a particular utterance which is more appropriate to it; and for every invocation there is a spiritual state, which is more suitable to it, as will follow. Just as the Qur'ān is better than the invocation, the invocation in some situations is better than it for the invoker, as in bowing during prayer.[13]

CHAPTER [FIVE]

The Gradual Advance of the Seeker by Means of the Invocations, and the Manner Wherein He Transfers from Degree to Degree, Stated by Way of Counsel and Summarization

WHOSOEVER perseveres in the invocation will find that lights come to him constantly and that the veils of invisible things are lifted from him. Whosoever is determined to seek guidance and follow a path of right conduct must search for a shaykh from amongst those who have realization, one who follows a path methodically, who has abandoned his passions, and who has firmly established his feet in the service of his Lord. How well said is the verse by a poet:

جَلَّ جَنَابُ الحقِّ أنْ يَراهُ　　مُسَافِرٌ يَصْحَبُهُ هَوَاهُ

The Divine Truth is too lofty to be seen and too august
By the traveller on the path accompanied by passion and lust.

When the seeker finds a guide, then let him obey what he orders him to do, and let him abstain from what he prohibits or restrains him from doing; otherwise, he will be lost. The seeker must enumerate the Names of God, adorn himself with the fundamental virtues, and abandon vices that arise from objectionable morals, deeds, and passional inclinations; he must be on his guard constantly, seek increased perseverance in devotional acts, and be sincere in desiring God Most High in every aim.

In the initiatic journey, there are diverse paths; you will not see any deviation or crookedness in a single one of them. I will begin now with an invocation of this way, which goes back to the Imām Abū Bakr aṣ-Ṣiddīq. I learned it from one of the realized sages. This way consists in the seeker's beginning by praying upon the Prophet ﷺ without any other type of invocation. For he ﷺ is the intermediary between God and us, our guide to Him, and our means of knowing Him through gnosis. Attachment to the intermediary precedes attachment to the One Who sent him. Also, the place of sincerity is the heart: it may be devoted to what is other-than-God Most High. The ego is turned toward creatures; it is the soul that commands evil (*an-nafs al-ammārah bi's-sū'*), that follows its passions, that inclines toward vanities. All of that consists of impurities that veil the heart from sincerity and from rightly turning towards God Most High.

The self is receptive to the commands of the devil. If it were not receptive to him, he would not find his way to the heart. Its receptivity towards the devil is a proof of its ignorance and of its absence from God Most High. Absence is a thick veil that hides the soul from its Creator. The veil is a darkness. So the seeker needs to dispel this darkness and remove these impurities. The darkness disappears with light. It is related that the Prophet ﷺ said, 'Prayer upon me is a light'. The elimination of impurities is through ritual purification. It is related in a *ḥadīth* that he ﷺ said, 'The hearts of believers are made pure and cleansed of rust through prayer upon me'.

For that reason, in the beginning, the seeker is commanded to pray upon the Prophet ﷺ in order to purify the locus of sincerity, for there can be no sincerity so long as defects abide within us. Through the remembrance of God's beloved ﷺ comes the cessation of tribulations. Frequent prayer upon him yields as its fruit the capacity to love him from the heart. The capacity to love him from the heart results in intense devotion to him and care for the qualities, character, and spiritual distinction he possesses. When we know that we cannot get to the point of following his deeds and virtues except after intense devotion to him, that we cannot reach that except through the utmost love for him, that we cannot attain to the utmost love for him except through the frequency of praying upon him—for whoever loves something remembers it frequently—then, the seeker, because of that, begins with prayers upon the Prophet ﷺ. They combine both the remembrance of God and the remembrance of His Messenger ﷺ.

It is related that the Prophet ﷺ said, 'God Most High has said to me, "O Muhammad, I have made you an invocation that is of My invocation. Whosoever remembers you, remembers Me and whosoever loves you, loves Me".' So the Prophet ﷺ said, 'Whosoever remembers me, remembers God, and whosoever loves me, loves God.'

When the worshipper utters the phrase 'O God' (*Allāhumma*), he is pronouncing an invocation of God. Know that invocation is of two types: one which does not comprise intimate conversation and one which does. The latter has a deeper, more far-reaching effect on the heart of the novice than does the invocation which does not include intimate discourse, because the one engaged in such intimate conversation makes his heart feel near the one whom he addresses. That is one of the things influencing the heart, clothing it with fear. Verily, one's utterance of 'O God, pray . . .' (*Allāhumma ṣalli . . .*) is an invocation and an intimate talk, because one is asking for prayers upon the Prophet and that is an intimate conversation. Naught but you are present before Him.

Perhaps the secret of the religious prescription of prayers upon the Prophet is that the spirit of man is weak and unprepared to receive divine lights. So when the connection between his spirit and the Spirit of the Prophets becomes deep-rooted through prayers upon them, then the lights flowing forth from the Invisible World upon the Spirit of the Prophets will reflect upon the spirit of those praying upon them.

Section [One]

If many misdeeds and sins have been formerly committed by the seeker, then let him begin his path by frequently asking God for forgiveness until the fruit of so doing is apparent to him. For every invocation has its own fruit and sign which are well-known by the sages of the path. The fruit characteristic of invocations is of two kinds: the first is that which is visible to the heart in the waking state, and the second is that which the seeker sees during sleep.

With regard to the production of these fruits, seekers belong to one of three categories—by which I mean the fruits which grant them progress from one invocation to another. One seeker advances after the fruit that is manifested in the waking state; another advances because of what is manifested to the Spirit during sleep; and a third combines the fruits of waking and sleeping, and that is the most perfect of the categories. Fruits vary according to individuals; but they derive from one source. Thus, by virtue of a person's familiarity with nearness to God, there is made manifest to him what is not manifest to another; and there is made manifest to another what is not manifest to him. Each one of them has produced fruit because that which has manifested itself to both stems from one source.

Fruits differ in accordance with the blessing bestowed on seekers, and those blessings revolve around immutable principles which are held as invariable by sages having realization. No seeker advances from one invocation to another until its particular fruit is manifest to him. When the signs of humility are evident in him, and when the traces of contrition and submission are manifest on his face, he should then be ordered to engage in an invocation that polishes the heart, and that is the prayer upon the beloved Prophet. This is the case if he had formerly employed his limbs in transgression and his soul had previously been inclined toward sins. As for the one who had formerly made efforts in virtue and who was not seduced by the soul that commands evil (*an-nafs al-ammārah bi's-sū'), the first thing given to him is the prayer upon the Messenger; for by it he will reach the hoped-for goal.

Then the question should be posed: Is this seeker from amongst the common people or from amongst the knowledgeable? If he is from amongst the common people, he should begin with the complete prayer upon the Prophet and persevere in it until he understands its reality and until its hidden meaning appears to him. Then will he advance to another state.

If the seeker is from amongst the knowledgeable, he is not to be ordered to begin with the entire prayer, for his tongue is already moist from repeating it over and over again and from the frequency of usage. However, he will not grasp its hidden meaning because he cannot master the light of prayer upon the Prophet ﷺ. So it behoves him to recite the entire prayer upon the Prophet eleven times at the end of every ritual prayer (*farīḍah*), making it a litany (*wird*) until his intellect (*baṣīrah*) discerns its meaning. And let him persevere in the aforementioned prayer day and night.

Be careful not to neglect to pronounce the word *sayyid* (master), for it contains a mystery which appears to whosoever persists in this devotion. When that mystery emerges and manifests itself, the seeker proceeds to an invocation higher than the previous one. So he invokes, saying: 'O God, bless Your beloved, our master Muḥammad' (*Allāhumma ṣalli ᶜalā ḥabībika sayyidinā Muḥammad*). The invocation attaches him to the Creator and therein distinguishes him by the highest degrees of love above created beings. In order to advance to the loftiest degrees, the seeker must have both intention and resolution.

Let us mention now the sitting posture for the invocation. We say: It is in accordance with the rules of conduct (*adab*) to sit in front of one's master in a submissive, humble, and unpretentious manner; to put one's head between one's knees; and to close one's eyes to all sensory perceptions. It is through this manner of sitting that the heart is recollected and cleansed of impurities and that lights, flashes, and mysteries come to it.

When you are seated in this fashion, take refuge in God from the accursed devil, then say: 'In the Name of God'. Then say immediately afterwards: 'O God, I ask blessings upon our master Muḥammad' such-and-such a number of times, and you state the number you intend to do, with faith and expectation of a reward from God Most High, magnifying the proper due of the Messenger of God ﷺ with honour and veneration. Then begin the prayer upon the Prophet ﷺ.

When you have finished the number, or when, with a rosary (*subḥah*) in hand, you have arrived at the place wherein you began, renew your intention, as we have previously mentioned. It could be that, with repetition, the mysteries contained in the words will appear; for there is no word that does not have a hidden mystery within it. Before the break of dawn or after it, let the seeker recite: 'God testifies, as do the angels and the possessors of knowledge, that there is no divinity save Him, standing on justice. There is no divinity save Him, the Mighty, the Wise.'[1]

Let him say after that:

> I testify of God what He has testified of Himself and what the angels and possessors of knowledge among His creatures have testified of Him. I entrust this testimony with God until the time of my death, my entering the grave, my departing from it, and my meeting with my Lord. Verily, He does not fail that which is entrusted with Him.

The seeker repeats that three, five, or seven times every day. Within the depths of this utterance lies a blessing which sincerity towards God Most High brings forth. It has a result that perseverance reveals.

You must mention to your shaykh whatever states and the like that come upon you and whatever you see in dreams. When the heart shines with the lights of prayer upon the Prophet and is purified of unclean desires, the fruit of your prayers become evident to you, the foundations of sincerity come to your heart, esoteric truths manifest themselves and furnish you with gifts from the Unseen World. Wisdom appears on your tongue, and your listener is amazed by your eloquence.

The novice should adopt two litanies (*wird*), one litany after the morning prayer and the other after the sunset prayer. As for those who are firmly established and are at the end of the path, invocation occupies their hearts at all times. Guard against haste in proceeding from the prayer upon the Prophet ﷺ before its fruit reveals itself to you. Add to it the invocation of negation and affirmation; that is to say: *Lā ilāha illa'llāh*, *Muḥammadun rasūlu'llah*; that will be your tireless pursuit and occupation the rest of the time. It is a powerful invocation, more powerful than the first one; only the strong can bear it.

If the invoker is of mature mind, of a balanced disposition, sure-footed, and of a strong constitution, he is instructed to invoke frequently. If he is disturbed, weak, and hot-tempered, he is to be led with gentleness and a well-known litany assigned to him, based on the foregoing, until it imposes itself on his soul and strength flows to him bit by bit. At that point he can invoke frequently, because he has entered into the ranks of the strong. If he should increase the invocation before the appropriate time for him, then, with his hot temper, the invocation would burn him and he would be cut off from his goal.

So, persist in that invocation until the unity of the world is subsumed for you in a single sphere, so that with the eye of your heart you will see naught in the two worlds save the One. Then, you will pray the prayer for the dead for all beings, and you will utter *Allāhu Akbar* (God is Most Great) four times for them. Praise and blame will be equal to you: you will see their criticism as a discipline and a reprimand for you, and their praise will be for you a trial. For it is by His command that their tongues move in praise or in blame of you. Whenever there remains any support for the ego within, even if it be only an atom's weight, then you are pretentious and have a devil who leads you astray.

When the fruit of the invocation of 'negation and affirmation comes over you',[2] then occupy yourself with the invocation of transcendence (*tanzīh*), which is that you say: 'Glory be to God the Supreme' (*subḥāna 'llāha'l-ʿAẓīm*); and with an invocation praising the Prophet: 'O God, bless our master Muḥammad and his family' (*Allāhumma ṣalli ʿalā sayyidinā Muḥammadin waʿalā ālihi*). When the fruits of this have become apparent and its mysteries made clear to you, at that time will you become worthy of invoking the simple invocation; then you will say *Allāh*, *Allāh*, *Allāh*—that permanently.

Be extremely careful not to neglect the remembrance of the Prophet ﷺ for it is the key to every door with the permission of the Generous, the Giver. (We have been made most fortunate because we have come to understand this extraordinary method and have taken our share therein. Praise be to God, the Near, the Responder!)

Another method is the way of al-Junayd. It has eight conditions: maintaining one's ritual purity constantly; fasting constantly; being silent constantly; being in spiritual retreat constantly; invoking constantly, that is, invoking *Lā ilāha illa'llāh*; attaching one's heart to one's shaykh constantly and benefitting from his knowledge of spiritual events by extinguishing one's free will in that of the shaykh's; rejecting self-centred thinking constantly; and abstaining constantly from resisting God Most High in whatever happens to one, whether good or bad, and from asking questions about Paradise and taking refuge from hell-fire.[3]

Another method is to decrease the intake of food gradually; for verily, both the devil and the ego derive their reinforcement from food. So, when food is decreased, their power decreases.

Another method is to entrust a reliable shaykh with authority over one's soul, so that he might choose whatever will reform the seeker. For verily, the novice bent on the path is like a child or youth or spendthrift: each must needs have a guardian or counsellor or judge or authority who will assume responsibility for his affairs.

CHAPTER [SIX]

On the Invocation During the Spiritual Retreat

THE RETREAT (*khalwah*) is in reality the conversation of the innermost being with God in such a manner that no one else is perceived. As for its form, it is that which allows one to reach this goal of devoting one's life to God Most High and withdrawing from all else.

With regard to retreat of the outer being, it polishes away from the mirror of the heart the forms engraved upon it ever since it forgot and mingled intimately with the world and whatever is in it. These forms are darknesses enveloped one within the other and assembled together. From them comes the heart's rust, which is forgetfulness. By means of the retreat, the invocation, fasting, ritual purity, silence, rejecting wrong thoughts, steadfastness, and oneness of purpose, the mirror of the heart is polished of its rust. For the retreat is like a pair of bellows, the invocation is like the fire, the file, and the hammer. Fasting and ritual purity are the instruments of polishing. Silence and rejecting wrong thoughts banish the inspirations coming from the darknesses. Steadfastness is the student and oneness of purpose the teacher. This retreat is a means to the real retreat mentioned previously.

Know that if you wish to enter into the presence of God,

obtaining knowledge from Him without the intermediary of secondary means, and being intimate with Him, then that will not be possible for you so long as an other-than-God lords it over your heart, for verily, you belong to whosoever has authority over you. Therefore, you must withdraw from mankind and prefer the retreat to crowds. Indeed, your degree of closeness to the Truth is in proportion to your distance outwardly and inwardly from creatures.

You must rectify your religious creed (*ʿaqīdah*) to bring it into line with the doctrine of the initiates and you must learn what constitutes acts of worship. Before the retreat, engage in spiritual discipline, namely, in refining moral character, in avoiding levity, and in bearing wrong. It is rare that any good fortune can come from him whose illumination precedes his spiritual discipline. Thus, you must repent of sins, requite wrongs capable of being restored through honour and money, purify your inner self of every objectionable trait, and restrict your inner being from wandering about in the degrees of existence. Rational thinking is the most injurious thing in all retreats: it neither provides good fruit to the one in retreat nor does it help the soul in its words and deeds in the degrees of existence.

Seclusion from the world, silence, and reducing one's food are necessary as is striving to avoid drinking water. Thus, when the soul is accustomed to solitude, enter the retreat at that point. When you seclude yourself from people, beware of their making for you and drawing near to you; for the purpose in withdrawing from people is to leave their company behind; the purpose is not in renouncing their very forms.[1] Rather, the goal is that your heart and ears should not become a receptacle for the excessive chatter that people bring; otherwise the heart would not be purified of the senseless jabber of the world. So, close your door to mankind and the door of your room to your family, and occupy yourself with the remembrance of the Lord of the world. Whosoever withdraws but opens a door, people will make for him. That is a seeker of leadership and fame, one who is driven away from God's door: perdition is closer to him than the lace of his sandal.

Watch out for self-deception in this station, for most people have perished therein. The person in retreat should be courageous, bold, immovable upon hearing a great outcry or the tumbling down of a wall or the sudden appearance of a frightful thing. He should be neither cowardly nor reckless, but be given to much silence and always meditating; he should neither rejoice when praised nor suffer when blamed. He should carry out the necessary conditions of his retreat; for no one else will undertake to do that for him.

Hence, if he is of such a nature, he should enter the retreat; if not, so be it. Then let him use the solitude to discipline himself until he gets used to it and the ego no longer takes notice of him just as it no longer takes notice of acts of worship. Following on that, let him enter the retreat relaxed, eager, good-natured, free of striving and difficulties, ready to devote himself exclusively to the invocation and to give up any desires. For indeed, striving and effort in the retreat eliminate concentration—which is its spirit—for they are a distraction in time; hence, no inspiration will come upon you. Do your striving, therefore, in solitude before entering the retreat until your soul is familiar with it. And when, in your retreat, you are burdened by anything, such as sleeplessness, hunger, thirst, cold, heat, mental distractions, or loneliness, then leave it for your solitude until you become stronger. When you want to re-enter, perform a major ritual ablution, clean your clothes, and formulate the intention of drawing near unto God Most High.

As for the physical structure of the cell for your retreat, let its height be as tall as you are, its length as long as your prostration is, and its width as wide as your sitting posture. There should be no hole in it through which light can penetrate into the retreat; and in a house inhabited by people, it should be far from noises, and its door should be solid and small. It is best that one spend the night close to the door of the cell and not move around very much inside. It has been said: 'Do not exceed the required prayers and supererogatory devotional exercises.' And also: 'Rather, one should limit oneself to the required prayers and to two prostrations at each ritual purification from impurity; one should face the direction of prayer and remain in a state of ritual purity.'

Let the water-closet be close to your cell; and be on your guard against any unusual air current when you emerge therefrom, for this creates a dispersing influence in you for a long time. Do not vary the discipline you are following. If you go out to take care of a call of nature, close your eyes and ears. Have your food with you already prepared or kept behind the door of your cell.

Amongst the conditions for undertaking a spiritual retreat is that no one know that you are doing it. But if that is unavoidable, then let it be the person closest to you. He should ignore what you are doing and not be aware of what your intention is, because people would expect him to divulge the reason why he has gone out to see you; and this is a major obstacle which chases illumination away.

With regard to eating during spiritual discipline, solitude, and retreat, you should take a morsel of food and invoke the Creator's name over it with humility, need, presence of mind, vigilance, and attentiveness until you are aware that it has reached the stomach. At that moment take another morsel and do the same with it as with the first; and continue in such a manner until your meal is finished. You should sip your water and interrupt your breathing several times in the process. Do not fast excessively or overeat to discomfort. As soon as your stomach is empty, hasten to obtain food in such a manner that no man suffers harm thereby through inconvenience or, for that matter, any animal. Let no one else but you prepare food for you.

If you are unaware of your constitution, then submit yourself to an examination by physicians, who will prescribe food for you that will agree with your nature and improve your constitution. Tell them what you wish to do in the way of minimizing your daily needs, avoiding excess, and the heaviness that leads to sleep and sluggishness. They will prescribe food for you that will permit you to live on it for many days, during which time you will need no further food nor have to go forth to get it. The whole point is that you not use anything but light food which is suitable to your nature, slow to digest, and filling, which requires no effort on your part. Stick to whatever brings about a balanced temperament; if its dryness is excessive, it leads to fantasies and delirium; but if an inspiration itself produces the indispostion, then that is desirable.

Wear clothes that permit your body to be harmonious therein and that are of a type creating no misgivings in you, as in the case when you observe the rules for eating. You should have a clean cloth with which to handle your private parts and which you should wash often. Neither lie down nor sleep except when you are overcome by fatigue. Kill no animal – not an ant or anything else. If you fear getting vermin in your hair, shave your head. Dress with your cleanliness in view, changing your clothes often before any vermin can attach itself to them and trouble you. Tarry not an instant without being in a state of ritual purity.

The difference between an angelic inspiration and a satanic one is that coolness and bliss follow the angelic inspiration; you experience no pain nor do you see any form undergo a change; and it leaves behind knowledge. Agitation of the body, pain, and confusion follow the satanic inspiration; and it leaves behind bewilderment. A suggestive thought (*al-khāṭir*) is that which comes to the heart from the 'speech' of the inspiration wherein the servant plays no role.

Whatever is a 'speech' can be classified into four categories. One, divine speech; it is the first of the suggestive thoughts, and Sahl (may God be pleased with him!) called it 'the first cause' and the 'abode' of suggestive thoughts; it never errs, and it may be known by its power, authority, and immovability when one seeks to repel it. Two, angelic speech; it is the motive for doing what is recommended or required or, in general, everything in which there is good; it is called 'inspiration' (*ilhām*). Three, physical speech; it is that wherein the self has its share; it is called 'notion' (*hājis*). Four, satanic speech; this is that which provokes opposition to the Truth. God Most High has said, 'The devil promiseth you destitution and enjoineth on you lewdness . . .'.[2] The Prophet ﷺ has said, 'The call of the devil leads to the denial of Truth and threatens one with evil.' It is called 'a diabolic suggestion' (*waswās*) to be weighed with the scales of the sacred Law.

So when there is proximity to God, then it is of the first two categories; and when there is aversion or opposition with regard to the sacred Law, then it is of the last two categories; but it is of a doubtful nature with respect to things permitted (*al-mubāḥāt*). To the first two categories belongs that which is nearer to opposing the self; and to the last two belongs that which is nearer to passion and to agreement with the self. The distinction between the two is easy for the one who is truthful, pure-hearted, ever-present with God. But God knows best!

Let your invocation be the all-embracing Name, which is *Allāh*, *Allāh*, *Allāh*, or if you so wish, *Huwa*, *Huwa*, *Huwa*; and do not violate this remembrance. Be careful lest your tongue pronounce it while other-than-He is in your heart. Let your heart be the one who utters, and your ear the one who is attentive to this invocation until the 'speaker' (*an-nāṭiq*) emanates from your Self (*sirr*). When you feel the emergence of the Speaker within you through the invocation, do not abandon the spiritual condition wherein you find yourself.

CHAPTER [SEVEN]

The Oneness of God

THE IMĀM AL-GHAZĀLĪ (may God Most High have mercy on him!), said,

> Affirming the unity of God (*tawḥīd*) is that one see all things as coming from God Most High in a vision preventing one from giving undue consideration to intermediate causes. Thus, one does not see good or evil except as coming from Him. The fruit of that is trust in God, refraining from complaining about people, avoiding anger toward them, contentment, and resignation to the judgment of God Most High. It is as if the affirmation of God's Oneness were a rare jewel having two coverings, one of which is farther from the essence than the other; people devote themselves to the name of the covering and neglect the essence.

The first covering is to say *Lā ilāha illa'llāh* (There is no divinity but God) with your tongue. This is called 'affirming the Oneness of God', because it is opposite to the doctrine of the Trinity which the Christians declare; but the affirmation might emanate from a hypocrite whose interior contradicts his exterior.[1]

The second covering is that one not have in one's heart any opposition to or rejection of the content of this formula. Rather, the literal meaning of the formula embraces both the adherence to it as a dogma and the belief in it. It is the profession of God's

Oneness to which most people adhere. The theologians are the watchmen who protect this covering from the confusion of innovators.

The third covering,[2] which is the essence, is that one see all things from God Most High in a vision preventing one from giving undue consideration to intermediate causes; and to worship Him with a devotion that isolates Him from all else, so that one does not worship other-than-Him. Following passion is a deviation from the affirmation of God's Oneness, inasmuch as everyone who follows his passion has taken it as his god. God Most High has said, 'Hast thou seen him who chooseth for his god his own passion . . .'[3] The Prophet ﷺ has said, 'For God, the most hateful deity worshipped in the world is passion.'

Section [One]

Whosoever reflects deeply will find that all creatures affirm the Oneness of God Most High in accordance with the subtleness of their 'breaths'. Were that not the case, punishment would have overwhelmed them. For in each one of the atoms of the world, and in whatever is smaller than that, there is one of the mysteries of the Name of God Most High. It is by virtue of that mystery that each one, according to the species wherein it finds itself, understands and acknowledges the Oneness of God, knowingly or unknowingly, as God Most High has said, 'And unto God falleth prostrate whosoever is in the heavens and the earth, willingly or unwillingly, as do their shadows in the morning and the evening hours.'[4] Each one affirms God's Oneness in every station with whatever befits His Lordship and with whatever the attributes of servanthood are capable of, in accordance with the destiny allotted all creatures for the realisation of the Oneness of God.

A gnostic has said:

> He who glorifies God (*al-musabbiḥ*) glorifies with his inner Self the reality within the pure attributes of his meditation in

the domain containing the marvels of the Realm (*al-Malakūt*) and the minute subtleties of the world of Power (*al-Jabarūt*). The seeker (*as-sālik*) glorifies God by invoking Him in the oceans of the heart. The novice (*al-murīd*) glorifies God with his heart within the oceans of meditation. The lover (*al-muḥibb*) glorifies God with his Spirit in the oceans of his longing. The gnostic (*al-ʿārif*) glorifies God with his inner being in the oceans of the Unseen. The veracious (*aṣ-ṣiddīq*) glorifies God with the Self of his inner being in the 'mystery' of holy lights which move about within the prototypes of the names of God's attributes; and this he does with steadfast surefootedness at different times.

CHAPTER [EIGHT]

Gnosis

GNOSIS (*ma'rifah*) is the perception of something as it is in its essence and attributes. The gnosis of the Creator, (may He be glorified and exalted!) is one of the most difficult of all types of gnosis, for God has no likeness. Yet in spite of that, God Most High has enjoined on the Creation, including mankind, jinns, angels, and devils, the gnosis of His Essence, His Names, and His Atributes: it is affirmed with respect to both the animal and non-animal kingdoms. Everything which has being—except God Most High—is conscious of the Being of its Creator to the extent of its capacity.

God Most High has said, . . .'there is not a thing but hymneth His praise . . .'.[1] That includes man, angels, animals, minerals, plants, air, earth, and water. God Most High praises those who have gnosis of Him and censures those who are ignorant of Him and those who deny Him.

Gnosis is of two types: general and particular. General gnosis of God Most High, which is incumbent upon all who must observe the precepts of religion, is to affirm His Being, to declare Him to be holy in a manner worthy of Him, and to describe Him as He actually is and in the manner in which He describes Himself; for He is known even if He is not subject to conditions and cannot be encompassed.

The second type of gnosis is particular gnosis. It has been said that it is a state that arises from contemplation. The gnostic (*al-ʿārif*) is the one whom God Most High causes to contemplate His Essence, Attributes, Names, and Acts, while the knower (*al-ʿālim*) is the one to whom God Most High makes that known, not through contemplation, but rather through certitude. It is said that gnosis is a type of certitude that occurs through serious effort in religious devotions.

The Imām al-Ghazālī (may God Most High have mercy on him!), has said:

> God is much too great for the senses to reach Him or for reason and logic to plumb the depths of His Majesty. Indeed, He is much too great for anyone but Himself to plumb the depths of His Majesty or for anyone but Himself to know Him. Verily, no one knows God but God. The highest degree of gnosis that His servants can attain is the realization that true gnostic knowledge of Him is impossible for them. Furthermore, no one can know that in its totality except a Prophet or a righteous saint (*siddīq*). As for the Prophet, he has clearly expressed this by saying, 'I cannot enumerate the ways of praising Thee; Thou art as Thou has praised Thyself'. As for the righteous saint, he says, 'The incapacity to attain realization is a realization'.

It has been said that souls, after leaving their bodies, are not distinguished from one another save as regards the type of gnosis and knowledge imprinted upon them; nor will you be able, after that separation, to find any kind of gnosis or knowledge except what was there originally. Human nature will be raised on the Day of Judgment in accordance with the form of its knowledge; physical bodies will be resurrected in accordance with the form of their deeds, whether good or bad. When the soul leaves the world of religious commandments, the homeland for gaining the Hereafter and ascending thereto, it reaps the fruit of that which it has sown. Its discernment in the Hereafter is not greater than its discernment in this world except in terms of unveiling and clarity. Contemplation and vision will be commensurate with one's knowledge of God Most High, His Names and His Attributes, because gnosis in this world will be transformed in the Hereafter as a contemplative vision just as a seed is transformed into a spike of grain. Just as the one who has no seed will have no crops, so too the one who has no gnosis in this world will have neither vision nor contemplation in the Hereafter. The difference of vision as regards the degrees of illumination are due to the differences in the degrees of gnosis.

Subtle point: Whosoever wants to light a lamp needs seven things: flint, stone, tinder, sulphur, a lampstand, a wick, and oil. So when a servant seeks the lamp of gnosis, he must have the flint of effort: 'As for those who strive in Us, We surely guide them to Our paths . . .',[2] and the stone of humility: 'Call upon your Lord humbly . . .'.[3] As for the tinder, it is the burning of the soul. God Most High has said,' . . . and restrained his soul from passion'.[4]

The fourth is the sulphur of turning to God repentantly: 'Turn often in repentance unto your Lord . . .'.[5] The fifth is the lampstand of patience: ' . . . But be patient! Verily God is with the patient'.[6] The sixth is the wick of gratitude: ' . . . and be grateful for the blessings of your Lord . . .'.[7] The seventh is the oil of contentedness with the decrees of God, Who has said, 'Bear calmly the judgment of thy Lord'.[8]

It was related that there was a good man whose brother had died. He saw him in a dream and said to him, 'What did God do with you?' He answered, 'He had me enter Paradise where I eat, drink, and mate'. The other said, 'I did not ask you about that. Have you seen your Lord?' He answered, 'No one sees Him except the one who knows Him'.

Section [One]

On Whether the Invocation or Reciting the Qur'ān Is Better.

The Imām al-Ghazālī (May God have mercy on him!), has said:

> Reciting the Qur'ān is the most excellent thing for all people except in all the beginning states of the traveller on the path to God Most High and in some of his states at the end. Indeed, the Qur'ān includes the categories of gnostic knowledge, spiritual states, and guidance along the way. As long as the servant is in need of improving his character and attaining gnostic knowledge, the Qur'ān is the more suitable for him.

If the Qur'ān is better for you, then you must recite it and reflect upon it. Consider in your recitation what qualities and attributes God praises therein, the ones with which He describes those servants of His whom He loves, who are characterized by them. And see what God Most High reproves in the Qur'ān regarding the qualities and attributes characteristic of the one whom He hates, and avoid them. God Most High did not mention them to you nor reveal them to you in His Book nor present them to you except to have you act accordingly. Strive to be as mindful of the Qur'ān in deed as you are mindful of it in your recitation. Indeed, no one will be more severely chastised on the Day of Judgment than the person who has memorized a verse then forgotten it. Likewise, whosoever has learned a verse by heart, then neglected acting upon it, that verse will be a witness against him and a source of grief for him on the Day of Judgment.

The Prophet ﷺ has said, 'The likeness of the believer who recites the Qur'ān is the citron: its fragrance is sweet'.[9] By that he means chanting and recitation; they are indeed breaths flowing out, which he likens to fragrances; their scent is the breaths. Then he continues: '. . . and its taste is delicious'. By that he means faith. Therefore, the Prophet said, 'He who is content with God as Lord, with Islam as his religion, with the Qur'ān as his model, and with

Muhammad ﷺ as Prophet and Messenger has tasted the flavour of faith.' He linked flavour to faith. Then he said, 'The likeness of the believer who does not read the Qur'ān is like the date: its taste is good' (insofar as he is a nominal believer), 'but that has no fragrance' (insofar as he is not conforming in his behaviour to that which he reads, even if he is one of those who have memorized the Qur'ān).

Then the Prophet said, 'The likeness of the hypocrite who reads the Qur'ān is sweet basil: its fragrance is good' (because the Qur'ān is good and because during the time of the chanting and the state of recitation there is nothing but the breaths of the chanter and reciter), but 'its taste is bitter' (because hypocrisy is inward disbelief, for sweetness belongs to faith and is considered delicious). Then he said, 'The likeness of the hypocrite who does not read the Qur'ān is the colocynth: its taste is bitter and it has no fragrance' (because in this case he is not even reading).

In this regard, the form of every good word, whether from believer or hypocrite, and with which God Most High is pleased, is as the form of the Qur'ān, comparatively speaking. However, the rank of the Qur'ān is not hidden: for no utterance that draws us close to God is comparable to the Word of God. It behoves the invoker to take his invocation from those invocations mentioned in the Qur'ān in order to invoke God therewith and to be a reciter during the invocation. He should neither praise God nor glorify Him nor say 'There is no divinity but God' except with what is to be found in the Qur'ān, holding fast to it.

Al-Ghazālī said,

> When the servant is not in need of refining his character and attaining gnostic knowledge, but rather has gone beyond that to the point where discernment has taken hold of his heart, so that it is hoped that this will lead him to immersion in God, then perseverance in the invocation of God is more suitable.

Indeed, the Qur'ān addresses his mind and carries him off to the gardens of Paradise. The novice travelling to God should not turn his attention to Paradise and its gardens. Rather, he should make his aspirations one aspiration and his invocations one invocation until he realizes the degree of extinction and immersion, neither persisting nor abiding therein. When he is brought back to himself, then reciting the Qur'ān will benefit him. This state is very rare and precious like 'red sulphur' (*al-kibrīt al-aḥmar*): it is spoken of but is not to be found.

Reciting the Qur'ān is the most excellent thing in an absolute sense because it is the best act in every state, except in the state wherein the Divine Interlocutor distracts one from His Word, since the point of the Qur'ān is gnosis of the One Who uttered the Qur'ān and gnosis of His Beauty, and immersion in Him. The Qur'ān goes before one to God and guides one toward Him. Whoever is close to the Goal pays no attention to the path.

Previously, it was said that the reality of the invocation is when the Invoked takes possession of the heart, and He is One. Separation and multiplicity exist before that for as long as the invoker is in the station of invoking with the tongue or with the heart. At that point, the invocation is divisible into what is preferable or otherwise: its excellence depends on the qualities which are expressed through the invocations and attributes.

The Names belonging to God Most High are divided into those that are real with respect to servants but figurative in relation to God Most High, like the Patient, the Grateful, the Compassionate, and the Avenger; and into those that are real when pertaining to Him but figurative when employed in regard to others. Among the greatest of invocations is *Lā ilāha illa'llāh al-Ḥayyu'l-Qayyūm* (There is no divinity but God the Living, the Self-Subsistent), because the most supreme Name of God is found therein. The Prophet ﷺ said, 'The most supreme Name of God is found in the verse of the Throne and in the Family of ʿImrān'.[10]

The two Names[11] are not associated except in regard to this Supreme Name. It contains a mystery the mentioning of which is too subtle for your understanding. The extent to which symbolic allusion to it is possible is that your saying *Lā ilāha illa'llāh* causes you to perceive the Unity of God. The meaning of the Oneness of God in essence and degree is real with respect to God Most High and is not to be interpreted. However, with regard to other-than-Him, the meaning is figurative and interpretable; and the same holds true for *al-Ḥayy* (the Living).

The meaning of *al-Ḥayy* (the Living) is 'the one who is aware of himself', while the dead person is one who has no awareness of himself. The meaning is also real in regard to God Most High, not figurative. *Al-Qayyūm* (the Self-Subsistent) perceives His Being as self-subsisting. Indeed everything is sustained by Him. *Al-Qayyūm* is also real in regard to God Most High, not figurative, nor is it to be found in something else.

Apart from those two, the other Names which indicate Acts, like the Merciful (*ar-Raḥīm*),the Equitable (*al-Muqsiṭ*), the Gatherer (*al-Jāmiʿ*), the Just (*al-ʿAdl*), and so forth, are subject to whatever denotes the Attributes because the sources of Actions are the Attributes. The Attributes are the principles; the Actions are the consequences. As for the other Attributes which indicate Power, Knowledge, Will, Speech, Hearing, and Vision, it is understood that what they affirm regarding God Most High is the intelligible contents of their literal meaning. It is quite wrong to say that the intelligible contents of their literal meaning are realities that go with the attributes of man, his speech, his power, his knowledge, his hearing, and his vision. Instead, the intelligible contents are realities that are impossible to affirm of men. Therefore, some form of interpretation has to be construed for these terms.

Almost in the same category are such statements as 'Glory be to God' (*subḥāna'llāh*), 'Praise be to God' (*al-ḥamdu li'llāh*), 'There is no divinity but God' (*Lā ilāha illa'llāh*), and 'God is Most Great' (*Allāhu Akbar*). 'Glory be to God' is a declaration of His Holiness, which is real with regard to Him: the truly Most Holy (*al-Quddūs*) is not to be conceived except in regard to Him. Your expression

'Praise be to God' connotes the ascription of all blessings to God; it is real inasmuch as He is really alone in all His actions without this having to be interpreted. He (exalted and blessed be He!) alone is deserving of praise, since absolutely no one ever has any association with Him in His deeds, just as the pen has no association with the writer in deserving praise for good handwriting. Any blessing seen to come from someone else is subject to His use, like the pen; so He alone is deserving of praise.

Your Saying 'God is Most Great' does not mean that He is greater than something else, since there is nothing else alongside of Him, so that it could be said that He is greater than it. Rather, everything other-than-He is one of the lights of His Omnipotence. Sunlight has no rank in juxtaposition with the sun, so that it could be said that the sun is greater than it; instead, it has the rank of subordination. Rather, the meaning of *Allāhu Akbar* is that He is much too great to be perceived by the senses or for the depths of His Majesty to be reached by reason and logic, and indeed, that He is much too great to be known by an other-than-Him for truly, no one knows God but God.

Section [Two]

The Prophet ﷺ said, 'The best thing that I and the Prophets before me have said is *Lā ilāha illa'llāh*'.[12] God Most High has mentioned it in His Noble Book in thirty-seven passages. It is a formula which combines negation and affirmation: the division is an all-encompassing one that alternates between negation and affirmation. Only he who knows what this formula contains can know its value, as shown in the following discussion; for it is the expression of Unity.

Nothing resembles Unity, for if anything resembled it, it would not be One, but two or more. There is nothing that can measure it. Only that which is of equal value or of analogous nature can measure it. But there is nothing of equal value or of analogous nature. That is the obstacle which prevents *Lā ilāha illa'llāh* from being measured. The majority of religious scholars view associationism (*shirk*) as that which opposes the Oneness of God. It is not correct, on the part of the servant, to hold to that view while maintaining the existence of God's Unity. Man is either a polytheist or a monotheist. Hence, only polytheism can take the measure of Unity, but they cannot meet in the same scale.

As for the angel who records man's deeds, he cannot make the scale incline on the Day of Judgment except with the scroll (*biṭāqah*) that bears the Testimony of Faith. That is what the balance encompasses because *Lā ilāha illa'llāh* is both written and created in speech; and were it given to everyone, then whosoever pronounced it would not enter hellfire. However, God wishes that its excellence be seen only by those who have a certain standing with the angel who records men's deeds. God wills that some monotheists not see it and that it not be put in the balance except after they have entered hellfire. For when no monotheist remains standing in judgment, one whom God has decreed should enter hellfire and emerge therefrom as a result of the intercession of Divine Providence, then the recording angel is summoned. So no one remains standing in judgment then except the one who will enter Paradise, who has no share in hellfire; and he will be the last creature to have his deeds weighed. Indeed, the formula *Lā ilāha illa'llāh* has a beginning and an end. For the angel who records men's deeds, its beginning might very well be its end.

Section [Three]

In general, only the best of all things, the most widely beneficial, or the most significant has been imposed upon us by God, because He compares those things to many opposites. Inescapably, in that very thing imposed on us, there must in general be found a power that can counter any opposite. The Prophet ﷺ said, 'The best thing that I and the Prophets before me have said is *Lā ilāha illa'llāh*'.[13]

From this, it is evident that a certain probability attaches to the claim of the person who holds that saying *Allāh*, *Allāh* or *Huwa*, *Huwa* is the most special invocation, for it is among the sum of expressions of which *Lā ilāha illa'llāh* is the best, according to the knowers of God. So you must invoke *Lā ilāha illā'llah*, for it is the most powerful invocation and possesses the most radiant light: no one is aware of that save he who perseveres in it and acts in accordance with it until he masters it. (For, indeed, God Most High has not sent His mercy except to cover all creatures and to help mankind reach the hoped-for goal.) This is according to the belief of some people. For those who see a hierarchy in the invocations that conforms to the hierarchy of stations and states, the best invocation in any situation will be that which is compatible with it, as was previously said.

Know that among the gnostics are those who choose silence over the invocation in the end. It is related that he ﷺ said, 'Whoever knows God has a tongue that is wearied'. It is related that al-Junayd (may God have mercy on him!), was speaking when ash-Shibli screamed and said, '*Allāh*!' So al-Junayd said, 'Absence (*al-ghaybah*) is prohibited!' The meaning is that if you are absent (*ghā'ib*), then the invocation of the Unseen (*al-Ghā'ib*) is absent; but if you are present (*ḥāḍir*), then mentioning the Name in a state of presence (*al-ḥaḍrah*) is bad manners.[14]

Take note: Beware of showing enmity towards the people who invoke *Lā ilāha illa'llāh*; for verily, God has put universal sanctity in it. They are God's saints, and if they were to err with a quantity of mistakes equal to the earth's weight, while not associating anyone with God, He would meet them with an equal amount of forgiveness. It is forbidden to wage war against someone whose sanctity is established. God has mentioned the punishment in this world and the next for the one who wages war against God. You must not take as your enemy anyone whom God has not informed you of his being an enemy of God. If you are not aware of his situation, then the least of your responses should be to disregard his affairs. When you have come to realize that he is an enemy of God – and this is nothing but polyetheism – then wash your hands of him, as did Abraham, the friend of God عليه السلام with respect to his father Āzar.

God Most High has said, '. . . but when it had become clear unto him that he [his father] was an enemy of God, he [Abraham] disowned him . . .'.[15] That is your standard of measurement. God Most High has also said, 'Thou wilt not find a people who believe in God and the Last Day loving those who oppose God and His Messenger, even though they be their fathers . . .', as did Abraham the friend of God عليه السلام, '. . . or their sons or their brethren or their clan'.[16]

Until you know that, show no enmity toward the servants of God, so far as is possible, even by word. You should hate the action, not the person himself, whereas with regard to the enemy of God, he himself is to be hated. The Prophet ﷺ said that God says, 'Whosoever shows Me his hostility towards a righteous person, then I shall declare war on him'.[17]

Indeed, when one does not know someone and treats him as an enemy, he does not fulfil his duty to God regarding His creatures. He does not know what God will do to him until he turns away from that person and takes him as his enemy. If that person's outward state is known, even though he might be in fact an enemy of God – which you do not know – assist him, nevertheless, in performing his duty to God and be not hostile toward him; otherwise, the Divine Name *aẓ-Ẓāhir* (the Outward) will oppose you before God.[18] Do not cause God to have proof against you, for you will perish. Indeed, '. . . to God belongs the most far-reaching proof . . ..'[19]

Treat the servants of God with compassion and mercy, since God has provided for them in their state of unbelief in spite of His knowledge of them. He does not give them sustenance except as a result of His knowledge that the state in which they are is not actually due to themselves. Rather, it is due to God, as we have previously mentioned in a general manner. Verily, God is the

Creator of everything; their unbelief is created in them. To speak more precisely, no condition appears in any existent being except in so far as it corresponds, in the pre-existential state, to its immutable prototype to which it conforms and belongs and out of which it emerges. Thus, to God belongs 'the far-reaching proof' against everyone.

Encompass with your mercy and compassion all animals and creatures. Do not say, 'This is inanimate and has no awareness'. Indeed, it does; it is you yourself who have no awareness! So let existence be as it is, and be merciful towards it with the mercifulness of the Creator in the midst of His creation.

SECTION [FOUR]

There are ten dangers in journeying to God Most High which may block some travellers on their way: seeing one's own deeds; prolonging hope; having egocentric notions about reaching sanctity; being dependent on the attention of mankind; being content with the vision of dreams; delighting in the litany (*wird*); taking pleasure in inspiration (*wārid*); being reassured by promises; being satisfied with pretense; and being inattentive to God.

The signs of falling from the sight of God are three: being content with oneself; not being content with God; and competing with mankind by fate and divine decree.[20]

The signs of nearness to God Most High are three: abandoning chance; carrying out one's duty; and humility toward God amongst creatures.

The signs of reaching God Most High are three: understanding God Most High; listening closely to God Most High; and learning from God.

The signs of devotion to God are three: abandoning choice; rejecting self-determination; and deny self-willing.

The signs of acting on behalf of God Most High are: exchanging ephemeral attributes for permanent ones; transitory qualities for permanent ones; and effacing the ephemeral essence in the eternal Essence. '. . . God bestoweth His sovereignty on whom He will. God is all-encompassing and all-knowing.'[21]

The signs of the soundness of the servant's love for his Lord are three: absence of self-willing; pleasure in every event which takes place through divine decree; and seeing the perfection of the Beloved in everything and being content with Him in everything through submission to Him in all things.

The signs of the permanency of God's love for His servant are three: His contentment with him in all that he does; His permitting him to speak about Him; and His revealing the divine mysteries to him by virtue of His far-reaching wisdom, which guides the servant to Him.

CHAPTER [NINE]

What Initiates on the Path Must Impose Upon Themselves and Practice Constantly

KNOW THAT God's path is far from discord and from manifestations of the ego's inclinations. There is no excuse, pardon, or peace of mind in whatever causes one to leave the path. Among themselves, the initiates censure verbally and do not pardon whatever the sacred Law does not permit; but they are tolerant of the rights of others and give them their due.

Among the conditions imposed on the followers of this way are: that they treat people justly of their own accord but not demand justice from anyone; that they accept excuses from outsiders but not excuse themselves; that they offer assistance but not take sides; that they treat people with mercy and compassion; that they give good counsel in whatever transpires among them; and that no one among them should hand over to his companion whatever is not required by their order. This is the case if they are equal in rank; but if the one who made the move is of higher rank, then handing it over is obligatory. There should be no hatred or grudge among them, nor should they envy each other with respect to the gifts of God. None of them should say, '*I* have' or '*I* own' or '*my* property' or '*my* slipper' or '*my* robe'. They are all equal with respect to whatever God bestows on them. None among them should own possessions not had by his companions.

It is part of their discipline to renounce keeping company with women, sitting with them, and being fraternal with them; and to renounce the comradeship of youth and conversing with them. One of their obligations is that they not make promises, for whosoever errs and makes a promise is obligated to keep it, to be true to his word, and to be scrupulous in speech, food, sight, and so on. He must not practice dissimulation but must observe the code of conduct of the Law, both in its minor and major points, if he knows them. If he does not know them, then with respect to every situation in which he finds himself, he asks, 'What does the Law prescribe therein?' Whosoever betrays the code of the Law is more likely to betray the divine secrets. God Most High only bestows His secrets on the trustworthy.

It is part of their discipline that they not choose, because they go along with God's choice for them; and that they not dwell on indifferent actions,[1] because it is a waste of time. Whosoever embarks upon this path while married should not divorce, or while single should not marry until he perfects himself. When he has perfected himself, then he will act in this matter in accordance with what his Lord inspires him to do.

One of the conditions binding upon the seeker is that he should not take charity, even though he has demonstrated piety while asking; nor should the seeker accept it in order to give it to someone else. For indeed, that would be a veil for him. As for the perfected person, he may take or refrain from so doing, if he wishes, because he acts in accordance with what God inspires him to do in the circumstances, as in the example of the disciple with his shaykh: just as the disciple is not to be opposed in carrying out whatsoever his shaykh instructs him to do, likewise the shaykh is not to be opposed in whatsoever he does, because it issues from God, if he is, in truth, a shaykh.

Another of their conditions is to renounce opposition unless the one opposing is higher in rank, because then it is a discipline. If the seeker is subordinate to him in rank, then he should keep silent; if he refuses, then he has nullified a fundamental principle in his order that he had agreed to observe. For they are the people of truth who speak only about what they contemplate.

When the novice visits a shaykh, let him empty his heart of everything that is within him so that he may be receptive to what the shaykh gives him and in order that no rejection occur. If there should occur whatsoever is unacceptable to him, he should blame himself and say, 'This is a station which I have not reached', and not attribute the mistake to the shaykh. Whosoever goes to see a shaykh in order to test him is ignorant indeed. He should not ask of the shaykhs just anything he likes; rather, he should ask of them knowledge about the deceptions of the ego and their remedies and about the things revealed in the states of the novices, not the states of the gnostics.

When initiates see someone in a state of disobedience, they should not believe that he is that way persistently; they should say, 'Perhaps he will repent inwardly', or 'Perhaps he is among those who are not harmed by sins due to the Creator's providential care of him with respect to his behaviour.' They should not believe that there is evil in anyone except in the case of the person about whom God has made known to them the consequences of his behaviour; however, they do not reproach anyone.

The people of this way do not see themselves as better than anyone else. Whosoever views himself as better than someone else without knowing his own rank and that of the other person ultimately, and not just momentarily, is ignorant of God, deceived, and no good is to be found in him, whatever gnostic perceptions he might have been given. Contempt of knowledge from the point of view of Reality is contempt of God Most High, and it is the antithesis of sanctity.

Among their attributes: purifying the soul of every base disposition, adorning it with every sublime disposition; enduring injury but not inflicting it; bearing all mankind but not goading all of them against anyone; helping others obtain righteousness; and aiding the distressed. They guide the lost, teach the ignorant, and alert the heedless. They neither veil themselves nor have others who veil them: all who seek them find them, and all who want them reach them. They do not hide from anyone nor do they refuse a beggar. They receive a guest hospitably and put the stranger at ease; they reassure the fearful, satiate the hungry, give drink to the thirsty, clothe the naked and help the servant. They neglect no virtue and commit no vice.

Among their attributes: physical efforts in the way of hunger, thirst, nakedness, and the four rigours: white death, which is hunger; red death which is opposition to passion; black death, which is bearing injury; and green death, which is the wearing of a frock with patches one over another.[2]

Among their attributes: renouncing both worlds from their hearts, and preferring their brethren among God's creatures to what they possess; relying upon God Most High in all their affairs; being content with everything that happens to them which the ego detests; and bearing patiently sufferings and separation from one's homeland. They dissociate themselves from creatures without believing that there is evil in them, but rather out of preference for the Creator over creatures. They sever relationships, surmount obstacles, and strive in fulfilling the needs of people after emptying themselves: for whosoever strives to do that before emptying himself is actually seeking leadership and a good reputation.

Among their virtues: being satisfied, which means that their souls should be content with what has been provided in the way of sustenance without expecting more; and not shaving a hair or cutting it, nor clipping a nail, nor taking off a garment to be given to someone else unless they are ritually pure, for it is their intention that nothing leave them without their being in a state of ritual purity. The angels say, 'We left them while they were praying'.[3]

Among their attributes: supplication to God Most High by way of fulfilling the duty of servanthood (*ʿubūdiyyah*); spiritual poverty, submissiveness, humility, obedience, modesty toward God Most High in order that the Divine Names which correspond to these qualities may be manifested. Indeed, only he who is characterized by these attributes can know the mystery of these Names, for they are the spirit of servanthood.

Among their states: examining their defects and occupying themselves with their own souls, while being blind to the faults of people. They believe in nought but the good in everyone, and therefore habituate their tongues to the good. They abstain from being curious, walk quickly, keep silent except with regard to the good, command good deeds, and prohibit kings who are feared and in whom others place their hope from committing evil deeds. They are at peace with all of creation and pray for Muslims secretly. They serve their fellow seekers and have compassion and mercy for all God's servants, whether human or non-human living things.

It is related that in Bukhāra there was a governor who was one of the most tyrannical of men. One day he was riding and saw a mangy dog. That day was extremely cold, so he said to one of his men, 'Pick up that dog!' It was taken to his house, and he was kind and friendly to it. When night came, a voice called out in his sleep, 'You were a dog, so we gave you to a dog'.

Among their states: they spread about the good qualities of people and hide their faults, except for heretics: everyone is under obligation to make known their state so that people can be on their guard against them.

Among their states: looking with the eye of appreciation, not with the eye of contempt. They do not see themselves as better than anyone else, nor do they see themselves as having a superiority or right over anyone; rather, it is creatures who have rights over them. They do not lend anything to anyone, but if someone who is in need requests something of them, they give it to him; nor do they tell themselves that they will take anything from him; but if it is returned, they persuade him gently to keep it. If he refuses, they take it from him and give it to some other needy person, since it can never be added to their property; for verily, once they abandon anything, they do not go back to reclaim it. If they drop something in the street, whether clothing or money—even if it be one thousand dinars—which they might have left behind as they walked on, they neither search for it nor return to search for it nor ask about it. If on account of that loss, their minds are distraught, then they have a weakness, and the world has a share in their hearts. So let them take steps to remove this weakness. If someone returns what was lost to them without being asked, then if they wish, they may keep it or if they wish, they may give it away.

Among their attributes: giving preference to the poor over the rich and to those concerned with the Hereafter over those concerned with the here and now. It is not one of their conditions that they not have wealth; rather, among them are those who have wealth and those who have nothing.

Among their attributes: taking pleasure in acts of obedience both during spiritual retreat and in public; keeping an eye on their moments with God Most High; preserving their thoughts fixed on God Most High when receiving inspirations from time to time; being content with God Most High in all states; and praising God for every state.

Whosoever breaks a habit within himself of the type that everyone else amongst mankind continues to have, then God Most High, in return for that, will similarly break a habit for him, and this is called a miracle (*karāmah*) by the masses. As for the élite, to them this miracle is the Divine Providence which bestows on them success and strength, so that they can break their habits themselves.

PART TWO OF THE BOOK

ON EXPLAINING INVOCATIONS

Herein Are Sections and a Conclusion Which Are Part of the Total Number of Principles

Section [One]
Discussions on the Phrase *Lā ilāha illa'llāh*

First Discussion
Grammarians have said: When *lā* (no) is joined to an indefinite noun, it signifies a general negation. If you say, 'There is no man in the house,' you negate both the few men and the many. Therefore, it is not correct to say after that, 'but one or two men'.

Second Discussion
A number of grammarians claim that the phrase *Lā ilāha illa'llāh* (There is no divinity but God) has elision and ellipsis, the meaning being, 'We have no divinity but God,' or 'There is no divinity in existence but God.' This calls for reflection, because if the meaning were, 'We have no divinity but God,' then 'There is no divinity but God' would not have the meaning of True Unity. It is conceivable that one may say, 'Suppose that we have no divinity but God. Then would you say that there is no divinity but God for all creatures and possibilities?' Accordingly, when God Most High

said, 'Your God is One God,' He said afterwards, 'There is no god save Him, the Compassionate, the Merciful.'[1]

There remains for a proponent to say, 'Suppose that our God is One. Would you then say that the God of all is One'? He removed that possibility by His saying, 'There is no divinity but Him'; otherwise it would be pure repetition.

There is a second meaning to 'There is no divinity in existence but God', and it also has to be considered, because there is no need for this ellipsis. If we assess it correctly, it negates the existence of the Divinity. Even if we did not assess it correctly and simply took the literal meaning of the phrase, it would negate the essence of the Divinity. It is known that the negation of the essence is more powerful in affirming Unity than the negation of existence.

If it be said: The negation of essence is absurd, for the statement, 'Black is not black' is a judgment to the effect that black has been transformed into its opposite. Now, that something should become its opposite is preposterous. While if we say, 'Black is non-existent', then that is reasonable.

The response: We do not concede that the negation of the essence is absurd. When you say, 'Black is non-existent', you have negated existence, but existence insofar as it is an essence. When you negate absolute essence, you negate the essence which is called existence. Hence, negation of the essence is intelligible; therefore, it is possible to interpret the phrase *Lā ilāha illa'llāh* in a literal sense. When you say, 'Black is non-existent', you negate the essence, but you do not negate existence. You only negate the essence whose attribute is existence. So, is this essence whose attribute is existence something that is different from essence and existence or not? If it differs from the two, then that difference is an essence. Hence our statement, 'Black is non-existent', is a negation of that essence which is called 'attribution' (*mawṣūfiyyah*); and at that point we return to the previous discussion. But if we say that the essence whose attribute is existence is not something that is different from essence and existence, then applying the negation to both is not possible. When that is impossible, negation remains directed either at essence or at existence. At that point, we reach our aim of determining whether it is possible to negate the essence. Thus, our statement, *Lā ilāha illa'llāh*, without ellipsis, is correct.

Third Discussion

Our saying '*Allāhu*' in the phrase *Lā ilāha illa'llāh*[2] is in the nominative case because it is an appositive standing for *lā* with its noun. For if you say, 'No man came to me except Zayd', your saying 'except Zayd' is in the nominative case in apposition, because in apposition one rejects the first part of the phrase and accepts the second. So the meaning becomes, 'None but Zayd came to me'. This is logical, because it conveys the negation of the coming of all except Zayd. In your saying, 'The people came to me except Zayd', apposition is not possible, because the meaning then is, 'They came to me except Zayd', which necessitates that everyone but Zayd came to him; and this is absurd.

Fourth Discussion

Grammarians agree that the place of *illā* in this expression is the same as *ghayr*, so the implied meaning is *Lā ilāha ghayru'llāh* (There is no divinity other than God). A poet once said,

وَكُلُّ أَخٍ مُفَارِقُهُ أَخُوهُ   لَعُمْرُ أَبِيكَ إِلاَّ الْفَرْقَدانِ

And every brother quits his brother
By your father's life, except (*illā*) the two stars (*al-farqadān*)[3]

The meaning: Every brother other than (*ghayr*) the two stars quits his brother. God Most High has said, 'If there were, in the heavens and the earth, other gods besides (*illā*) God', meaning: If there had been deities other than (*ghayr*) God—'then verily, there would have been confusion in both [the heavens and the earth] . . .'.[4]

For if we interpret *illā* as exception, then *Lā ilāha illa'llāh* would not be pure Unity, because the meaning would become, 'There are no divinities from which God is to be excluded'. It would be the negation of deities from which God has been excluded and indeed this is affirmed by those who hold to the actual meaning of the statement, and that is disbelief. Accordingly, it has been proved that if the expression *illā* be construed as exception, then the phrase *Lā ilāha illa'llāh* would not be pure Unity. The sages agree that it conveys the meaning of pure Unity; so it is necessary to ascribe to *illā* (except) the meaning of *ghayr* (other than), so that the meaning of the phrase would be *Lā ilāha ghayru'llāh* (There is no divinity other than God).

Fifth Discussion

A number of theologians have said, 'The exception from a negation is not an affirmation'. They advanced as an argument that exception (*istithnā'*) is derived from the saying, 'I diverted something from its direction',[5] which means, 'I kept it away from it'. When you say, 'There is no scholar' (*lā ʿālim*), then this is both a judgment of non-existence as well as the negation of non-existence; then, when you say, immediately afterwards, 'except Zayd', this exception might conceivably go back to the judgment of non-existence; and upon the elimination of the judgment of non-existence, the exception remains undiscussed and unevaluated as either negative or affirmative; so no certainty results.

However, if the influence of the exception is in its removal of non-existence and in precluding it, then certainty results necessarily. This is so because, when non-existence is removed, existence results necessarily, for there is no intermediary between the two opposites. When that is ascertained, then referring the exception to the judgment of non-existence is more appropriate than referring it to non-existence itself, because the words were devised with reference to conceptual judgments, not to external existent things. Hence, ascribing that exception to the judgment of non-existence is more appropriate than ascribing it to non-existence itself. Moreover, both the non-existence of something in itself and its essence are not subject to the control of an evaluator; rather, it is the evaluator who judges of that existence and non-existence. So, referring the exception to the judgment is better than referring it to the thing adjudged to be non-existent.

The second proof in elucidating that the exception from a negation is not an affirmation is that many illustrations have come down through the Prophetic traditions and customs regarding the exception from negation, even though they do not necessarily lead to certainty, as in the words of the Prophet ﷺ 'There is no marriage except through a legal guardian' and his other words, 'There is no prayer save through ritual purity'. It is customarily said, 'There is no power except through wealth and no wealth except through men'.

The meaning of each of these statements is conditional. Even though other illustrations have come down to us indicating that the exception from the negation is affirmation, we say: A figurative expression must be in one of the two parts of the sentence. Otherwise, we say that when it is not decreed that whatever is excluded from the negation is affirmation, the meaning might be just that, whatever the wording indicates. If we say: If it be decreed that whatever is excluded from the negation is affirmation, and such is not the case, then we must require the non-observance of whatever the wording indicates. It is known that the former is more appropriate because the affirmation of an additional matter through additional proof is not a contradiction to the general meaning; but abandoning whatever the wording might be is a contradiction to the general meaning. Thus, the exception from the negation is not affirmation.

Accordingly, our statement *Lā ilāha illa'llāh* (There is no divinity but God) is a declaration negating the remaining deities. It is not a recognition of the existence of God Most High, which would not suffice in terms of sound faith. Also, it has been established that *illā* (except) has the meaning of *ghayr* (other than), so that our phrase *Lā ilāha illa'llāh* means *Lā ilāha ghayru'llāh* (There is no divinity other than God). Then the meaning becomes the negation of a divinity differing from God Most High. It does not follow that the negation of that which differs from something is an affirmation of the former; for ambiguity would then return.

The response: The affirmation of the Divinity was agreed upon among the intelligent, for God Most High says, 'And if thou ask them who created them, they will surely say God . . .'.[6] except that they used to affirm associates and peers alongside Him. Thus, what was intended by *Lā ilāha illa'llāh* was the negation of associates and peers, for the affirmation of Divinity is one of the necessary attributes of intelligence. We have admitted that the phrase *Lā ilāha illa'llāh* indicates the negation of the other deities and the affirmation of the divinity of God Most High, except that this comes about through the regulation of the Sacred Law, and through the grasp of a principle of language.

Sixth Discussion

It may be said, 'There is no man in the house,' or 'There is no man except in the house.' As for the first example, it necessarily negates all men totally; for when *lā* (no) is joined to an indefinite noun, it conveys the meaning of general negation; it is not, therefore, correct to say thereafter, 'but one or two men'; for it is the negation of the essence, and negation of the essence necessitates the negation of all its constituent parts. As to our statement, 'There is no man except in the house,' it is the opposite of 'There is no man in the house.' But our statement, 'There is no man except in the house,' conveys the certainty of one man. When we say, 'There is no man in the house', it necessarily conveys the meaning of general negation, and thus a mutual contradiction between the two statements is confirmed. It is evident that 'There is no man in the house' is more forceful in indicating general negation than is the phrase 'There is no man', in spite of the fact that each one of the two examples conveys the meaning of general negation. Inasmuch as the accusative construction is stronger in indicating generality, scholars agree upon it in the statement, *Lā ilāha illa'llāh*.[7]

Seventh Discussion

It is said that the concept of affirmation has priority over the concept of negation because of the possibility of conceiving affirmation, even though the idea of negation and non-existence does not occur to the mind of one. The concept of non-existence and negation is impossible before the concept of affirmation, because non-existence is unintelligible except in relation to a specified thing. Since the concept of affirmation precedes the concept of negation, why, then, should negation, which is subordinate, be made antecedent?

The answer is that there are many reasons for its precedence. The first: The negation of divinity from other than God Most High and then its affirmation in regard to Him are much more emphatic than affirming it of Him without negating it in other-than-Him. Our statement, 'There is no scholar in the town other than Zayd' is much more praiseworthy than 'Zayd is the town scholar'.

The second: Every man has one heart and one heart cannot be occupied with two thing at the same time. When it is occupied with one of two things, it is excluded from the other thing, and this to the extent of its pre-occupation with the first. Thus, it behoves the one who says *Lā ilāha illa'llāh* that he intend by *Lā ilāha* the expulsion of what is other-than-God from his heart. When the heart is empty of what is other-than-God, and when the authority of God is present therein, its light shines with a complete radiance, and His possession of it is perfect.

The third: Negation is analogous to ritual purity and affirmation is analogous to prayer. Just as ritual purity precedes prayer, so too does *Lā ilāha* precede *illa'llāh*. Negation is analogous to seeking refuge in God prior to reading the Qur'ān.[8] Just as cleaning a house of dirt precedes the arrival of a king therein, likewise is it the case here. And in this regard, realized sages have said: The first half of this expression is cleansing the heart, and the second is the advent of illumination through the presence of *al-Jabbār* (the Compeller); the first half is separation and the second is union; the first half points to His Words (may He be exalted!), 'Therefore flee unto God'[9] and the second to His Words, '. . . Say *Allāh*. Then leave them . . ..'[10]

Eighth Discussion

Someone might say: Whosoever knows that the world has a Wise, Powerful Creator, described by passive and dynamic divine Attributes, knows God with complete gnosis. His knowledge of the non-existence of a second divinity does not increase his knowledge of the reality of the Divinity and His Attributes, because the non-existence of a second deity is not equivalent to the existence of the first Divinity nor to any of His Attributes. Knowledge of the Essence of the Divinity and His Attributes does not suffice for the realization of salvation; rather, as long as the non-existence of a second divinity is not known, valuable knowledge about salvation is not attained.

If you ask: Why is gnosis of the Essence of God Most High and His Attributes not sufficient for the realization of salvation, while the knowledge of the non-existence of a second deity is important for the realization of salvation? The answer is this: Assuming there were two divinities (may God be exalted!), the servant would not know if he were the servant of this one or the servant of that one or of both together. It is possible that he may be the worshipper of one who is not his Creator. But when he knows that *Lā ilāha illa'llāh*, then he is absolutely certain of the fact that he is the worshipper of his Lord and Creator. Consequently, salvation cannot be attained save through Unity.

I say: For me, the supposition of the existence of two deities is rationally impossible, because the Divinity is the One Who has the Attributes of Majesty and Beauty, both dynamically and passively.

Then who is there other-than-He? In the 'other-than He', those attributes are acquired from Him. Thus, the Divinity is naught but One, and He is *Allāh*, as is evidenced through His Words (may He be exalted!). 'If there were, in the heavens and the earth, gods besides God, then verily, there would have been confusion in both . . ..'[11]

Ninth Discussion

On saying this phrase under different conditions: The most elementary of them is uttering it, which saves the life of the person who says it and protects his wealth. The Prophet ﷺ said, 'I have been commanded to fight people until they say, *Lā ilāha illa'llāh*. When they say it, they safeguard their lives and property from me, except as is rightfully due; and their reckoning is with God.'[12]

Both the sincere ones and the hypocrites share therein; thus all who attach themselves to this phrase obtain its blessings and gain a share of its benefits. Whosoever asks for the world through it gains safety and peace therein; and whosoever asks for the Hereafter has already combined two shares and has gained happiness in both worlds. And yet confessing with the tongue is but one degree!

The second condition[13] is to add to the saying belief in the heart in keeping with traditional conformism; for the conformist is not a scholar or gnostic. Rather, there is a difference of opinion: is he a Muslim or not? Belief in the heart has several degrees according to the strength of belief and to the greater or smaller number of its articles of faith.

The third condition is to add to belief in the heart knowledge of the convincing arguments that strengthen that belief. Mankind differs therein with a difference that is difficult to ascertain.

The fourth condition is to back up his belief with decisive proofs, unless he is not from amongst the people of contemplation, unveiling, and revelation.

The fifth condition is to be from amongst the people of contemplation, unveiling, and revelation. Their relationship to the people with decisive proof is like the relationship of the people of proofs to the generality of mankind.

Know that the science of unveiling has no end to it, for it consists in the journey of the intellect in the stations of Majesty, Beauty, Sublimeness, Grandeur, and Holiness.

Note: He to whom the mysteries of *Lā ilāha illa'llāh* are revealed draws near to God, and his worship of God becomes sincere. He does not turn to anyone but to Him, nor does he have hope in or fear other than Him, nor does he see harm or benefit except as coming from Him. He abandons whosoever is not He and rids himself of inward and outward associationism (*shirk*).

Section [Two]
On Establishing Proof That He Is One Without Associate, Both Intellectually and Traditionally

As for intellectually, there are these aspects: First, the existence of two deities is absurd, since if we suppose the existence of the two, then each one would be master over all possibilities. If we suppose that onc of thc two wanted Zayd to move and the other wanted him to be still, either both desires would take place, which is absurd, due to the impossibility of combining two opposites, or one of the two would not occur, which is absurd, because preventing the occurrence of the desire of each one of them means achieving the aim of the other. Nor is the existence of one's desire to be prevented except when the existence of the desire of the other occurs or vice versa. Even if they both refrained together, they would both co-exist together, and that is impossible for two reasons:

The first: Inasmuch as each one of the two is master over that which is endless, it is impossible that one of them be more powerful than the other; rather, they are equal in power, so it is impossible that the desire of one of them become more worthy of occurrence than that of the other. This would require the predominance of one of the two equals without any predominating element; and this is absurd.

The second: If the desire of one of the two takes place without the other, then the one whose desire occurred is powerful, and the one whose desire did not occur is weak, and he is not the Deity of Creation.

If it be said: We do not accept that the contradiction of wills is a sound argument for two reasons. One of them is that since each one of them must be a knower of all things knowable, each of them is bound to know that one of the two opposites will take place while the other will not. Now the occurrence of that which a deity knows cannot take place is impossible; the knower of that which is impossible of occurrence does not, accordingly, desire it. Thus, each one wants naught but the occurrence of one thing.

The second reason is that since each one of them must be wise, each knows what is good and not good, and both agree in willing the good; thus, contradiction is impossible. We accept the validity of the argument, but we say it is merely conceivable, not real; so it is not necessarily absurd.

The answer: If knowledge of the good were the cause for willing it, then the deity would be the result of his deeds, not the creator of them out of free will. The doctrine on Unicity is subordinate to the doctrine that affirms the powerful, the free of will.

The second proof: If we assume that there are two deities, each of them would have power over all possibilities, which would lead to the occurrence of two possibilities emanating from two independent powers; and that is impossible. Hence, the existence of two deities is impossible.

The proof of inseparableness is that, if each one of them were subject to the other, and they agreed on a possible creation, then the power of one of them would not be worthier to create than the other, because each one is independent in creating and is willing to do it, and there is no predominance in either one of them. We only said that the occurrence of two possibilities emanating from two independent powers is impossible, because that deed is in need of both and yet is in no need of both; thus, it would need and yet not need both of them; and that is a union of opposites.

The third proof: If we assume that there are two deities, then either it is true that they will disagree, so that one of them must be weak; or it is not true, and this leads to the weakness of one of them also, for each one of them must be weak in regard to the opposition manifested by his counterpart. Thus, the matter goes back to the point already made, that each one of them is weak. Now, the weak cannot be a deity.

When you know that, you know that all created beings and things that are in the higher and lower world are proofs of the Unicity of God Most High. Indeed, if one of the two deities had wanted it to be summer and the other winter, or if one of them had wanted this person to be well and the other wanted him sick, then what we had previously established would crop up again. I would say in verse:

سماءٌ وأرضٌ وشُمُّ الجبال كذاك البحارُ له شاهدُ
وعَجْزُ جميعِ الوَرَى عن أقَلّ ذُبابٍ له عابدُ
وفي كُلِّ شيءٍ له آيةٌ تَدُلُّ على أنّه واحِدُ

Heaven and earth and the highest of mountains,
as these oceans, witness to Him.
And all of mankind are unable to create
the least insect, which worships Him.
And in everything there is a sign that points
to the Oneness of Him.

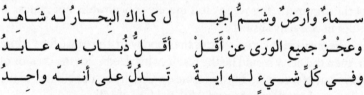

The fourth proof: If we assume two existents as having necessary self-existence then each would have to be a partner to the other in existence and at variance with him in himself. Now, that through which the partnership comes about is other than that through which the variance occurs. Each one is a compound made up of existence, which the other shares with him, and of dissimilarity through which he is at variance with the other. Each compound needs every one of its parts, but its parts are other-than-it. Thus, every compound is in need, and everything needful is a possibility. Maintaining that Necessary Existence is more than one is therefore absurd.

The fifth proof: If we assume two deities, each of them having necessary self-existence, then each one must be distinguished by a certain characteristic; otherwise, multiplicity could not occur. So, wherein lies the distinction? Either it is an attribute of perfection or it is not. If it were an attribute of perfection, then the one devoid of it would be devoid of an attribute of perfection, and it would be imperfect. Now, the imperfect cannot be a god. If it is not an attribute of perfection, then it is an attribute of imperfection; and the imperfect cannot be a god.

The sixth proof: Wherein lies the distinction? Either it is of considerable importance in the ascertainment of his divinity, or it is not. If it were of considerable importance, then the one devoid of it would not be a god. But if it were not of considerable importance, then being distinguished by it is not necessary. Hence, he is in need of a distinguishing trait; he who is in need is one who lacks and is not a deity.

The seventh proof: If we assume two deities, then inevitably the servant would be able to distinguish between them. That distinction, in our minds, would come about through place, time, or power; and such restrictions for a god are impossible.

The eighth proof: If we assume two deities, then one of them is either sufficient for directing and creating the world, or he is not. If he were sufficient, then the other would not be needed, and that is an imperfection; or if he were not sufficient, then he is imperfect, and the imperfect cannot be a god.

The ninth proof: Intelligence makes the judgment that an act is in need of an agent, and a single agent is enough. With regard to what is greater than one, we say that the need for two is no more valid than for three, and the need for three is no more valid than for four, and so on endlessly. Thus, declaring that there are two deities is absurd.

The tenth proof: One of the two deities either has the ability to distinguish himself and delimit himself, or he does not. First: this is absurd, because the proof for affirming a creator is based on the contingency of created beings and their possibility; and nothing therein indicates delimitation. Second: This is false because it leads to positing weakness in the deity.

The eleventh proof: One of the two deities either has the ability to hide some of his deeds, so that the veiled deity must be ignorant, or he is unable to, and thus he must be weak.

The twelfth proof: The totality of both their powers is stronger than the power of each one individually; hence, the power of each one is limited, so each one is weak.

The thirteenth proof: Number is imperfect because of its need for the number 'one'; and likewise 'the one' which is created out of the same species and type as number is imperfect, because the total sum of quantity is greater than it; and the imperfect cannot be a god.*

The fourteenth proof: If we assume two deities, and we assume that a non-existent can exist, then if one of the two deities cannot create, they are both weak; but if one of them can, then the weak one is not a god. If they both can together and if they create through mutual co-operation, then each one is in need of the other; so each one is weak. If each one can create independently, then when one of them does create, either the second one has the power to do so – and that is impossible, because the creation of what exists is absurd – or else he does not have the power, in which

* The author is speaking of 'one' in a quantitative sense in contrast to the qualitative Oneness of God.

case the first has eliminated the second's power and weakened him. So he is vanquished and is not a god.

If it be said: As for the first deity, when his creation comes into being, his power ceases, so he must of necessity have made himself weak. We answer: When his creation comes into being, his power is exhausted; but exhaustion of power is not weakness. As to his partner, his power has not been exhausted; rather it has vanished because of the power of the first; and that is a weakening.

The fifteenth proof: We say that if we assume two deities, then either each one of them has the ability to produce movement in a particular body in place of repose, and vice versa, or each does not. If one does not, he is weak; and if he does, then when he produces movement in it, it would be impossible for the second one to produce repose in it. So the latter is weak and not a god.

The sixteenth proof: If we assume two deities that were knowers of all things knowable, then the knowledge of each one of them would be dependent upon the very thing known by the other. Hence, similarity would inevitably result; the receiver of one of two similar things would then be the same as the receiver of the other. It would then be conceivable for beings possessed of such-and-such a knowledge, rather than the possibility of another, to be distinguished by that very knowledge. That requires a restriction for each one of the two deities as regards his own knowledge and power. So each one is imperfect, needing a deity, which is absurd.

The seventeenth proof: Partnership in sovereignty is a flaw in any textual proof in as much as the quality of being unique, the affirmation of Unity, and independence of rule are attributes of perfection. Kings loathe partnership in this lower kingdom. The greater the kingdom, the stronger is the aversion to partnership; so what must be your thought about the Kingdom (*mulk*) of God Most High and His Realm (*Malakūt*)? Thus, when one of the two deities has power to take a kingdom for himself, the other is weak.

The eighteenth proof: If we assume two deities (may God be exalted!), then either each one is in need of the other or is not in need, or else one of them is in need and the other is not. If the first part of the condition applies, then both are needful; if the second part applies, then each one is in no need of the other, so the other is imperfect. Do you not see that when a country has a chief, but the people do what is best for that country without either consulting or taking the chief into consideration, that this is the extreme of baseness and meanness? The deity that is self-sufficient cannot be dispensed with; and if one of them needs the other without the opposite being true, then the one in need is imperfect, and the independent one is the deity. Some of these viewpoints are decisive and some are convincing.

As for the traditional proofs, the first ones are His Words:

> 'Your God is One God; there is no deity save Him . . ..'[14]
> 'Say: "He is God, the One!"'[15]
> 'God says: "Do not take two gods, for He is only One God . . .".'[16]

The second is His words (may He be exalted!), 'He is the First and the Last . . .'.[17]

The First is the One without antecedent, so that if someone were to say, 'The first slave I buy will be freed', and then buys firstly two slaves; he will free neither of them because the first must be a single person. Even if he were to buy one after that, he would not free him either, because the first must be prior to the others. For when God Most High described Himself as being First, it is incumbent that He be unique and prior to all else; hence, this requires that He not have a partner.

The third is His words (may He be exalted!), 'And with Him are the keys of the Invisible. None but He knoweth them . . .'.[18] If He had a partner, surely the partner would know them, but the text decrees that no one knows them except Him.

The fourth is the phrase *Lā ilāha illa'llāh*; it is mentioned in thirty-seven passages in the Qur'ān.

The fifth is His words (may He be exalted!) '. . . Everything will perish save His countenance . . .'.[19] It was decreed that what is other-than-He should perish. Whatsoever is non-existent, and then comes into being, cannot be eternal; and that which has been ascertained as eternity cannot possibly be non-existence. What is not eternal is not a god.

The sixth is His words (may He be exalted!), 'If God touch thee with affliction, there is none that can relieve therefrom save Him . . .'.[20] The affirmation that there is a partner alongside God is false. The partner is either higher or lower. The higher are the stars, the sun, and the moon; but God has nullified these by the argument of Abraham, when he said, ' . . . I love not things that set'.[21] God has nullified the argument of those who allege that the partner is either light or darkness by His words, ' . . . He hath appointed the darkness and the light . . .'.[22] God Most High has nullified whosoever says that there are two deities by His words, 'If there were, in the heavens and the earth, gods beside God, then verily there would have been confusion in both . . .'.[23] and His words, '. . . then had they sought a way against the Lord of the Throne',[24] and His words '. . . some of them would assuredly have overcome others'.[25]

The lower partner is said to be the Messiah, but God nullified it by His words, 'The Messiah will never scorn to be a servant unto God . . .'.[26] It is also said to be an idol, but God nullified this by His words, 'Is he who creates like he who createth not? . . .'.[27]

The seventh: God (may He be glorified!), has mentioned three proofs on the validity of Oneness:

[1] 'If there were, in the heavens and the earth, gods beside God, then verily there would have been confusion in both . . ..'[28]

[2] '. . . and some of them would assuredly have overcome others'.[29]

[3] '. . . then had they sought a way against the Lord of the Throne'.[30] Glory be to God, Lord of the Throne.

That is a warning to the effect that being occupied with the glorification of God is of benefit only after establishing proof that

His existence is incomparable. He said, '. . . Glory be to God, the Lord of the Throne, from all that they ascribe unto Him.'[31] He did not say, 'Glory be to God from all that they ascribe unto Him', as a warning: that how is it possible for the intelligent person to make the inanimate, which neither lives nor discerns, a partner in divinity with the Creator of the Supreme Throne and the Originator of the heavens and the earth?

Conclusion: Know that faith is composed of the gnosis occurring in the heart, which is the foundation, for God Most High has said, 'Know that there is no divinity but God . . .'[32] and of confessing Oneness with the tongue, for God Most High has said, 'Say: He is God, the One!'[33] Indeed, 'say' is an imperative for the one under obligation to declare with his tongue whatsoever denotes Unicity. The words of the Prophet ﷺ confirm that: 'I have been commanded to fight people until they say, *Lā ilāha illa'llāh*'.[34]

Pronunciation with the tongue is an obligation, because faith has precepts which pertain to the inward, and these are the precepts of the Hereafter; and the inward is subordinate to the knowledge which is hidden from Creation. It also has precepts which pertain to the outward, which are the rules of this world. Determining them is not possible for us except after we have come to know of the submission to God (*islām*) of the one under obligation to observe the religious precepts, and this we know only through words. Knowledge is a basic support with regard to God Most High, while speech is a canonical support with regard to mankind. That is what His words allude to in the verse: 'Wed not idolatresses till they believe . . .'.[35]

The Prophet ﷺ said, 'Whosoever says *Lā ilāha illa'llāh* sincerely with his heart will enter Paradise'. Ad-Daqqāq said, 'Whosoever says it sincerely in his speech enters Paradise as he is'. God Most High has said, 'But for him who feareth the standing before his Lord, there are two Paradises',[36] the Paradise of the present moment, which is the Paradise of gnosis, and the Paradise in the end, which is the Paradise of the Hereafter.

Section [Three]

It was related on the authority of Muḥammad al-Hakīm at-Tirmidhī that Muʿadh ibn Jabal said, 'The Messenger of God ﷺ said, "Not a soul dies witnessing that there is no divinity save God and that I am the Messenger of God – with that stemming from a believer's heart – but God pardons it".'

The Shaykh[37] said,

This is because this testimony of faith is attested to at death when passions have died out in him, his rebellious soul has softened, his desire has left, he has cast himself before the power of the Lord of the Worlds, and both the inward and the outward have become alike for him. He meets God sincerely by that testimony of faith, and He pardons him through that true testimony of faith, the exterior of which corresponds to the interior. As for the one who says it while still healthy, that is a confused statement, because he bears witness to this testimony while his heart is filled with passions and his soul is reckless and arrogant. This, then, is the difference between remembering the testimony of faith in a state of health and remembering it at the end of one's life.

The Imām Fakhru'd-Dīn elaborated on it by saying:

Indeed, the heart of man is tempted by his world, fettered by the power of passions, intoxicated away from the Hereafter, and perplexed with regard to God Most High. Certitude will never take place in him, because his heart is filled with the tendency towards what is other-than-God Most High; so the tendency towards God Most High does not take place.

When certitude about God Most High does occur in the heart, the situation is the reverse of what was said, for certitide is called certitude (*yaqīn*) because of its settling (*istiqrār*) in the heart; and it is the light. It is said, 'The water in the hole was clear' (*tayaqqana*), when it settles (*istaqarra*)

> therein. So when light settles in, it is lasting; and when it lasts, the soul becomes discerning. The heart becomes tranquil through the Majesty of God; then it abstains from what is other-than-God. So, it stands weak and is compelled to cry out to God for help. Then He who responds to the necessitous when they cry out to Him, responds to it. That radiant light settles into the heart and the darkness of preoccupation with what is other-than-God is extinguished therewith. Then the reality of the Realm (*al-Malakūt*) becomes visible to it, and that is what Ḥārithah meant when he said to the Messenger of God ﷺ : 'It is as if I see the Throne of my Lord distinctly.' And the Messenger of God ﷺ said, 'The Light of God Most High is faith in one's heart.'

Tradition mentions that Idrīs ﵇ and Moses and Muḥammad, the blessings of God be upon them all!, each of them in his own time practiced this supplication constantly: 'O Light of everything, Thou art He whose Light dispels the darkness'. The words of the Prophet ﷺ substantiate that:

> For whosoever says, 'There is no divinity but God alone; He has no associates; to Him belong dominion and praise; He gives life and causes death; and He has power over everything,' sincerely in his spirit, believing in his heart and with his tongue, the heavens will rend asunder so that the Lord sees the one speaking among the people of the world.

Zayd ibn Arqam transmitted the following:

> The Messenger of God ﷺ said, 'Whosoever says *Lā ilāha illa'llāh* sincerely, enters Paradise'. He was asked, 'O Messenger of God, how can one say the words sincerely?' He answered, 'By keeping away from things forbidden.' The Prophet ﷺ said, 'Be sincere! Even a little will suffice you!'

Zayd ibn Arqam said,

> The Messenger of God ﷺ said, 'Verily, God has enjoined upon me that no one from my community should come to me with *Lā ilāha illa'llāh*, without mixing anything in the words, but that Paradise is incumbent upon him.' They said, 'O Messenger of God, and what is that which one might mix with the words?' He answered, 'Desire for this world, amassing wealth for its sake, and defending it; he professes the teachings of the Prophets while behaving like tyrants.'

In short, certitude is inevitable upon uttering this phrase, so that it become beneficial. But certitude does not occur through it except through the death of passions; and the death of passions is not reached except through one of two ways: one, that he discipline himself until his passions die while he is alive; and two, that his passions die at his death. Then his hopes and fear of his Lord become great, and his view of the world as a whole is severed by force. When he utters these words in that state, he merits forgiveness. For this reason, the pious ancestors used to prefer teaching them to the dying person. The Prophet ﷺ said 'Teach your dying *Lā ilāha illa'llah*'.[38]

For the human being near death, his passions are extinguished, the light of certitude comes to him; then this sacred phrase on his part becomes acceptable. As to the first category, which is the one who disciplines his soul, God opens for him a small window to the invisible world. Then the terrors of the Lord of Majesty master him, so he utters the phrase from a pure heart, which makes him more deserving of forgiveness.

Section [Four]

Since this sacred phrase is the most excellent invocation, both the saint and the enemy of God seek refuge therein at the moment of tribulation. Thus Pharaoh, when near drowning, '. . . he exclaimed: I believe that there is no god save Him in whom the Children of

Israel believe . . .'[39] That is, there is no deity who has the ability to make fire a comfort as was the case with the Friend (*al-Khalīl*),[40] or make water a torture as was the case with Pharaoh: 'save Him in whom the Children of Israel believe . . .'[41]

And to Jonah ﵇ God Most High said, '. . . he cried out in the darkness that there is no god but Thou . . .'.[42] That is, indeed it is Thou who art able to keep a human being alive in the stomach of a whale, and no one other than Thou canst do that. So He accepted Jonah's appeal but did not accept Pharaoh's, because Jonah had had prior knowledge. God Most High has said, '. . . and be not like him of the fish, who cried out in despair',[43] and He Most High has said, 'And had he not been one of those who glorify [God], he would have tarried in its belly till the day when they are raised'.[44]

This is a warning that whosoever is mindful of God in seclusion is mindful of Him in public. However, Jonah ﵇ remembered this phrase with presence of mind, contemplation, and contrition, then said, '. . . there is no god but Thou . . .'[45] while Pharaoh said it with absentmindedness: '. . . there is no god save Him in whom the Children of Israel believe . . .'.[46] With regard to Pharaoh, polytheism preceded him, so he did not mention the phrase out of veneration but rather to seek deliverance from drowning, due to His Words (may He be exalted!), '. . . till, when the drowning overtook him, he exclaimed: I believe that there is no god save Him in whom the Children of Israel believe . . ..'[47]

God Most High commands you to perform many acts of obedience, but it is impossible that he fulfill your wish in any one of them; and He commands you to say *Lā ilāha illa'llāh*, but He fulfills your wish therein, for he said, 'God is witness that there is no god save Him . . .'.[48] The command to repeat this phrase in the verse is a command to repeat it throughout your life.

It is related that Joseph ﵇ desired to have a minister. Gabriel ﵇ said, 'Verily, God commands you to take so-and-so as your minister'. Joseph ﵇ then looked at him, and the man was extremely ugly; so he asked Gabriel the reason for choosing him.

He answered, 'Indeed, he has witnessed for you; for it is he who has testified, ". . . If his shirt is torn from the front . . .".'[49]

The allusion therein is that the one who bore witness to a fellow creature found his ministry in this world; and thus how can the one who bears witness to the Oneness of God here and now not find His mercy in the Hereafter? A *ḥadīth* states: 'Verily, God has angels who guarantee the protection of a leader (*imām*); now he whose protection is in agreement with the guarantee of the angels is forgiven all his former sins.' He whose protection corresponds to the guarantee of the angels one time is forgiven. He whose testimony of faith corresponds to the Unity of God Most High and witnesses to God one thousand times is even more deserving of being forgiven.

It was reported that al-Ḥajjāj ordered the death of a man who said, 'Do not kill me until you take my hand and walk with me.' So he acceded to his wishes. Then the man said, 'By the sacredness of my companionship with you this hour, do not kill me.' Thus, he pardoned him. Companionship with God Most High happens to the believer during the testimony of *Lā ilāha illa'llāh*; therefore, forgiveness of him is to be expected.

The phrase *Lā ilāha illa'llāh* ascends to God by itself, while other forms of obedience ascend by way of the angels. God Most High has said, '. . .Unto Him good words ascend, and the pious deed doth He exalt . . .'.[50] Some have said that the pious deed ascends by way of the angels. All acts of obedience disappear on the Day of Judgment, but the utterance of the formulas *Lā ilāha illa'llāh* and *al-ḥamdu li'llāh* (praise be to God) do not.

God Most High has said, relating the words of those in Paradise, 'And they say: Praise be to God Who hath put grief away from us . . .',[51] and 'They say: Praise be to God Who hath fulfilled His promise unto us . . .'.[52] 'Their prayer therein will be: Glory be to Thee, O God! and their greeting therein will be: Peace . . ..'[53]

There is no divinity but He, to whom belongs all praise in this world and the next. It is reported in a tradition that whosoever says

Lā ilāha illa'llāh that He Most High will grant him pardon equal to the number of every unbelieving male and female who ascribe to God an opponent or an antagonist or an associator. Certainly, he deserves a reward equal to their numbers. It is said, 'When it is the end of time, there will be no excellence to anything of the pious deeds like the excellence of *Lā ilāha illa'llāh*, for the prayers and fasting of people will be vitiated by hypocrisy and reputation, and their almsgiving by what is unlawful.' *Lā ilāha illa'llāh* is a remembrance, and the believer does not remember God except out of a sincere heart.

Section [Five]
On the Excellence of *Lā ilāha illa'llāh*

It was related that the Prophet ﷺ said, 'The best remembrance is *Lā ilāha illa'llāh* and the best supplication is *al-ḥamdu li'llāh*'.[54]

According to Ibn ᶜUmar (may God be pleased with both of them!),[55] he said,

> For the people of *Lā ilāha illa'llāh*, there is neither loneliness at death nor at the Resurrection. It is as if I were looking at the people of *Lā Ilāha illa'llāh* at the moment of the Outcry,[56] shaking off the dirt from their hair and saying, 'Praise be to God who hath put grief away from us'.[57]

It was related that when al-Ma'mūn departed from Merv in the direction of Iraq, he passed through Nīshāpūr. At his vanguard was ᶜAlī ibn Mūsā ar-Riḍā. A group of shaykhs went to him and said, 'We ask you, because of your relation to the Messenger of God ﷺ to tell us a *ḥadīth* that will be beneficial to us'. So he narrated on the authority of his father and his forefathers that the Prophet ﷺ said, 'God Most High has said, '*Lā ilāha illa'llāh* is My fortress; whosoever enters My fortress is safe from My chastisement'.

Ibn ᶜAbbās related that the Prophet ﷺ said,

> God opens the gates of Paradise and a herald calls out from

beneath the Throne, 'O Paradise and every bliss that is within you, to whom do you belong?' Paradise and all therein exclaim, 'We belong to the people of *Lā ilāha illa'llāh* and we long for the people of *Lā ilāha illa'llāh*. No one takes possession of us except the people of *Lā ilāha illa'llāh*, and we are forbidden to anyone who does not say *Lā ilāha illa'llāh* and who does not believe in *Lā ilāha illa'llāh*.' At this, hellfire with all the chastisement that is therein says, 'No one enters me except the one who disavows *Lā ilāha illa'llāh*; I seek only those who deny *Lā ilāha illa'llāh*; I am forbidden to whosoever says *Lā ilāha illa'llāh*; I am not filled except by those who reject *Lā ilāha illa'llāh*; and my wrath is only toward the ones who disavow *Lā ilāha illa'llāh*.'

The Prophet continued,

> The forgiveness and mercy of God come and they both say, 'Verily, we belong to the people of *Lā ilāha illa'llāh*; we help those who say *Lā ilāha illa'llāh*; we love those who say *Lā ilāha illa'llāh*; and we honor those who say *Lā ilāha illa'llāh*.' God says, 'I have made Paradise lawful for those who say *Lā ilāha illa'llāh*; I have declared hellfire forbidden to those who say *Lā ilāha illa'llāh*; I pardon every sin of those who say *Lā ilāha illa'llāh*; I conceal neither mercy nor forgiveness from those who say *Lā ilāha illa'llāh*; I have not created Paradise except for the people of *Lā ilāha illa'llāh*; so, do not mix the people of *Lā ilāha illa'llāh* with anything but that which is in conformity with *Lā ilāha illa'llāh*.'

The Prophet ﷺ has said,

> I have been commanded to fight people until they say *Lā ilāha illa'llāh*. When they say it, they safeguard their lives and property from me except as is rightly due; and their reckoning is with God.[58]

Section [Six]

Gnostics, in commenting on *Lā ilāha illa'llāh*, have mentioned various aspects. One of them: Ibn ʿAbbās said, '*Lā ilāha illa'llāh* means there is no benefactor, no harmer, no exalter, no debaser, no giver, and no preventer except God.'

The second of them: '*Lā ilāha illa'llāh* means whose grace is hoped for, whose chastisement is feared, whose oppression one can feel safe from, whose sustenance is consumed, whose command is revealed, whose pardon is asked, whose prohibition is not transgressed, and whose favour is not forbidden, if it be not God's?'

Likewise, the phrase *Lā ilāha illa'llāh* is a sign of knowledge and an affirmation of Unity with the tongue of praise, testifying to the glorious King. When the servant says *Lā ilāha illa'llāh*, it means that there is no deity who has blessings, favour, power, permanence, majesty, splendour, might, praise, displeasure, and contentment except God, Who is Lord of the Worlds, Creator of the first ones and the last, and Judge of the Day of Judgment.

Also, the phrase means, 'There is no divinity of desire and no divinity of fear except God, remover of grief.' Similarly, the expression *Lā ilāha illa'llāh*[59] consists of twelve letters, so certainly there are twelve religious obligations, six exoteric and six esoteric. As to the exoteric, they include ritual purity, prayer, almsgiving, fasting, the pilgrimage to Makkah, and holy war. As to the esoteric, they include trust in God, committing things to Him, patience, contentment, detachment, and repentance.

Some have said, 'The wisdom in the interrogation of the two angels[60] is that the angels discredited the offspring of Adam with their words, '. . .Wilt thou place therein one who will do harm therein?'[61] So God Most High said, 'Surely I know that which ye know not.'

When the believer dies, God sends two angels to his grave who say to him, 'Who is your Lord and what is your religion?' He answers, 'My Lord is God and my religion is Islam.' Then God

Most High commands the two angels, saying, 'Bear witness to what ye two have heard', because the smallest number of witnesses to a deed is two.[62] Then God Most High says to the angels,

> Look at My servant from whom I have taken his spirit, wealth, and wife. Others have taken his wealth, his wife is under the protection of someone else, and I have caused him to perish at the hands of another. Then the angels question him in the bowels of the earth, but he does not remember anything except My Unicity and My Transcendence, and this, that they may know that 'surely I know that which ye know not'.[63]

Also in this regard, God Most High said in the very beginning:[64] '. . . Am I not your Lord? They said: Yea, verily . . .'.[65] God testifies about them; for when they came into this world, they bore witness to His Oneness, and the Prophets and believers bore witness about them on that point. When someone dies and is laid in his grave, the two angels question him about this testimony of faith. He bears witness to it in his grave and they hear that testimony. Then when the Day of Judgment comes, Iblīs[66] comes, wanting to take him by saying, 'This is one of my people, because he used to follow me in disobedience to God'. But God says,

> Thou hast no power over him, because I heard his declaration of Unicity from him in the beginning and at the end, and the Messengers heard that from him in the interim, and the angels heard that from him at the end. So how canst he be of thy people and how canst thou have power over him? Take him to Paradise!

Section [Seven]
On the Names of *Lā ilāha illa'llāh*

The first: the word *tawḥīd* (the affirmation of the Oneness of God) because it indicates the absolute negation of polytheism (*shirk*), and its significance without question is that He Most High said, 'Your God is One God . . .'.[67] Perhaps it would occur to someone to say, 'Suppose that our God is One, but it may be that others have a god who opposes our God.' However, God has removed this delusion by His words, 'There is no god save Him . . .'.[68]

Because our saying, 'There is no man in the house', necessitates negation of the essence, and when the essence is negated, all its constituent parts are negated. Then, even if one of the constituent parts of that essence were to exist, certainly that essence would have existed, because each one of its parts includes that essence. If the essence exists, then that contradicts negation of the essence. Thus, it is established that our saying 'There is no man in the house' allows of a comprehensive, general negation; and when after that one says, 'except Zayd', that conveys a complete meaning of oneness.

This word yields two fruits: the first is that the substance of man was originally created noble and honourable. God Most High has said, 'Verily We have honoured the children of Adam . . .'.[69] Inasmuch as there was honour in the original prototype, then man's being purified is in accordance with his prototype, while his being defiled is in opposition to his original prototype. Then, when we see that man, when associating partners with God, becomes impure, this is due to His words (may he be exalted!). 'The polytheists are unclean . . ..'[70] Impurity is in opposition to the prototype, and his being one who affirms the Oneness of God necessitates purity to begin with, because he is in conformity with the prototype. For he who professes God's Unity is among the élite of God, due to His words (may He be exalted!), '. . .Good women are for good men, and good men for good women . . .'.[71]

The second fruit is that polytheism is a cause for the ruination of the world: God Most High has said, 'Whereby almost the heavens are torn therefrom . . .'.[72] If polytheism is a cause for the destruction of the world, then the Oneness of God is a cause for the well-being of the world, because two opposites diverge in rule. If the expression of Oneness is a cause for the well-being of the world, then it is all the more so a cause for the well-being of the heart, which is the place of Unicity, and for the well-being of the tongue, which is the place for the invoking of Unicity. That is in keeping with God's forgiveness of the people of Oneness.

The second name: the word *ikhlāṣ* (sincerity) is so-called because the principle in it involves action of the heart, which is man's knowing with his heart the Unicity of God Most High. It is impossible that this gnosis resulting in the heart should be achieved by man for any other purpose than to obey God, love Him, and worship Him. This gnosis should be sought for the sake of God, not for any other reason whatsoever, unlike the remaining external acts of devotion. Since they can be performed to glorify God Most High, they can also be performed for other worldly interests, such as hypocrisy, praise, and commendation. That is why the word *ikhlāṣ* is so designated.

The third name: the word *iḥsān* (virtue).[73] God Most High has said, 'Is the reward of virtue aught save virtue?'[74] That is, is the reward of faith other than faith? Know, O man, that the covenant of servanthood is incumbent upon you, and that the covenant of Lordship is incumbent upon His magnanimity, as He Most High has said, '. . . and fulfill your covenant, I shall fulfill My covenant'.[75]

The covenant of your servanthood is that you be a servant to God, not to someone else, and that you know that everything except God is a servant to God, as He Most High has said, 'There is none in the heavens and the earth but cometh unto the Compassionate as a servant'.[76]

The phrase *Lā ilāha illa'llāh* indicates one's recognition that everything except Him is His servant; so it is established that saying *Lā ilāha illa'llāh* is virtue (*iḥsān*) on the part of the servant; hence His words, 'Is the reward of virtue aught save virtue?'[77] That is, is the reward of one who produces the statement *Lā ilāha illa'llāh* other than his being put under the protection of *Lā ilāha illa'llāh*?

God Most High has said, 'For those who do good is the best reward, and even more . . .'.[78]

The meaning in His saying 'those who do good' is the phrase *Lā ilāha illa'llāh*, according to what the principal commentators have agreed upon, because if one were to say that and die, one would enter Paradise. God Most High has said, 'And who is better in speech than him who prayeth unto God . . .'.[79] It is agreed that the verse was revealed with reference to the excellence of the call to prayer, because it includes *Lā ilāha illa'llāh*.

God Most High has said, 'Those who hear the word and follow the best thereof . . .'[80] and the best word is *Lā ilāha illa'llāh*. He Most High has said, 'Lo! God enjoineth justice and virtue . . .'.[81] It is said that justice is avoiding what is other than God and virtue is drawing near to God. He Most High has also said, 'If ye do good, ye do good for your own souls . . .'.[82] Doing good is saying *Lā ilāha illa'llāh*.

Abū Mūsa al-Ash ͨarī transmitted the following: 'The Messenger of God ﷺ said, " For those who do good is the best reward,[83] that is, those who say *Lā ilāha illa'llāh*".' 'Doing good' is Paradise and even more is seeing His noble face.[84] Wherever an act is better, its agent is more virtuous. The best invocation is *Lā ilāha illa'llāh*, and the best gnosis is the gnosis of *Lā ilāha illa'llāh*. This gnosis and this invocation are virtue (*iḥsān*).

The fourth name is *da ͨwat al-ḥaqq* (the call of the Truth). God Most High has said in the Surah of *ar-Ra ͨd* (The Thunder), 'Unto Him is the Call of the Truth . . .'.[85] That means delimitation, namely, that this call of the Truth belongs to Him, not to someone else, as God Most High has said, 'Unto you is your religion and unto me is my religion'.[86] In other words, you have your religion which is not for someone other than you.

The reason for its meaning the delimitation is that Truth is the opposite of falsehood. Truth is Being and falsehood is non-being. Inasmuch as the Truth (may He be glorified!) is real in His Essence because of His Essence and His Atrributes, and inasmuch as alteration of His true nature is impossible, gnosis of Him is true gnosis, remembrance of Him is true remembrance, and calling to Him is true calling. As for what is other-than-He, it is a possibility because of its essence. But knowledge of it is not necessary to ascertain nor is remembrance of it nor calling out to it. The call of the Truth is sometimes from the Truth for the Truth to the Truth and sometimes it is from mankind for the Truth to mankind.

As for the call of the Truth being from the Truth, verily it is He who calls the heart to His presence. Were it not for His call to that presence and the granting of His success in that union, then from whence is the human intelligence able to unite with the Majesty of the presence of God Most High? Moreover, the principles of movement and the beginnings of life ultimately lead to the power of God Most High and His decrees. God Most High has said, '. . . God's is the decision in the past and in the future . . .'.[87]

As for that being the call of the Truth, God Most High has said, '. . .Whose is the sovereignty this day? . . .'.[88] As for that ultimately leading to the Truth, God Most High has said, 'And that thy Lord, He is the goal'.[89] As for the call of the Truth sometimes being from mankind, He has said, 'And who is better in speech than him who calleth unto God and doeth right . . .'.[90]

The fifth name: the word *ᶜadl* (justice). God Most High has said, 'Lo! God enjoineth justice and virtue . . .'.[91] A *ḥadīth* states, 'Indeed, Gabriel said, O Muḥammad, Lo! God enjoineth justice and virtue.'[92]

Ibn ᶜAbbās said, 'Justice is the testimony that there is no divinity but God, and virtue is the practice of servanthood.' It is said, 'Justice is a testimony that 'There is no divinity but God', and virtue is sincerity therein.' It has also been said, 'Justice is toward people and virtue is *vis-à-vis* oneself in obedience'. Most High has said, 'If ye do good, ye do good for your own souls . . .'.[93]

It is said, 'He commands justice with the bodily members and virtue with the heart so that He may nurture it with the food of Oneness and the drink of Love.' It is said that through justice comes the vision of being in need of the Truth, and through virtue comes the contemplation of virtuous conduct of the Truth towards everything in the Creation.

There are several reasons for giving the Testimony of Faith this name of 'justice' First: justice in everything is attaining that which leads to equilibrium therein and perfection of its state. Perfection of the state of the sensorial faculties is in the awareness of sensorial things. Perfection of the state of the psychic faculties is in seeking beneficial corporeal things. Perfection of the state of nervous strength is in rejecting things incompatible with the body. As for the intellectual faculty, the perfection of its state and its ultimate felicity lies in having the forms of the inner realities and the images of intelligible things engraved upon it as they are until such time as the intellectual faculty becomes like a mirror wherein the forms of faces are revealed perfectly. The noblest and the loftiest of intelligible things are the gnosis of the Majesty of God, His Sanctity, His Sublimeness, and His Might. He is the goal of justice and equilibrium for human spirits and intellectual faculties; and He created them to be receptive to this state and absorbed in it.

The second reason: the gnosis of God is intermediate between immoderation, which is ascribing human characteristics to God (*tashbīh*), and negligence, which is denying any attributes to God (*taʿṭīl*). Whosoever exaggerates in the way of affirmation (*ithbāt*) falls into anthropomorphism; and whosoever exaggerates in the way of negation (*nafy*) falls into denial of all attributes. The Truth lies in the balance between the two extremes.

The third reason: whosoever abandons reasoning and argumentation in regard to the gnosis of God and turns to the idea that the Truth is what he feels and imagines falls into error. As for the one who penetrates deeply into investigation, desiring union with the depth of Infinity, he becomes confused and hesitant—rather, he becomes blind. Verily, the light of the Majesty of the Divinity blinds the eyes of human reasoning. These two extremes then become objectionable. It is better to look for equilibrium and to abandon going too deeply into things as the Prophet ﷺ said, 'Reflect on the Creation, but do not reflect on the Creator'. God Most High commanded justice in Oneness and said, 'Ye will never be able to deal justly between (your) wives, however much ye wish to . . .'.[94] He made the weak impotent and placed the highborn in a position of power so that each might know that everything is from Him.

The sixth name is *at-ṭayyib min al-qawl* (the good in speech). God Most High has said, 'They are guided unto the good in speech . . .'[95] that is, to *Lā ilāha illa'llāh*. The definite article is for the sake of comprehensiveness,[96] as if He had said, 'There is nothing delicious or good except this', because the good of something else in relation to His goodness is as if it were not good at all. What word is sweeter or purer than the affirmation of Oneness (*tawḥīd*)? Unbelief is a cause for seventy years of impurity, which is removed by the remembrance of this phrase one time. That is, because the good is sweet and the sweet is the awareness of what is appropriate. That which is appropriate for the sensorial faculties is what is perceived through the senses. That which is appropriate for intellectual faculties is the awareness of the Majesty of God Most High and His Sanctity and the awareness of the sensorial faculty.

As for what the sensorial faculties grasp, it is the accidents found in existing, corruptible bodies; and what the intellectual faculties grasp is the Essence of God Most High and His Sublimeness. The stronger the comprehension and the nobler what is grasped, the nobler and loftier is the joy reached because of that awareness. With regard to this, the relationship of intellectual pleasure to the sensorial in terms of honour and power is as the relationship of the Essence of God Most High in His Attributes, in Glory and Exaltedness, to existing accidents and matter. Just as there is no end to the relationship which occurs between these two types of discernment and what is discerned, so likewise there is no end to the relationship occurring between intellectual pleasures obtained from the discernment of the Majesty of God and from the pleasures obtained through the awareness of food and fragrances and the rest of the senses. It is evident that the absolute good is the gnosis of *Lā ilāha illa'llāh*, the remembrance of *Lā ilāha illa'llāh*, and immersion in the Light of the Majesty of *Lā ilāha illa'llāh*.

The seventh name is *al-kalimat aṭ-ṭayyibah* (the good word). God Most High has said, '. . . God sets forth a parable—a good word . . .'.[97] It is called that because it is free from anthropomorphism and from denying to Him all attributes, since it is an intermediate way between the two, differing from each one of them, as milk differs from phlegm and blood, and is therefore free from each one of them.

Commentators have said, 'The good tree is the date palm'. It resembles the affirmation of Oneness (*tawḥīd*) because it grows in some countries but not in others: the affirmation of Oneness flows on the tongue of some people but not on those of others, and the gnosis of Oneness occurs in one heart but not in another; because the date palm is the tallest of trees,[98] just as the utterance of Oneness is the loftiest of words; and because the roots of the date palm are firmly in the ground while its branches are in the heavens, just as the roots of the good word are firmly in the heart—and this is gnosis—while its branches are in the heavens: '. . . Unto Him good words ascend . . .'.[99]

The eighth name is *al-kalimat ath-thābitah* (the firm word). God Most High has said, 'God confirmeth those who believe by a firm word in the life of this world and in the Hereafter . . .'.[100] It is called that because the Invoked, the Known, is firm, necessarily immutable on account of His Essence, and incapable of non-being due to His Essence; hence likewise His 'word'.

The ninth name is *kalimat at-taqwā* (the word of piety). God Most High has said, '. . . and He imposed upon them the word of self-restraint . . .'.[101] It is called that because the one who says *Lā ilāha illa'llāh* protects himself against unbelief, and because the phrase is a protection for your body from the sword, for your property from plunder, and for your children from captivity. If the tongue is united with the heart, the phrase becomes a protection for your heart from unbelief; and if it is successful, it becomes a protection for your limbs from sin.

The tenth name is *al-kalimah al-bāqiyah* (the everlasting word). Many Qur'ānic commentators have said, regarding His words (may He be exalted!), 'and he[102] made it an everlasting word among his progeny . . .'[103] that 'it' refers to the phrase *Lā ilāha illa'llāh* due to His words in the preceding verse, '. . . Lo! I am innocent of what ye worship, save Him who did create me, for He will surely guide me'.[104] The meaning of 'Lo! I am innocent of what ye worship' is an exclusion of the Divinity from among the things which they used to worship. Then he said, 'Save Him who did create me . . .': therein is affirmation of the Divinity of the One who created him; and the totality of that is *Lā ilāha illa'llāh*.

The eleventh name is *al-istiqāmah* (uprightness). God Most High has said, 'Lo! those who say; Our Lord is God, and afterwards are upright . . .'.[105] It is the saying of *Lā ilāha illa'llāh*; and their saying 'Our Lord is God' is a confirmation of the existence of the Lord Most High. However, among mankind are those who affirm that He has an equal and partner – may God be exalted! And among them are those who deny that, and they are the ones who are upright, following the straight path. Uprightness at the resurrection is in proportion to uprightness in denying partners to God.

The twelfth name is *kalimatu' llāh al-ʿulyā* (the Most Supreme Word of God). He Most High has said, '. . . and He made the word of those who disbelieved the lowest, while God's Word it was that became the highest . . .'.[106] That is due to the fact that when the light of this Word is revealed in the heart, it comes after the attainment of strength through God. Consequently, the gnostics who are immersed in the light of the Majesty of God look down on worldly conditions and mighty kings as contemptible. They are not concerned about warfare, nor do they give any consideration to the pleasures and beauties of this world whatsoever.

Do you not see that when the light of this Word appeared to the magicians of Pharaoh, they did not notice the cutting of their hands and feet? And do you not see that our master Muḥammad ﷺ when he was immersed in this light, did not notice the world of Dominion (*al-Malakūt*), as He Most High has said, 'The eye turned not aside nor yet was overbold'.[107] In this world the Word of God towers above the rest of the religions: God Most High has said, '... that He may cause it to prevail over all religions ...'.[108] And it rises above all sins, for verily, it effaces all sins, but no sin can efface it.

The thirteenth name is *al-mathal al-aʿlā* (the sublime similitude). Qatādah said in reference to God's words (may He be exalted!), '... and God's is the sublime similitude ...'[109] that 'Its meaning is the phrase *Lā ilāha illa'llāh*'. The meaning of 'similitude' here is 'attribute'; such is what the linguists say; and its analogue is in His words (may He be exalted!), 'The similitude of the Garden which is promised unto those who keep their duty ...'[110] that is, the attribute of Paradise.

The fourteenth name is *al-ʿahd* (the covenant). Ibn ʿAbbās said in regard to His words (may He be exalted!), 'They will have no power of intercession save him who hath made a covenant with the Compassionate.'[111] The covenant is the phrase *Lā ilāha illa'llāh*.

The fifteenth name is *maqālīd as-samāwāt wa'l-arḍ* (the keys of the heavens and the earth). Ibn ʿAbbās said, 'It is the phrase *Lā ilāha illa'llāh*, because polytheism (*shirk*) is a cause for the corruption of the world.' God Most High has said, 'Whereby almost the heavens are torn and the earth is split asunder and the mountains fall into ruins that they ascribe unto the Compassionate a son'.[112]

Since that is the case, the affirmation of the Oneness of God (*tawḥīd*) is the well-being of the world. The gates of heaven do not open upon supplication except through saying *Lā ilāha illa'llāh*. Neither are the gates of Paradise opened except through this phrase nor are the gates of hell closed except through this saying. The gates of the heart are not opened except by these words, and various kinds of evil suggestions are not repelled except by this phrase. Hence, it is the noblest key of the heavens and the earth and the mightiest key of spirits, souls, bodies and intellects.

The sixteenth name is the word *al-Ḥaqq* (the Truth) due to His words (may He be exalted!), 'And those unto whom they cry instead of Him possess no power of intercession, saving him who beareth witness unto the Truth knowingly',[113] that is, the phrase *Lā ilāha illa'llāh*.

The seventeenth name is *al-ᶜurwah al-wuthqā* (the firm handhold). God Most High has said, '. . . And he who rejecteth false deities and believeth in God hath grasped a firm handhold . . .',[114] that is, saying *Lā ilāha illa'llāh*.

The eighteenth name is the word *aṣ-ṣidq* (veracity) due to His Words (may He be exalted!), 'And whoso bringeth the Truth and believeth therein . . .'.[115]

The nineteenth name is *kalimat as-sawā'* (the word of common agreement). God Most High has said, '. . . Come ye to an agreement between us and you'.[116] Abu'l-ᶜĀliyah said, 'It is the words *Lā ilāha illa'llāh*'.

Section [Eight]

The word *al-ilāh* (the deity) is a name given to anything worshipped, whether rightly or wrongly; then it prevailed as the name given to the One rightly worshipped. As for the word *Allāh* (God), it is said to be a derivative;[117] scholars have different opinions regarding it. It is said to be taken from *aliha ila'r-rajul* (he took refuge with the man) which means to take refuge with someone from something that has happened. But then *alahahu* (he protected him) means to give someone sanctuary; the protector is named *ilāh* just as the one who leads people in prayer (*amma*) is called *imām*.

It is said to be taken from *waliha*, *yawlahu*;[118] originally it was *walaha* but the *waw* was replaced by a *hamzah*,[119] just as one says *ishāḥ* for *wishāh* (sash). *Al-walah* is intense love. It should have been necessary to say *ma'lūh*[120] (adored), just as one says *ma ʿbūd* (worshipped); but that was changed, just as one says *kitāb* (piece of writing) for *maktūb* (what is written) and *ḥisāb* (calculation) for *maḥsūb* (what is counted).

It is also said to be taken from *lāha, yalūhu,*[121] meaning 'to be covered', that is, 'He veiled the mind from His Reality'; and it is said to be from *lāha, yalūhu,* which means 'to arise'; one says *lāhat ash-shams,* 'the sun arose'. According to some, the word comes from *alihtu bi'l-makān,* I dwelt in a place, when one remains there; that is an indication of the duration of one's stay. A poet has said,

أَلِهْنا بدارٍ مــــا تَبِينُ رُسُومُهــــا   كـأنَّ بقـايـاهـا وِسـامٌ عَلَى اليَدِ

We took refuge (*alihna*) in a house whose outline was not clear
As if its remains were a tattoo mark on the hand.

The word *Allāh* is said to be from *aliha, ya'lahu,* which means 'to be confused'; that is an indication of the confusion of the intellect in understanding the essence of His Reality. It is also said to be from *at-ta'lluh,* which is devoting oneself to the service of God (*ta ʿabbud*). One says *alaha, ya'lahu, ilāhah,* that is, *ʿabada, ya ʿbudu, ʿibādah* (he worshipped, he worships, worshipping). Ibn ʿAbbās recited: '. . . and flout thee and thy gods (*ilāhatak*)? . . .'[122] that is *ʿibādatak* (thy acts of devotion).

At-Tilimsānī said, 'It is closer to His words (may He be exalted!), 'And ask those of Our messengers whom We sent before Thee: Did We ever appoint gods (*ālihah*) to be worshipped beside the Compassionate?'[123]

The meaning of *Lā ilāha illa'llāh* is 'There is no one worshipped except God'. It is said: The word *Allāh* is not a derivative; however, it takes the place of a proper noun because it is described by the rest of the Names while it does not describe itself, description being the characteristic of the proper noun. We only say it is not a proper noun due to the lack of canonical permission. It is a noun for the true Being that contains the Attributes of the Divinity; it is qualified by the qualities of Lordship, the one who is uniquely possessed of real Being. Everything other-than-He derives its being from Him. This Name is greater than the Ninety-Nine Names[124] because it refers to the Essence that contains all the Attributes of the Divinity. The origin of the rest of the Names indicates only their origin from an idea, such as knowledge or the like.

Amongst the Arabs, it is not mentioned before the time of the Prophet ﷺ nor after him that the pronunciation of this Name was used in its present form, let alone its being used as an attribute for someone other-than-Him. In the oral traditions, it is mentioned that, in pre-Islamic times (*al-Jāhiliyyah*), the Arabs used to put down in their writings, 'In thy name, O God (*Allāhumma*)'; and He Most High has said, '. . . Knowest thou one that can be named along with Him?'[125]

For this reason al-Junayd (may God be pleased with him!), said, 'No one knows God but God and He gave the Names to His creatures, veiling them thereby.' He Most High said, 'Therefore, praise the Name of thy Lord, the Supreme'.[126]

For, by God, no one knows God but God in the two existences and the two worlds, and in the two 'days'.[127] God Most High has contracted the expansion of intellects, spirits, and hearts into the domain of this Name just as He has expanded them in the domain of the Names. Consequently, no insolence can take place nor does it occur to the mind to designate others by this Name, in spite of the presence of infidels and despotic pharoahs and the intensity of their disbelief. For that reason, each of the Names is good to emulate except this Name. Verily, it is for devotion.

The servant's part in this Name must be in adoring God. I mean by this that his heart and aspiration should be absorbed in God Most High, seeing neither other-than-Him nor being attentive to anything but Him, neither hoping for nor fearing aught but Him. Attachment to this Name is not valid save after emulating the totality of Names in words, deeds, and states, outwardly and inwardly.

Whosoever desires proximity to God through this Name should follow seven principles: to regard what is other-than-God as contemptible without delay; to glorify the commandments of God through illumination; to efface the worlds through contemplation; to extinguish oneself in everything totally; to devote one's zeal to God indefatigably; to be inwardly vigilant over one's breathing;[128] and to invoke the most supreme Name outwardly and inwardly until one is ardently devoted to God – that is, until one's inner being is immersed in His Being in the reality of one's contemplation, neither seeing other-than-Him nor perceiving anything but Him. Then God will watch over one and one's states and protect one's secrets (*asrār*) from alterities (*aghyār*).

According to ash-Shiblī (may God have mercy upon him!), 'No one has truly said *Allāh* save *Allāh*, and whosoever has said it has done so out of good fortune.' Abū Saᶜīd al-Kharrāz said, 'Whosoever goes beyond the boundary of self-forgetfulness falls into the forgetfulness of his good fortune from God and forgetfulness of his need for God. For if his limbs could speak, verily they would say *Allāh, Allāh*.' These are they whose innermost being ardently loves God; their forms are obliterated in the essence of Oneness; God makes creatures subservient to them and makes the mysteries subject to them. Who, then, is the one who will enter a retreat with this Name until he becomes ardently immersed in it?

The reality of adoration (*tawalluh*) is that one be so immersed that he does not sense whether he is invoking or being silent, whether he is existent or non-existent, until the invocation overcomes him and he hears every member of his body saying *Allāh, Allāh*, in a tongue which he hears. Even if his blood were shed, verily it would spell out *Allāh, Allāh*, and so forth.

Know that in every atom among the atoms of the world and even in what is smaller than an atom, there is a mystery among the mysteries of God's Name. By virtue of that mystery, every knower – whatever his kind might be, and whether he knows it or not – understands Him and affirms Oneness of Him, as God Most High has said, 'And unto God falleth prostrate whosoever is in the heavens and the earth, willingly or unwillingly . . .'.[129]

The first *alif*[130] refers to the Essence; the first *lām* refers to the Attributes of the Essence; the second *lām* refers to the names of the Acts; the third *lām*[131] refers to the names of Qualities based on the names of the Attributes; and the *hā'* refers to the demonstrative pronouns within the hidden Names.

Section [Nine]

It is related that a man was standing on ʿArafāt[132] and in his hand were seven stones. He said, 'O ye seven stones, bear witness that I bear witness that there is no divinity but God, and I bear witness that Muḥammad is the Messenger of God.' Later he slept and dreamt that the Day of Judgment had come, that he had been examined and that hellfire had been decreed for him. When he was led to one of the doors of hell, one of these seven stones came and threw itself against that door. The angels of chastisement gathered to remove it but they could not. Then he was led to the second door, but the same thing occurred there as with the first, and so on for seven doors. So he was led to the Throne, and God (may He be glorified!) said, 'My servant, you made the stones bear witness; hence, thou wilt not forfeit thy rights; and I am a Witness to thy testimony of faith in My Oneness. Enter Paradise.' When he approached the doors of Paradise, lo, they were closed. So the testimony of *Lā ilāha illa'llāh* came and opened the doors, and the man entered Paradise.

It is mentioned that the water in Baghdad rose until the city was on the verge of being submerged. One of the righteous said,

> This night I dreamt that I saw myself standing on the edge of the Tigris River, saying, 'There is no power or strength save

> in God! (*Lā ḥawla wa lā quwata illā bi'llāh*) Baghdad is flooded!' A handsome man came and I knew that he was an angel, and another angel came from another direction. One of them said to the other, 'What have you been commanded to do?' He said, 'I was commanded to drown Baghdad, then I was prohibited from doing it.' The other asked, 'Why?' he answered, 'The angels of the night reported that seven hundred girls had been deflowered yesterday in Baghdad. So God became angry and commanded me to drown it. But the angel of the day reported in the morning nine hundred calls to prayer (*ādhān*) and introductory formulas to the prayers (*iqāmah*). So God pardoned the former through the latter.'

The one who had dreamt said, 'I awakened and went to the Tigris, and lo! the water had receded'.

Someone has said, '*Lā ilāha illa'llāh, Muḥammad rasūlu'llāh* (There is no divinity but God, Muhammad is the Messenger of God) consists of twenty-four letters; the hours of the day and night are of the same number. It is as if it were said,"Every sin which I have committed, whether great or small, secretly or openly, accidentally or intentionally, by word or deed during these hours is pardoned by these words".'

Also the phrase *Lā ilāha illa'llāh, Muḥammad rasūlu'llāh* consists of seven words. The servant has seven organs and hellfire has seven doors. Each of these seven words closes one of the seven doors to one of the seven organs.

It is said that the phrase *Lā ilāha illa'llāh* consists of twelve letters; so inevitably twelve obligations are enjoined – six outward and six inward. As for the outward ones, they include ritual purity, prayer, almsgiving, fasting, the pilgrimage, and holy war. As for the inward, they include trust in God, commitment, patience, contentment, asceticism, and repentance.

As for *Huwa* (He), it is composed of two letters[133] They are the realities of the inhalation and exhalation, whether or not you pronounce it. The inhalation is the *hā'* and the exhalation is the *waw*, which is expansion. The *hā'* pertains to the breath of life and the *waw* comes out of the fire of inner emotions. Indeed, God Most High made the interior the seat of emotions, among which are the fervour of love for God Most High, the eagerness of seeking, the enthusiasm of invoking, the intensity of meditating, and the warmth of one's nature. Contraction and expansion of one's spiritual state will not disappear until the servant's appointed time: thus, God comes between the *hā'* and the *waw* by means of a veil hidden from the illusions of the mind; and indeed, by means of what God Most High decreed in His eternal, pre-existing knowledge.

All created beings exist because of God Most High in accordance with their subtle breaths, and all are subject to His power; were it not for that, chastisement would have overcome them. God spares the inner being of men from being overwhelmed by emotions through the selfsame inward Name, which is *Huwa*. For if the gnostic says *Huwa*, those burning passions gather and are expelled by the same breath to the spirit of the air. Then the breath returns with the coolness of the air, which is *Huwa*, except that it is coolness outwardly and heat inwardly, because it is air. The secret of the *alif* which has been added to the *Huwa*[134] is that it connotes intensification of life, because it is a combination of the inward *Huwa* and the outward *alif* with respect to the affirmation of Oneness.

As for the invocation of transcendence, it is 'Glory be to God and in praise of Him' (*Subḥāna' llāh wa bi-ḥamdih*). The meaning of glorification (*tasbiḥ*) is transcendence (*tanziḥ*), and the saying 'Glory be to Him' (*subḥānahu*) is in the accusative as a verbal noun. You say, 'I praise God with all glory' (*sabbaḥtu 'llāha tasbīḥan wa subḥānan*). The meaning of 'Glory be to God' (*subḥana 'llāh*) is that transcendence belongs to Him and He is free of every imperfection and attribute of creatures. Saying 'and in praise of Him' (*wa bi-ḥamdih*) that is, 'in praise of Thee I glorify Thee' means 'by Thy bounty toward me and Thy gifts and blessings upon me, I glorify, not by my power or strength'. Therein is gratitude towards God Most High for this blessing and recognition of it and commitment to God Most High. Verily, all deeds belong to Him Most High.

CONCLUSION OF THE BOOK

It Includes What Has Been Mentioned in the Way of Remembrance in All Situations and Times During the Day and the Night

Ḥadīth: When something distressed the Prophet (may God bless him and grant him peace!), he would say 'O Living, Everlasting God, by Thy mercy, I seek help'.[1]

Ḥadīth: When something used to concern him, he would look up at the sky and say, 'Glory be to God, the Supreme'.[2]

Ḥadīth: He also said, 'When worry or sadness befalls one, let him supplicate with these words:

> O God, I am Thy servant, son of Thy servant, son of Thy bondwoman, in Thy grasp. My forelock is in Thy hand, Thy judgment is carried out in me, Thy decrees toward me are just. I ask Thee by every Name which is Thine, by which Thou hast designated Thyself or hast revealed in Thy Book, or which Thou has taught to anyone of Thy creatures or hast kept for Thyself in the knowledge of the Unseen World, that Thou maketh the Qur'ān the light of my mind, the springtime of my heart, the departing of my sadness, the disappearance of my worry.

A man among the people said, 'O Messenger of God, one who is deceived is the one who forgets these words'. He answered, 'Yes, indeed! So say them and teach them, for whosoever says them as a petition, seeking what they mean, God will make his sadness disappear and prolong his happiness.'[3]

Ḥadīth: According to ʿAlī (may God honour him!), 'The Messenger of God ﷺ taught me these words and instructed me that, if any sorrow or misfortune befell me, to say the following:

> There is no divinity but God, the Supreme, the Most Generous. Glory be to Him; may God, the Lord of the Great Throne be blessed. Please be to God, Lord of the Worlds'.[4]

ʿAbd Allāh ibn Jaʿfar used to teach these words and utter them over the ill, and he used to teach them to the unmarried among his daughters.

Ḥadīth: He said, 'The words of the distressed are: "O God, I hope for Thy mercy. Do not entrust me to myself for the twinkling of an eye, and make right all of my affairs for me. There is no divinity but Thou".'[5]

Ḥadīth: 'Verily, I know an utterance which someone in distress cannot say but God will comfort him. It is the utterance of my brother Jonah ﷺ "He cried out in the darkness that there is no divinity but Thou; may Thou be glorified! Verily, I have been amongst the wrongdoers".'[6]

Ḥadīth: 'Whosoever reads the Verse of the Throne[7] and the concluding verses of *Sūrat al-Baqarah*[8] during times of distress, God will help him.'[9]

Ḥadīth: 'When you fear a power or something else say:

> There is no divinity but God the Clement, the Generous. Glory be to God, Lord of the Seven Heavens and Lord of the Supreme Throne. There is no divinity but Thou. May he in Thy charge become strong and Thy praise exalted.'[10]

Ḥadīth: ʿAbd al-Mālik wrote to al-Ḥajjāj ibn Yūsuf, 'Look after Anas ibn Mālik, the servant of the Messenger of God ﷺ go to his assemblies, elevate him, give him a good reward and honour him.'

Anas said, 'I went to al-Ḥajjāj and he said to me the same day, "O Abū Ḥamza,[11] I would like to show you a horse, tell me how it compares with the horses belonging to the Messenger of God ﷺ ".'

'So he showed it to me and I said, "What a difference between them! The very dung and urine and forage of the Prophet's horses would have been a reward!".'

Al-Ḥajjāj said, 'If it were not for the fact that the Commander of the Faithful wrote to me about you, I would have struck you on the head!'

I said to him, 'You cannot do that'.

He said to me, 'And why not?'

I answered, 'Because the Messenger of God ﷺ taught me a prayer, which, when I utter it, makes me fear no devil or power or any beast of prey.'

Al-Ḥajjāj said, 'O Abū Ḥamza, teach your nephew Muḥammad ibn al-Ḥajjāj.'

I refused him. So he said to his son, 'Go to your Uncle Anas, and ask him to teach that to you'.

Abān said, 'He explained it, for when death was approaching Anas, he called for me and said, "O Aḥmar,[12] indeed, you have devoted yourself to me, so out of esteem for you, I shall teach you the prayer which the Messenger of God ﷺ taught me, but do not teach it to anyone who does not fear God (may He be powerful and exalted!"), or something approximating that. He said,

> God is Great, God is Great, God is Great: May 'In the Name of God' be upon my soul and my religion: May 'In the Name of God' be upon everything which my Lord hath bestowed upon me: 'In the Name of God' is the best of Names: 'In the name of God', with Whose Name nothing on earth can cause harm, nor can any malady in heaven: 'In the Name of God' I begin and upon God do I rely. God, God, my Lord, I do not associate partners with Him whatsoever. O God, I ask Thee

out of Thy goodness from Thy goodness which naught but Thee giveth. May those in Thy charge be magnified and Thy praise be exalted! There is no divinity other than Thou. Put me in Thy protection from every evil and from the accursed devil. O God, by Thee I guard against the evil of all which Thou hast created that is possessed of evil, and by Thee I take heed of them; and I offer this in front of me: 'In the Name of God, the Compassionate, the Merciful, "Say: He is God the One! God the Eternal! he begetteth not nor was begotten. And there is none comparable unto Him"';[13] and I offer the same prayer behind me, the same on my right, the same on my left, and the same above me.

Ḥadīth: According to ʿAlī (may God be pleased with him!), 'When you are in a valley and fear predatory animals, say, "I take refuge in Daniel and the den from the evil of the lion".'

Ḥadīth: While the Prophet ﷺ was walking with his Companions, lo, the thong of his sandal broke. He said, '. . .Verily we belong to God and to Him we return.'[15] Those with him said, 'Is this a misfortune?'[16] He said, 'Yes, everything that troubles the believer is a misfortune.'[17]

Ḥadīth: 'One should ask for all of his needs; one should even ask Him for the thong of his sandal when it breaks.'[18]

On the authority of ʿĀ'isha (may God be pleased with her!), 'Ask God for everything, even for the sandal thong; for verily, if God does not make something easy, it will not be easy.'[19]

Ḥadīth: 'God does not bestow a blessing upon a servant who then says, "Praise be to God, Lord of the Worlds", without that which he has been given being better than that which was taken away.'[20]

Ḥadīth: On the authority of az-Zubayr ibn al-ʿAwwām (may God be pleased with him!), who related, 'I heard the Messenger of God ﷺ when he recited this verse: 'God is witness that there is no deity save Him, as do the angels and men of learning, maintaining

His Creation in justice. There is no deity save Him, the Almighty, the Wise'.[21] The Prophet ﷺ said, "And I am a witness, that is, to my Lord"'.[22]

Ḥadīth: 'God does not bestow the blessings of family or property or children upon a servant who recites, 'As God wills; there is no power save in God,' in order that he then see them come to harm before his death.'[23]

Section [One]

Ḥadīth: 'There is not a servant who commits a sin, then performs his ablution and prays two prostrations, asking God's forgiveness for that sin and reciting the following verse, but that He will forgive him: "Yet whoso doeth evil or wrongeth his soul . . .".'[24]

Ḥadīth: 'Whosoever asks pardon of God frequently, God will turn his every care into joy and provide a way out of every difficulty, and He will provide for him in such a way that he cannot calculate.'[25]

Ḥadīth: 'He is not a constant transgressor who asks God for forgiveness, even though he relapses seventy times a day.'[26]

Ḥadīth: 'Verily, I ask God for forgiveness and turn to Him in repentance one hundred times every day.'[27]

Ḥadīth: 'Whosoever asks God for forgiveness seventy times a day is not inscribed among the forgetful.'[28]

Ḥadīth: 'Our Lord (may He be mighty and exalted!) says regarding the last third of the night, "Whosoever calls to Me, I shall answer him; whosoever asks forgiveness of Me, I shall pardon him until daybreak appears".'[29]

Ḥadīth: 'O Messenger of God, how do I ask for God's forgiveness?' He answered, 'Say: O God, forgive us, have mercy upon us, restore us to Thy grace. Verily, Thou art the Most Forgiving, the Merciful.'[30]

Asking God's Forgiveness on Fridays

Ḥadīth: 'There is a time on Fridays during which if a servant asks forgiveness of God therein, He will pardon him.'[31]

When the Prophet ﷺ entered the mosque on Fridays, he would take hold of the two posts of the door of the mosque and say, 'O God, make me the one who turns to Thee the most often of all, the one who is the nearest of the near to Thee, and the one most preferred of those who ask of Thee and desire Thee.'[32]

Ḥadīth: 'Whosoever recites 'Say: He is God the One!'[33] and 'Say: I seek refuge in the Lord of the Daybreak',[34] and 'Say: I seek refuge in the Lord of Mankind',[35] seven times after the Friday prayer, God will protect him from harm with these verses until the next Friday'.[36]

Ḥadīth: 'It was related by ᶜAmr ibn Qays al-Malā'ī, who said,

> It has reached me that whosoever fasts Wednesdays, Thursdays, and Fridays, then performs the Friday prayer with the Muslims, then remains stationary while greeting others as the imām does,[37] then recites the first chapter of the Qur'ān and 'Say: He is God the One!'[38] ten times, then extends his hands up to God, saying, 'O God, I ask Thee by Thy Name, the Most High (*al Aᶜlā*), the Most High, the Most High: the Mightiest (*al-Aᶜazz*), the Mightiest, the Mightiest; the Noblest (*al-Akram*), the Noblest, the Noblest; there is no divinity but God, the Most Majestic (*al-Ajall*), the Most Majestic, the Supreme (*al-ᶜAẓim*), the Most Supreme (*al-Aᶜẓam*)' then asks something of God, He will certainly give it to Him sooner or later; but you are all in a hurry.[39]

Ḥadīth: 'Whosoever says, "Glory and praise be to God the Supreme" one hundred times after the Friday prayer has ended, God will pardon one hundred thousand sins for him and twenty-four thousand sins for his parents.'[40]

Ḥadīth: 'Ask God's blessings upon me often.'[41]

Ḥadīth: 'Whosoever hears me mentioned but does not ask God's blessings upon me is made miserable.'[42]

CHAPTER [TEN]

Incantations

IT WAS RELATED by ʿAlqamah ibn ʿAbd Allāh (may God be pleased with him!), who said, 'An incantation against snakes was mentioned to the Prophet ﷺ so he said, 'Recite it to me'. I then recited it to him: 'In the Name of God, the open wound of a sword on the head (*shajjah qaraniyyah*) is the salty wave of a sea (*malḥat baḥr*), a generous gift (*qafṭ*).' The Prophet said, 'These are the words of convenants that Solomon, the son of David (peace be upon them!), observed, in which I see no harm.' A man with ʿAlqamah was bitten by a snake, so ʿAlqamah used the incantation on him, and it was as if he had been freed from shackles.[1]

In another version, ʿAmr said, 'It has reached us that the Messenger of God ﷺ forbade spitting with the incantation.'[2]

Ḥadīth: The following was related by ʿUthmān ibn Abi'l-ʿĀṣ: 'I went to the Messenger of God ﷺ and said, 'O Messenger of God, I used to remember people, then something happened to me and I forgot some of them.' He put his hand upon my chest, then said, 'O God, expel the devil from him.' God expelled forgetfulness from me.'[3]

ʿUthmān said, 'Then I went to the Messenger of God ﷺ another time when pain afflicted me. He said to me, "Place your hand upon it and say: 'I take refuge in the might and power of God from the evil that I find', seven times.'" Then God lifted it from me.'[4]

Ḥadīth: ᶜUthmān ibn Abi'l-ᶜĀṣ said, 'O Messenger of God, verily the devil interferes between me and my prayers and my Qur'ānic recitation, making them obscure to me.' The Messenger of God ﷺ said, 'That is a devil who is called Khinzab. When you perceive him, take refuge in God from him and spit to your left three times.' So I did that and God made him depart from me.' Muslim transmitted it.[5]

Abū Rashīd said, 'I told Ibn ᶜAbbās, "There is nothing that I find in myself, that is, nothing of doubt." He said, "When you see such a thing, say: 'He is the First and the Last, the Outward and the Inward and He is the Knower of all things'".'[6]

Section [One]
On Invoking Morning and Evening

God Most High has said, 'O ye who believe! Remember God with much remembrance, and glorify him early and late.'[7] He said, '. . . Glorify thy Lord with praise evening and morning.'[8] He also said, '. . . Glorify thy Lord with praise before the rising of the sun and before its setting . . .'.[9]

Ḥadīth: Ṭalq ibn Ḥabīb related the following tradition:

> A man came to Abu'd-Dardā' and said, 'O Abu'd-Dardā', your house has burned down!' He answered, 'It has not; God would not do that because of the words I heard from the Messenger of God ﷺ. Whosoever says them at the beginning of his day will see no calamity befall him until evening and whosoever says them at the end of his day will see no calamity befall him until morning:
>
> > O God, Thou art my Lord. There is no divinity but Thou. Upon Thee do I rely and Thou art the Lord of the Supreme Throne. What God wills, will be and what He does not will, will not be. There is no power or strength save in God, the Lofty, the Supreme. I know that God has power over everything and that God's knowledge encompasses

> everything. O God, I take refuge in Thee from the evil in myself and from the evil in every beast whose forelock is in Thy hand. Verily, my Lord follows the straight path.[10]

Ḥadīth: 'Whosoever says "Glory and praise be to God" one hundred times in the morning and in the evening will find no one arriving on the Day of Judgment with better than that which he has unless it is someone who has said the same as he or who has said it more often.' Muslim transmitted it.[11]

Muslim also transmitted that when evening came, the Prophet of God ﷺ would say:

> We have entered into evening and the Kingdom (*al-mulk*) has become God's; praise be to God; there is no divinity but God alone; He has no associate; His is the Kingdom, His is the praise; and He has power over everything. My Lord, I ask of Thee the best of what there is in this night and the best of what comes after it. And I take refuge in Thee from the evil of what is in this night and the evil of what comes after it. My Lord, I take refuge in Thee from sloth and the evil of arrogance. My Lord, I take refuge in Thee from chastisement in hellfire and from chastisement in the grave.

When morning came, he would say that also: 'We have entered into morning and the Kingdom has become God's.'[12]

Ḥadīth: Master of pardon, O God, Thou art my Lord. There is no divinity but Thee. Thou hast created me and I am Thy servant. I am under Thy covenant and Thy promise as far as it is within my power. I take refuge in Thee from the evil that I have done. I acknowledge Thy bounty to me and I confess my sins, so forgive me, for verily, no one can forgive sins but Thou.

> Whosoever should say these words in the evening, then die that same night, will enter Paradise; and whosoever should say these words in the morning, then die that same day, will enter Paradise.' Al-Bukhārī transmitted it.[13]

Ḥadīth: 'Nothing can hurt the servant who says three times, "In the Name of God with whose Name nothing on earth or in heaven can be harmed, and He is the Hearer, the All-Knowing'. At-Tirmidhī verified it and found it to be a good *ḥadīth*.[14]

Ḥadīth: 'Whosoever says in the morning or evening, "O God, I have awakened; I bear witness to Thee and to the bearers of Thy Throne and Thy angles and all Thy creatures that verily, Thou art God than whom there is no divinity but Thou, and that Muḥammad is Thy servant and Thy Messenger," God releases one-quarter of him from hellfire. Whosoever says it twice, God releases one-half of him from hellfire. Whosoever repeats it thrice, God releases three-fourths of him from hellfire; and if he repeats it four times, God releases him completely from hellfire.' At-Tirmidhī said it was a good, but rare *ḥadīth*.[15]

Ḥadīth: 'Whosoever says, "There is no divinity but God alone; He has no partners. His is the Kingdom; His is the praise; He has power over everything,' one hundred times in a day, it is for him the equivalent in value of ten slaves, and one hundred good deeds are recorded for him and one hundred bad deeds are erased. It becomes a sanctuary for him from the devil that day until evening, and no one will bring anything better than what he brings forth save the man who has done more than he.' This *ḥadīth* is agreed upon by the authorities.[16]

Ḥadīth: 'Whosoever says, "Glory and praise be to God", one hundred times in a day will see his sins diminished even if they be as much as the foam on the sea.' This *ḥadīth* is agreed upon by the authorities.[17]

Ḥadīth: 'The most beloved of phrases to God Most High are four, any one of which you use will protect you from harm: Glory be to God, praise be to God, there is no divinity but God, and God is Most Great.' Muslim transmitted it.[18]

Ḥadīth: 'Say: He is God, the One![19] and the last two chapters on taking refuge in God[20] three times in the early morning and evening, and it will suffice thee from everything.' Abū Dā'ūd, at-Tirmidhī, and an-Nasā'ī transmitted it and Abu Da'ud verified it and found it to be a good *ḥadīth*.[21]

Ḥadīth: 'When the Prophet ﷺ wished to sleep, he would say, "In Thy Name, O God, I die and live." And when he awakened from his sleep, he would say, "Praise be to God who has revived us after having made us die and to Him belongs the Resurrection".' This is a *ḥadīth* agreed upon by the authorities.[22]

Ḥadīth: 'When he went to bed every night, he would put his palms together and blow upon them, then recite "Say: He is God, the One!"[23] and "Say: I take refuge in the Lord of Daybreak"[24] and "Say: I take refuge in the Lord of Mankind";[25] then he would rub his palms wherever he could reach on his body and pass them over his head and face and in front of his body. He would do that three times.' This is a *ḥadīth* agreed upon by the authorities.[26]

In a *ḥadīth* of Abū Hurayrah: 'When you go to bed, recite the Verse of the Throne: "*Allah*! There is no god save Him, the Living, the Eternal"[27] until you finish it; for indeed, a guardian angel from God will never leave you nor the devil approach you.' The Prophet ﷺ said, 'The devil will give credence to you while being a liar'. Al-Bukhārī transmitted it.[28]

Ḥadīth: 'Whosoever recites the last two verses from *Sūrat al-Baqarah*[29] at night is sufficed by them.' This is a *ḥadīth* agreed upon by the authorities.[30]

Ḥadīth: 'When one of you arises from his bed, then returns to it, let him shake it out by the end of its cover three times; for indeed, he does not know what might have been left upon it after him. When he reclines, let him say, "In Thy Name, my Lord, I lie down on my side and by Thee I arise. If Thou takest my soul, have mercy upon it, and if Thou releaseth it, protect it as Thou protecteth Thy pious servants".' This is a *ḥadīth* agreed upon by the religious authorities.[31]

Ḥadīth: According to ʿAlī (may God honour him!), Fāṭimah went to the Prophet ﷺ to ask him for a servant, but she did not find him. She saw ʿĀ'isha and informed her of this. ʿAlī said, 'The Prophet came to us as we were going to bed and said,

> Shall I not show you that which is better for you than a servant? When you go to your bed, say *subḥāna'llāh* (Glory be to God) thirty-three times and *al-ḥamdu lillāh* (Praise be to God) thirty-three times and say *Allāhu akbar* (God is Most Great) thirty-four times.[32] Verily that is better for you than any servant.

ʿAlī said, 'I have not quit reciting that since I heard it from the Messenger of God ﷺ.' He was asked, 'Not even the night of the Battle of Siffin?' He answered, 'Not even the night of the Battle of Siffin.' This is a *ḥadīth* agreed upon by the authorities.[33] It is said, 'Whosoever remembers these words will not be overtaken by exhaustion in whatever work or activity occupies him.'

Ḥadīth: When the Prophet ﷺ wished to sleep, he would place his right hand under his cheek, then say three times, 'O God, protect me from Thy chastisement the day Thou dost resurrect Thy servants'. Abū Dā'ūd and at-Tirmidhī transmitted it; the former verified it and found it to be a good *ḥadīth*.[34]

Ḥadīth: 'Whosoever says when he goes to bed, 'I ask forgiveness of God, the Supreme, than whom there is no divinity save Him, the Living, the Self-Subsistent, and to Him I repent', three times, his sins are forgiven even if they be as plentiful as the foam on the sea and even if they be as numerous as the shifting sands, and even if they be as numerous as the days of this world.' At-Tirmidhī said this is a good, rare *ḥadīth*.[35]

Ḥadīth: Al-Barā' ibn ʿĀzib said, 'The Messenger of God ﷺ said to me, 'When you go to bed, make your ritual ablution as for prayer, then recline on your right side and say,

> O God, I surrender myself to Thee, I turn my face to Thee, I entrust my affairs to Thee, and I commit my household to Thee out of both fear and love of Thee. There is no deliverance or refuge from Thee except in Thee. I believe in Thy sacred Books which Thou has revealed and in Thy Prophet whom Thou has sent.

If you should die, then you will die in accordance with primordial nature, so make these words the last thing you say.'[36]

Ibn as-Sunnī related,

> O God, Thou art my Lord; there is no divinity but Thee. Thou has created me and I am Thy servant. I am under Thy covenant and Thy promise as far as it is within my power. I take refuge in Thee from the evil that I have done. I acknowledge Thy bounty to me and I confess my sins, so forgive me, for verily, no one forgives sins but Thou.

And if he should die the same day, he would die a martyr, and if he should die the same night, he would die a martyr.'[37]

Ḥadīth: 'Say when you awaken,

> Glory and praise be to God, there is no strength save in God. Whatsoever He wills, will be and whatsoever He does not will, will not be. I know that God has power over everything and that God's knowledge encompasses everything.

Verily, whosoever says these words when morning comes is protected until evening; and whosoever says them when evening comes is protected until morning.' Ibn as-Sunnī transmitted it.[38]

He also transmitted the following, 'Whosoever says when morning comes, "I seek refuge in God the All-Hearing, the All-Knowing from the accursed devil" is protected from the accursed devil until evening.'[39]

He also transmitted from Ibn ʿAbbās (may God be pleased with them!),[40] that a man complained to the Messenger of God ﷺ that afflictions had befallen him, so the Messenger of God ﷺ told him, 'When you arise say, "In the Name of God for myself, my family, and my property"; otherwise, nothing will leave you'. So the man said these words and the afflictions left him.[41]

Ibn as-Sunnī also transmitted the following: 'Whosoever says when he arises, "O God, verily, I arise because of Thee, blessed, in good health, and protected. So bestow upon me Thy blessings,

Thy haleness, and Thy protection in this world and the next", three times when it becomes morning and when it becomes evening, will truly receive from God His blessings.'[42]

Ḥadīth: With respect to God's Word (may He be mighty and exalted!), 'And Abraham who fulfilled his obligations',[43] ʿAlī (may God be pleased with him!) transmitted this: 'The Prophet ﷺ used to say when it became morning and when it became evening:

> Glory be to God when ye enter the night and when ye enter the morning. Unto Him belongeth praise in the heavens and the earth! – and at sunset and noonday. He bringeth forth the living from the dead, and He bringeth forth the dead from the living, and He reviveth the earth after its death. And even so will ye be brought forth.'[44]

Ḥadīth: The Prophet ﷺ said, 'Whosoever says when it becomes morning, "Glory be to God when ye enter the night and when ye enter the morning, unto Him belongeth praise in the heavens and the earth."[45] (the entire verse), will make up for what escapes him that day and whosoever recites it when it becomes evening will make up for what escapes him that night.'[46]

Ḥadīth: 'Whosoever repeats three times when it becomes morning, "I seek refuge from the accursed devil", and recites three verses from the end of *Sūrat al-Ḥashr*,[47] seventy thousand angels will be assigned to him to pray for him until evening. If he should die that day, he dies a martyr, and if he says it when it becomes evening, he is of that rank.'

Ḥadīth: 'Whosoever says on Friday morning before the noon prayer, "I ask forgiveness of God the Supreme than whom there is no divinity but He, the Living, the Eternal and unto Him I repent," three times, is forgiven his sins, even though they be like the foam on the sea.'[49]

Ḥadīth: In his *al-Muʿjam al-Kabīr*, aṭ-Ṭabarānī narrated that Abu'd-Dardā' said, 'The Messenger of God ﷺ said, "Whosoever asks God's blessings upon me ten times when it becomes morning and when it becomes evening obtains my intercession on the Day of Judgment".'[50]

Ḥadīth: In the collection of forty *ḥadīths* of Muḥammad ibn Mūsā ibn Nuʿmān, he relates, 'A narrative was transmitted on the authority of Abū Hurayrah, who said, "The Messenger of God ﷺ said, 'Blessings upon me is a light upon the path; whosoever asks blessings upon me on Fridays eighty times is forgiven the sins of eighty years'".'[51]

Muḥammad ibn Mūsā ibn Nuʿmān said, 'Anas ibn Mālik related that the Messenger of God ﷺ said,

> Whosoever asks blessings upon me every Friday one thousand times will not die before he sees his place in Paradise; and whosoever asks blessings upon me once, and this has been accepted from him, God effaces the sins of eighty years from him.'[52]

Ḥadīth: 'Not a man leaves his house for prayer and says, "O God, verily I ask Thee by virtue of the right of those who can ask Thee and by virtue of this path of mine, verily, I do not go forth in insolence or arrogance or hypocrisy or good fame. I go forth in fear of Thy displeasure and seeking Thy contentment. I ask Thee to deliver me from hellfire and to forgive me my sins, for no one can forgive sins save Thee," but God appoints for him seventy thousand angels who ask forgiveness for him and God (may He be mighty and exalted!) draws His face near to him until he finishes his prayer.'[53]

Ḥadīth: 'When one of you enters the mosque or goes to the mosque, let him ask blessings upon the Prophet ﷺ and say, "O God, open the doors of Thy mercy to me"; and when he leaves, let him ask blessings upon the Prophet ﷺ and say, "O God, protect me from the accursed devil".'[54] Ibn Mukarram said in his version of the *ḥadīth*, 'O God, safeguard me'.[55]

Ḥadīth: 'A supplication is not refused between the call to prayer and the formula just preceding the ritual prayer (*iqāmah*), so supplicate.'[56]

Ḥadīth: 'He performed two short units of prayer[57] and I[58] heard him say three times while sitting, "O God, the Lord of Gabriel and Isrāfīl and Michael and Muḥammad ﷺ, I seek refuge in Thee from hellfire".'[59]

Ḥadīth: 'When the Prophet ﷺ used to perform the morning prayer, he would say, "O God, verily I ask of Thee beneficial knowledge, acceptable work and a good sustenance".'[60]

Ḥadīth: 'The Messenger of God ﷺ did not lead us in any prescribed prayer without turning his face toward us and saying,

> O God, verily I seek refuge in Thee from every deed which would dishonour me, and I seek refuge in Thee from every companion who would ruin me, and I seek refuge in Thee from every hope which would distract me, and I seek refuge in Thee from poverty which would make me forget, and I seek refuge in Thee from all wealth which would make me intemperate.'[61]

Ḥadīth: 'Whosoever recites the opening chapter of the Qur'ān and the Verse of the Throne[62] and the two verses from *Āl ʿImrān*: "God is witness that there is no deity save Him, as do the angels[63] . . ." and "Say: O God! Owner of Sovereignty!"[64] up to "and Thou givest sustenance to whom Thou choosest, without measure",[65] then verily, they are a means of attachment; no veil exists between them and God (may He be mighty and exalted!).'

'The verses said, "Are we to be sent down to Thy earth and to whosoever disobeys Thee?"'

'So God (may He be mighty and exalted!) answered,

> Verily, I have sworn that no one amongst My servants shall recite thee at the end of each prayer but that I shall make Paradise his abode in accordance with his deeds, or I shall make him dwell in the Garden, or I shall look at him with My

hidden eye seventy times every day, or I shall protect him from every enemy and deliver him.'[66]

Ḥadīth: 'Whosoever says three times after the morning prayer and three times after the afternoon prayer, "I ask forgiveness of God, the Supreme than whom there is no divinity but He, the Living, the Eternal, and unto Him I repent," is forgiven his sins, even though they be as the foam of the sea.'[67]

Ḥadīth: 'Whosoever says, "Glory and praise be to God, the Supreme, there is no power or strength save in God, the Exalted, the Supreme" three times as soon as he finishes his prayer, rises forgiven.'[68]

Ḥadīth: 'When you pray in the morning, say after the morning prayer, "Glory and praise be to God, the Supreme, there is no power or strength save in God," three times. God will safeguard you from four afflictions: from leprosy, the jinn, blindness, and semi-paralysis. This is in regard to your world here. As for your Hereafter, say, "O God, guide me Thyself and bestow upon me Thy bounty, spread forth upon me Thy mercy, and send down upon me Thy blessings".'[69]

Then the Messenger of God ﷺ said, 'If he has fulfilled them up to the Day of Judgment, never having abandoned them, they will assuredly open four gates of Paradise for him; he will be able to enter through whichever one he wants.'[70]

Another account says, '. . . never having abandoned them out of dislike or forgetfulness, he will not come to any one of the gates of Paradise but that he will find it open.'[71]

Ḥadīth: 'After saying the morning prayer, repeat seven times before speaking to anyone, "O God, protect me from hellfire"; for truly, if you should die that very day, God records for you safety from hellfire.'[72]

Ḥadīth: 'Whosoever repeats after finishing his noon prayer, "There is no divinity but God alone; He has no partner; His is the Kingdom, His is the praise; and He has power over everything," ten times before speaking to anyone, God records through them ten good deeds for him, and through them erases ten bad ones, and through them raises him ten degrees; and they are for him the equal of ten breezes; and they are his guards against the devil and his protection against adversity; no sin will affect him on that day except polytheism (*shirk*). And whosoever repeats these words when he finishes saying the afternoon prayer is given the same protection that night.'[73]

Ḥadīth: 'Whosoever says the morning prayer, then recites, "Say: He is the God, the One!"[74] one hundred times before speaking, every time he says, "Say: He is God, the One!" he is forgiven the sins of a year.'[75]

Ḥadīth: 'Whosoever prays at dawn, then sits invoking God (may He be mighty and exalted!) until the sun rises, Paradise is decreed for him.'[76]

Ḥadīth: 'Whosoever prays at dawn or in the early morning then sits at his place and does not speak nonsense about the things of this world, but remembers God (may He be mighty and exalted!) to the point that he has prayed four units, emerges from his sins like the day his mother gave birth to him.'[77]

Ḥadīth: 'Whosoever says in one of the marketplaces, "There is no divinity but God alone; He has no partner; His is the Kingdom; His is the praise; He gives life and takes it; He is Alive and does not die; in His hand is all good; and He has power over everything," one million good deeds are recorded for him and one million bad deeds are erased, and a house is built for him in Paradise.'[78]

In another account: 'Whosoever says, when he enters the market-place, "There is no divinity but God alone: He has no partner; His is the Kingdom; His is the praise; He gives life and takes it; in His hand is all good; and He has power over everything; there is no divinity but God; God is Great; praise be to God, glory be to God; there is no power or strength save in God," a million good deeds are recorded for him and a million bad ones are erased, and he is elevated one million degrees.'[79]

If you ask, 'For what reason should the reward of invocations be so great, given that they are so brief and easy on the tongue?', I respond, 'Because of their constant repetitions; for verily, all of them refer to faith, which is to the noblest of things; but God knows best.'

Ḥadīth: 'He who first greets another with the salutation of peace is worthier in the sight of God (may He be mighty and exalted!) and His Messenger ﷺ.'[80]

Ḥadīth: 'He who greets a people excels them by ten good deeds.'[81]

Ḥadīth: 'He who says, "Peace be upon you (*as-salāmu ʿalaykum*)" has ten good deeds recorded for him; and he who says, "Peace be upon you and the mercy of God (*as-salāmu ʿalaykum wa raḥmat-u'llāh*)" has twenty good deeds recorded for him; and he who says, "Peace be upon you and the mercy of God and His blessings (*as-salāmu ʿalaykum wa raḥmatu'llāh wa barakātuh*)" has thirty good deeds recorded for him.'[82]

Ḥadīth: 'When something startled him, he would say, "He is my Lord; He has no partner".'[83]

Ḥadīth: 'O ʿAlī! Shall I not teach you an expression to say when you fall into difficulty?' I said, 'Why, Of course, may God make me your ransom! How many good things you have taught me!'

He said, 'When you fall into difficult straits, say, "In the Name of God, the Compassionate, the Merciful; there is no power or strength save in God, the Exalted, the Supreme." For verily, through these words God disposes what He wills of the various kinds of afflictions.'[84]

Ḥadīth: 'When he feared a people, he would say, "O God, verily we place Thee in our breasts, and we take refuge in Thee from their evil".'[85]

Ḥadīth: 'We were with the Prophet ﷺ on a raid and the enemy was encountered. Then I[86] heard him say, "O sovereign of the Day of Judgment, Thee we worship and Thee we ask for help".' He continued, 'Then I came across men flung down on earth while the angels were striking them in front and from behind.'[87]

SECTION [TWO]
What to Say When Going on a Journey

Ḥadīth: 'Whosoever departs from his house, wishing to travel, should say when he leaves, "I believe in God, I take refuge in God, I put my trust in God; there is no power or strength save in God." Then God will bestow upon him the good of that departure and will avert from him the evil of that departure.'[88]

Ḥadīth: 'When the Prophet ﷺ travelled, he would say,

> O God, Thou art the Companion of the sojourn and the deputy (*khalīfah*) in the family. O God, accompany us on our journey and take our place in our family. O God, verily, I seek refuge in Thee from the hardships of travel and the sorrow of death, and from lean times after plenty, from the call of the tyrannized, and from the evil eye on one's family and wealth.'[89]

Ḥadīth: 'When the Messenger of God ﷺ travelled, riding his camel, he would say with his finger partially extended,

> O God, Thou art the Companion on the journey and the deputy in the family. O God, remove the distance of the land for us and facilitate the journey for us. O God, I seek refuge in Thee from the hardships of travelling and the sorrow of death.'[90]

Ḥadīth: 'Safety for my people from drowning when they ride on a boat is to say, "In the Name of God be its course and its mooring. Verily, my Lord is forgiving and merciful;[91] And they measure not the power of God in its true measure . . .".'[92]

Ḥadīth: Abū Hurayrah transmitted, 'Shall I not teach you something which the Messenger of God ﷺ taught me to say upon leave-taking?' I[93] said, 'Why, of course.'

He said, 'Say, "I command you to the protection of God who does not neglect those who are entrusted to him.'[94]

Ḥadīth: Abū Hurayrah said, 'Shall I not teach you an expression which the Messenger of God taught me? When you wish to travel or depart from a place, say to your family, "I have commended you to the protection of God who does not fail those who are entrusted to Him".'[95]

Ḥadīth: 'When an animal belonging to one of you escapes into the wilderness, call out three times, "O servants of God, apprehend it!"'[96]

Ḥadīth: Yūnus ibn ʿUbayd transmitted, 'There is not a man who rides a difficult animal and says in its ear, "Seek they other than the religion of God, when unto Him submitteth whosoever is in the heavens and the earth, willingly or unwillingly, and unto Him they will be returned",[97] without its becoming humble to him by the permission of God.'[98]

Ḥadīth: 'When the Messenger of God ﷺ would say the morning prayer and I[99] did not know it, he would raise his voice, so that his Companions could hear, and say, except when travelling, "O God, make my religion good for me, which Thou hast made as a protection for my affairs. O God, make my Hereafter good which Thou hast made my place of return", three times; "O God, I seek refuge in Thy contentment from Thy anger. O God, I seek refuge in Thee", three times; "There is no one who can restrain when Thou bestoweth, and there is no one who can bestow when Thou restraineth, and the good luck of anyone will not avail against Thee".'[100]

Ḥadīth: 'Verily, God (may He be mighty and exalted!) is a Friend who loves friendship. When you travel in a time of abundance, let your riding mounts have their fill of food, and do not go beyond the stopping-places on them; and when you travel in times of drought, then hurry. Make use of the end of the night. Verily, the earth is rolled up at night and if the desert demons seize you, then shout out the call to prayer. Beware of praying in the midst of main roads, for they are the crossings of predatory animals and the dwelling places of snakes.'[101]

Ḥadīth: 'Verily the Prophet ﷺ never saw a village which he wished to enter without saying upon seeing it,

> O God, Lord of the Seven Heavens and what they shelter, Lord of the Seven Earths and what they contain, Lord of the devils and that which they lead astray, and Lord of the breezes and what they scatter, verily, we ask of Thee the best for this village and the best for its people, and we seek refuge in Thee from its evil and from the evil of its people and from the evil therein.'[102]

Ḥadīth: 'Whosoever stops over at a place, then says, "I take refuge in the perfect words of God from the evil which He hath created," not a thing will harm him until he departs from that stopping-place of his.'[103]

Ḥadīth: Anas transmitted the following, 'When we stopped at a place, we would glorify God until the saddlebags were unfastened.' Shuʿbah said, 'That is, we glorified God verbally.'[104]

Ḥadīth: 'When he returned, he would say "God is Great (*Allāhu Akbar*)," three times, then say,

> There is no divinity but God alone; He has no partner; His is the Kingdom; His is the praise; and He has power over everything. We are those who are returning, worshipping, repenting, and prostrating ourselves to our Lord, and those who are praising. God has kept His promise and helped His servant and alone defeated the enemies.'[105]

Ḥadīth: 'When he went into his family, he would say, "Repenting, repenting to our Lord, returning. He has not left a sin upon us".'[106]

Section [Three]

Ḥadīth: One of the best ways of visiting the sick is to place your hand upon him and ask, 'How was your morning?' or 'How was your night?'[107]

Ḥadīth: 'When you visit someone sick, console him during the visit, for verily, that will not restore anything of his health, but it will put him in good spirits.'[108]

Ḥadīth: 'The Messenger of God ﷺ went in to visit a sick man who was near death. So he greeted him and asked, "How do you feel?" He answered, "Fine, O Messenger of God, I long for God and I fear for my sins." The Messenger of God ﷺ said, "The two will never join in the heart of a man in this world without God's bestowing upon him his wish and protecting him from what he fears".'[109]

Ḥadīth: 'The Messenger of God ﷺ went in to visit a sick man and asked, "Do you long for anything? Would you like some sweet bread?" He said, "Yes!" So he requested some for him.'[110]

Ḥadīth: 'When he visited someone sick, he would say, "Remove the injury, O Lord of Mankind. Heal, Thou art the Healer. There is no remedy except Thy remedy, a remedy that leaves no illness".' Ḥammād used to say, 'There is no remedy except Thy remedy.'[111]

Ḥadīth: 'There is not a Muslim who visits a sick man whose time has not yet come, and who says seven times, "I ask of God, the Supreme Lord of the Supreme Throne, to heal you", without the man's being restored to health.'[112]

Ḥadīth: 'Rub with your right hand seven times and say, "I seek refuge in the might of God and His power from the evil that I find."[113] I did that and God Most High removed what was the matter with me; and I have not ceased instructing my family and others to do the same.'

Ḥadīth: Abū Hurayrah said, 'The Messenger of God ﷺ and I went out, his hand in mine or my hand in his, to visit a man of shabby appearance. The Prophet said, "O so-and-so, what is it that I see that has happened to you?" He said, "Sickness and harm, O Messenger of God." He said, "Shall I not teach you an expression which will remove harm and sickness from you?"'

Abū Hurayrah said, 'Teach me, O Messenger of God.' 'Say, O Abū Hurayrah, "I put my trust in the Living (*al-Ḥayy*) who does not die, and praise be to God who has not taken a son, who has no partner (*sharīk*) in the Kingdom, and who has no guardian over Him out of lowliness, and say God is Great".'

So the Messenger of God ﷺ went to the man, whose condition had improved and asked, 'How so?' He answered, 'I said the words, O Messenger of God. I have not forsaken the words which you have taught me.'[114]

Ḥadīth: 'When a man visits someone sick, let him say, "O God, heal Thy servant so that he may either overcome an enemy for You or else he may go to pray to You".'[115]

Ḥadīth: ʿUthmān ibn ʿAffān related, 'I became ill and the Messenger of God ﷺ came to visit me one day and said, "In the Name of God, the Compassionate, the Merciful, I protect you by the words of God, the One, the Eternal who 'begetteth not nor was begotten. And there is none comparable unto Him'[116] from the evil which you find." Then when the Messenger of God ﷺ rose to stand, he said, "O ʿUthmān, seek protection with these words, for there is none like unto them for you with which to seek protection".'[117]

Ḥadīth: 'Verily, the Messenger of God ﷺ used to teach his people to say for all their ailments and fever, "In the name of God the Great, we seek refuge in God the Supreme from the evil of a gushing wound and from the evil of the heat of hellfire".'[118]

Ḥadīth: Khawwāt ibn Jubayr related, 'I became ill and the Messenger of God ﷺ visited me, saying, "Your body is healed, O Khawwāt." I said, "And your body, O Messenger of God." He said, "Fulfill what you promised to God (may He be mighty and exalted!)", I said, I did not promise Him anything." He said, "Verily, you did! There is not a servant who becomes ill without offering some good to God (may He be mighty and exalted!). So fulfil the pledge which you made".'[119]

Ḥadīth: 'When misfortune befalls someone, let him remember his misfortune with Me, for it is the greatest of misfortunes.'[120]

Ḥadīth: The Prophet ﷺ said, 'Moses said to his Lord, "What is the recompense for one who consoles a mother who has lost a child?" He answered, "I shelter him in My Shade on the day when there is no shade but My Shade".'[121]

Ḥadīth: 'When some matter distresses you, pray to your Lord for proper guidance (*istikhārah*)[122] regarding it seven times, then look to that which spontaneously comes to your heart; for the good lies therein.'[123]

Ḥadīth: 'When the Messenger of God ﷺ had some matter in view, he would say, "O God, choose for me and select for me".'[124]

This is the conclusion of what we had wished to cite in this book in a concise manner. The door has now been opened to whosoever wishes to ponder thereon; for the best of speech is that which is concise and clear, not long and tedious. Praise be to God, Lord of the Worlds; prayers and blessings upon our master Muḥammad, the opener (*al-fātiḥ*) and sealer (*al-khātim*),[125] and upon his family and his Companions, the possessors of outstanding virtues and noble qualities. 'God is sufficient for us! Most excellent is He in Whom we trust.'[126]

NOTES

APPENDIXES

BIBLIOGRAPHY

SUGGESTED READINGS

INDEXES

NOTES

TRANSLATOR'S INTRODUCTION

1. Carl Brockelmann, *Geschichte der Arabischen Litteratur*, vol. ii (Leiden: E. J. Brill, 1949), p.143; George Makdisi, 'Ibn ᶜAṭā' Allāh', *Encyclopaedia of Islam*, vol. i (Leiden: E. J. Brill, 1971), p.722; F. Wustenfeld, *Geschichtschreiber der Araber und ihre Werke* (New York: Burt Franklin, n.d.), p.154; ᶜAbd al-Wahhāb b. Aḥmad ash-Shaᶜrānī, *Aṭ-Ṭabaqāt al-Kubrā*, ed. by ᶜAbd al-Qādir Aḥmad ᶜAṭā' (Cairo: Maktabat al-Qāhirah, 1970), section 2, p.19; Ibn al-Ḥayy b. Aḥmad b. al-ᶜImād, *Shadharāt adh-Dhahab fī Akhbār Man Dhahab*, vol. vi (Beirut: Al-Maktab at-Tijārī li'ṭ-Ṭibāᶜah wa'n-Nashr wa't-Tawzīᶜ, n.d.), p.19; ᶜAbd Allāh b. Asᶜad al-Yāfiᶜī, *Mir'āt al-Janān wa ᶜIbrat al-Yaqẓān*, vol. iv, 2nd ed. (Beirut: Mu'assasat al-Aᶜlamī, 1970), p.246. Jalāl ad-Dīn ᶜAbd ar-Rahmān as-Suyūṭī, *Ḥusn al-Maḥāḍarah fī Tārīkh Miṣr wa' l-Qāhirah*, vol. i, ed. by Muḥammad ᶜAbu' l-Faḍl Ibrāhīm (N.P: Dār Iḥyā' al-Kutub al-ᶜArabiyyah, n.d.), p.524, gives the *kunya* Abu'l-ᶜAbbās, whereas Ibrāhīm b. ᶜAlī b. Farḥūn, *Ad-Dībāj al-Mudhhab fī Maᶜrifat Aᶜyān 'Ulamā' al-Madhhab*, vol. i, ed. by Muḥammad al-Aḥmadī Abu'n-Nūr (Cairo: Dār at-Turāth, 1972), p.242, gives both Abu'l-ᶜAbbās and Abu'l-Faḍl. Abu'l-Mahāsin Yūsuf b. Taghribirdī, *An-Nujūm az-Zāhirah fī Mulūk Miṣr wa'l-Qāhirah*, vol. viii, p.280, and Yūsuf b. Ismāᶜīl an-Nabhānī, *Jāmiᶜ Karāmāt al-Awliyā'*, vol. i, ed. by Ibrāhīm A. ᶜAwḍ (Cairo: Muṣṭafā al-Bābī al-Ḥalabī, 1962), p.525, refer to his *nisbah* of place as as-Sakandarī. Victor Danner, 'Ibn ᶜAṭā' Allāh: A Sufi of Mamlūk Egypt' (unpublished Ph.D. dissertation, Harvard University, 1970), p.197, cites Ibn ᶜAṭā' Allāh's full name according to Aḥmad Zarrūq in an unpublished manuscript in the Escorial, No. 738, folio 9b, as Tāj ad-Dīn Tarjumān al-ᶜĀrifīn Abu'l-Faḍl

Aḥmad b. Muḥammad b. ᶜAbd al-Karīm b. ᶜAbd ar-Raḥmān b. ᶜAbd Allāh b. Aḥmad b. ᶜĪsā b. al-Ḥusayn b. ᶜAṭā' Allāh al-Judhāmī al-Mālikī al-Iskandarī al-Qarāfī aṣ-Ṣūfī ash-Shādhilī.

2. Ibn Farḥūn, *ad-Dībāj*, vol. II, p.43; as-Suyūṭī, *Ḥusn al-Maḥāḍarah*, vol. I, p.456; Aḥmad b. Muḥammad b. ᶜAṭā' Allāh, *Laṭā'if al-Minan*, ed. by ᶜAbd al-Ḥalīm Maḥmūd (Cairo: Ḥassān Publishers, 1974), p.191, refers to taking his grandfather's place and gives Shaykh Abu'l-ᶜAbbās al-Mursī's comments about him. Abu'l-Wafā at-Taftazānī, *Ibn ᶜAṭā' Allāh as-Sakandarī wa Taṣawwufuh* (Cairo: Maktabat al-Angalū al-Miṣriyyah, 1969), pp.14–16.

3. Ibn ᶜAṭā' Allāh, *Laṭā'if*, p.141, mentions that when his father went to see Shaykh Abu'l-Ḥasan ash-Shādhilī, he heard the shaykh say, 'You have asked me a question for which I have no answer, but I see the answer written upon the inkwell, the mattress, and the wall.' As-Suyūṭī, *Ḥusn al-Maḥāḍarah*, vol. I, p.520; Danner, 'Ibn ᶜAṭā' Allāh,' p.135. According to the *Laṭā'if*, p.138, the full name of Shaykh Abu'l-Ḥasan is Taqi'd-Dīn Abu'l-Ḥasan ᶜAlī b. ᶜAbd Allāh b. ᶜAbd al-Jabbār b. Tamīm b. Hurmuz b. Ḥātim b. Qusayy b. Yūsuf b. Yusha' b. Ward b. Battāl b. Aḥmad b. Muḥammad b. ᶜĪsā b. Muḥammad b. al-Ḥasan b. ᶜAlī b. Abī Ṭālib. However, Danner, 'Ibn ᶜAṭā' Allāh', p.118, gives the following preferred alternatives, based on al-Kattāni's *Salwat al-Anfās* (1898), vol. I, pp.84–5: Nūr ad-Dīn Abu'l-Ḥasan Aḥmad b. ᶜAlī b. ᶜAbd al-Jabbār al-Ḥasanī al-Idrīsī al-Miᶜmārī ash-Shādhilī az-Zarwilī, because Danner states, 'His lineage goes back to ᶜAlī b. Abī Ṭālib through Ḥassān b. al-Ḥasan not through Muḥammad b. al-Ḥasan, as is sometimes given, for that Muḥammad had no offspring.' Therefore, Danner says that 'in his *Laṭā'if* . . . Ibn ᶜAṭā' Allāh has the wrong descent also.'

4. Ibn Farḥūn, *ad-Dībāj*, vol. II, p.242; as-Suyūṭī, *Ḥusn al-Maḥāḍarah*, vol. I, p.524. Victor Danner, *Ibn ᶜAṭā' Allāh: The Book of Wisdom* (New York: Paulist Press, 1978), pp.19–20 (henceforth referred to as *The Book of Wisdom*).

5. Ibn al-ᶜImād, *Shadharāt adh-Dhahab*, vol. VI, pp.4, 20; Ibn ᶜAtā' Allāh, *Laṭā'if*, p.69; Danner, 'Ibn ᶜAṭā' Allāh', pp.144-145, 200; Taftazānī, *Ibn ᶜAtā' Allāh*, p.21; Ibn Taghribirdī, *an-Nujūm az-Zāhirah*, vol. VIII, p.198. His full name is Shihāb ad-Dīn Abu'l-Maᶜālī Aḥmad b. Isḥāq b. Muḥammad al-Mu'ayyad b. ᶜAlī b. Ismāᶜīl b. Abī Ṭālib al-Abarqūhī al-Hamadānī, an outstanding Qur'ān reciter and teacher and *muḥaddith*.

6. The order was founded by Shihāb ad-Dīn ᶜUmar as-Suhrawardī (d. 630 AH/1232 AD).

7. Ibn al-ᶜImād, *Shadharāt adh-*

Dhahab, vol. VI, p.12; Ibn Taghribirdī, *an-Nujūm az-Zāhirah*, vol. VIII, p.218, says he was learned in many disciplines. Ibn ʿAṭā' Allah, *Laṭā'if*, p.48; Danner, 'Ibn ʿAṭā' Allāh', pp.147-48, 200; Taftazānī, *Ibn ʿAṭā' Allāh*, pp. 21–2. His full name is given as Sharaf ad-Dīn Abū Muḥammad ʿAbd al-Mu'min b. Khalaf b. Abi'l-Ḥasan b. Sharaf b. al-Khidr b. Mūsā ad-Dimyāṭī ash-Shāfiʿī. He studied the seven schools of Qur'ānic recitation and became an expert in the Qur'ān and *ḥadīth*. He wrote works not only on *ḥadīth* and *fiqh* but also on language and linguistics.

8. Ibn al-ʿImād, *Shadharāt adh-Dhahab*, p.20; Aḥmad b. ʿAlī b. Ḥajar al-ʿAsqalānī, *ad-Durar al-Kāminah*, vol. I, ed. by Muḥammad Sayyid Jād al-Ḥaqq (Cairo: Dār al-Kutub al Ḥadīthah, 1385 AH/1966 AD), pp.109–10, 292; Danner, 'Ibn ʿAṭā' Allāh', pp.148–49, 201. His full name is given as Muḥammad b. ʿAbd Allāh b. ʿAbd al-ʿAzīz b. Muḥyi'd-Dīn al-Mārūnī Ḥafi Ra'sih al-Iskandarī. Taftazānī, *Ibn ʿAṭā' Allāh*, p.21, calls him al-Māzūnī.

9. Ibn al-ʿImād, *Shadharāt adh-Dhahab*, vol. V, p.381; as-Suyūṭī, *Ḥusn al-Maḥāḍarah*, vol. I, pp.173–74; Danner, 'Ibn ʿAṭā' Allāh', pp.150–54, 201; Taftazānī, *Ibn ʿAṭā' Allāh*, p.20. His full name is given as Nāṣir ad-Dīn Abu'l-ʿAbbās Aḥmad b. Muḥammad b. Abī Bakr Manṣūr b. Abi' l-Qāsim b. Mukhtār b. Abī Bakr ʿAlī b. al-Munayyir al-Judhāmī al-Iskandarī al-Mālikī. He is mentioned in the *Laṭā'if*, p.190, simply as Nāṣir ad-Dīn.

10. Ibn al-ʿImād, *Shadharāt adh-Dhahab*, vol V, p.421; as-Suyūṭī, *Ḥusn al-Maḥāḍarah*, vol. I, p.289; Ibn ʿAṭā' Allāh, *Laṭā'if*, pp.142, 175, 191, 224; Danner, 'Ibn ʿAṭā' Allāh', pp.158–59, 202. His full name is given as Makīn ad-Dīn al-Asmar ʿAbd Allāh b. Manṣūr al-Iskandarī. He became one of the early masters of the Shādhilī order and also taught Qur'ānic recitation.

11. Ibn al-ʿImād, *Shadharāt adh-Dhahab*, vol. V, p.406; al-Yāfiʿī, *Mir'āt al-Janān*, vol. IV, p.208; Tāj ad-Dīn as-Subkī, *Ṭabaqāt ash-Shāfiʿiyyah al-Kubrā*, vol. V, 1st ed. (Cairo: al-Maṭbaʿa al-Ḥusayniyyah al-Miṣriyyah, n.d.), p.41; Ibn ʿAṭā' Allāh, *Laṭā'if*, p.178; Taftazānī, *Ibn ʿAṭā' Allāh*, p.22; Danner, 'Ibn ʿAtā' Allāh', pp.155–6, 201. His full name is given as Shams ad-Dīn Abū ʿAbd Allāh Muḥammad b. Maḥmūd b. Muḥammad b. ʿAbbād al-Isfahānī. He is the author of several works such as *Kitāb al-Qawāʿid* and *Sharḥ al-Maḥsūl* and is also said to have had a great influence on Arabic language and poetry.

12. Other possible teachers include Ibn Daqīq al-ʿĪd (d. 702 AH/1302 AD), a renowned Shāfiʿī *faqīh* and disciple of both Shaykh Abu'l-Ḥasan ash-Shādhilī and Shaykh Abu'l-ʿAbbās al-Mursī; ʿAbd al-Ghaffār b. Nūḥ (d.708

AH/1309 AD), and Abū ᶜAbd Allāh b. an-Nuᶜmān (607–683 AH/1210–85 AD), both Mālikī authorities in their day.

13. Ibn ᶜAṭā' Allāh, *Laṭā'if*, p.185.

14. *Ibid.*, p.194; Yāfiᶜī, *Mir'āt al-Janān*, vol. IV, p.246; Ibn al-ᶜImād, *Shadharāt adh-Dhahab*, vol. VI, p.20; Danner, 'Ibn ᶜAtā' Allāh', p.24.

15. There is no record that Ibn ᶜAṭā' Allāh ever met Shaykh Abu'l-Ḥasan ash-Shādhilī. Since the latter died in 656 AH/1258 AD, Ibn ᶜAṭa' Allāh would probably have been a young boy.

16. Ibn ᶜAṭā' Allāh, *Laṭā'if*, p.194; Danner, 'Ibn ᶜAṭā' Allāh', pp.23–4; Danner, *Book of Wisdom*, p.23.

17. Ibn ᶜAṭā' Allāh, *Laṭā'if*, p.195.

18. *Ibid.*, p.196.

19. *Ibid.*, p.194; as-Suyūṭī, *Ḥusn al-Maḥāḍarah*, vol. I, p.524; Ibn Farḥūn, *ad-Dībāj*, vol. I, p.242; al-Yāfiᶜī, *Mir'āt al-Janān*, vol. VI, p.246; Ibn al-ᶜImād, *Shadharāt adh-Dhahab*, vol. VI, p.20; Ibn Ḥajar al-ᶜAsqalānī, *ad-Durar al-Kāminah*, vol. I, p.291; Danner, 'Ibn ᶜAṭa' Allāh', pp.135–36; Danner, *Book of Wisdom*, p.24; Shaᶜrānī, *Ṭabaqat al-Kubrā*, p.19, incorrectly states that Ibn ᶜAṭā' Allāh was the discipline of Shaykh Yāqūt al-ᶜArshī after the death of al-Mursī.

20. Ibn ᶜAṭā' Allāh, *Laṭā' if*, p.188.

21. *Ibid.*, p.189.

22. *Ibid.*, p.185.

23. *Ibid.*, p.190.

24. For his complete name, see note 9.

25. *Ibid.*, p.190.

26. *Ibid.*, p.196.

27. For an in-depth history of the Shādhilī order and its founder, see Victor Danner's unpublished dissertation, 'Ibn ᶜAṭā' Allāh'; and ᶜAbd al-Ḥalīm Maḥmūd, *Abu'l-Ḥasan ash-Shādhilī* (Cairo: Dār al-Kātib al-ᶜArabī, 1967).

28. Ibn ᶜAṭā' Allāh, *Laṭā'if*, p.187: Shaykh Abu'l-ᶜAbbās told one of his disciples to improve his ill-tempered nature because he had only one year to live, and according to Ibn ᶜAṭā' Allāh, the man did indeed die a year later.

29. *Ibid.*, p.170: 'This Abu'l-ᶜAbbās – since he penetrated to God, he has not been veiled and were he to ask for veiling, he would not find it.'

30. As-Suyūṭī, *Ḥusn al-Maḥāḍarah*, vol. I, p.523; Ibn ᶜAṭā' Allāh, *Laṭā' if*, pp.36, 164; Danner, 'Ibn ᶜAṭā' Allāh', pp.99 ff., 127; an-Nabhānī, *Karāmāt al-Awliyā'*, vol. I, pp.520-22, cites various miracles attributed to him; ash-Shaᶜrānī, *Ṭabaqāt al-Kubrā*, section 2, p.12 ff.

31. As-Suyūṭī, *op. cit.*, vol. I, p.523; cf. Ibn ᶜAṭā' Allāh, *Latā'if*, pp.168–71, 176 for Shaykh Abu'l-Ḥasan's praise of Shaykh Abu'l-ᶜAbbās; ash-Shaᶜrānī,

Ṭabaqāt al-Kubrā, section 2, p.4; an-Nabhānī, *Karāmāt al-Awliyā'*, vol. I, pp.341–44, for various miracles attributed to Shaykh Abu' l-Ḥasan.

32. That is, the spiritual axis of the religious community who is regarded as having pre-eminence over all other Sufi masters.

33. Ibn ᶜAṭā' Allāh, *Laṭā'if*, p.178, describes the circumstances when Shaykh Abu'l-ᶜAbbās began teaching as follows:

> Shaykh Abu'l-Ḥasan was in Cairo with a group of his disciples and companions at the home of az-Zakī as-Sarrāj, studying the *Kitāb al-Mawāfiq* by an-Niffarī. Shaykh Abu'l-Ḥasan asked where Abu' l-ᶜAbbās was. When he appeared, he said, 'O my son, speak. O my son, speak. God bless you! Speak and you will never be silent after this ever!' So Shaykh Abu' l-ᶜAbbās said, 'At that moment I was given the tongue of a shaykh'.

34. *Ibid.*, pp.178–79, 186, for the proof of his *quṭbiyyah*; see also p.169, where Shaykh Abu'l-Ḥasan states, 'O Abu' l-ᶜAbbās, I did not take you as a disciple except in order for you to become me and I you'.

35. *Ibid.*, p.20–1.

36. That is, the Ninety-Nine Beautiful Names of God.

37. *Ibid.*, pp.197–98: He adds, 'I heard that Shaykh Abu'l-Ḥasan said of him, "Abu'l-ᶜAbbās is more knowledgeable of the paths of heaven than he is of the paths of the earth".'

38. *Ibid.*, p.221.

39. See note 77; Ibn ᶜAṭā' Allāh wrote the *Kitāb al-Ḥikam*, which consists of aphorisms of a profound metaphysical nature, and presented it to Shaykh Abu'l-ᶜAbbās who heartily approved it. Before the latter died in Alexandria, Ibn ᶜAṭā' Allāh was already teaching in Cairo. Danner, *Book of Wisdom*, p.24.

40. Ibn al-ᶜImād, *Shadharat adh-Dhahab*, vol. VI, p.19, called him the spokesman of Sufism in his day, who also preached at the Azhar Mosque. He also cites the Shāfiᶜī Shams ad-Dīn adh-Dhahabī (d. 749 AH/1348 AD), who says that Ibn ᶜAṭā' Allāh spoke in a manner that would revive the spirit. The Shāfiᶜī as-Subkī, *Ṭabaqāt ash-Shāfiᶜiyyah*, vol. V, p.176, mentions his wondrous words; as-Suyūṭī, *Ḥusn al-Maḥāḍarah*, vol. I, p.524; al-Yāfiᶜī, *Mir'āt al-Janān*, vol. IV p.246, calls him 'the *imām* of both paths'; Ibn Taghribirdī, *an-Nujūm az-Zāhirah*, vol. VIII, p.280, mentions his eloquent public sermons; Ibn Farḥūn, *ad-Dībāj*, p.242, calls him 'the wonder of his time' in discussing Sufism; Ibn Ḥajar al-ᶜAsqalānī, *ad-Durar al-Kāminah*, vol. I, p.291, also cites him as the spokesman for Sufism in

his day and mentions his well-attended public sermons at the Azhar.

41. Ibn al-ᶜImād, *Shadharat adh-Dhahab*, vol. VI, p.19, and Ibn Ḥajar al-ᶜAsqalānī, *ad-Durar al-Kāminah*, vol. I, p.292, both cite adh-Dhahabī.

42. An-Nabhānī, *Karāmāt al-Awliyā'*, vol. I, p.525.

43. *Ibid.*, pp.525–26.

44. Ibn al-ᶜImād, *Shadharāt adh-Dhahab*, vol. VI, p.20; Ibn Ḥajar al-ᶜAsqalānī, *ad-Durar al-Kāminah*, vol. I, p.292, quoting adh-Dhahabī.

45. Ismāᶜīl b. ᶜUmar b. Kathīr, *Al-Bidāyah wa'n-Nihāyah*, vol. XIV (Cairo: Maṭbaᶜat as-Saᶜādah, n.d.), p.45; Ibn al-ᶜImād, *Shadharāt adh-Dhahab*, vol. VI, p.19; Ibn Ḥajar al-ᶜAsqalānī, *ad-Durar al-Kāminah*, vol. I, p.291; G. Makdisi, 'Ibn ᶜAṭā' Allāh', *E.I.*, III, p.723; Danner, *Book of Wisdom*, p.25.

46. Makdisi, 'Ibn 'Aṭā' Allāh', *E.I.*, III, p.722, and Brockelmann, *Geschichte der Arab. Lit.*, vol. II, p.143, give the date as 16 Jumada II 709 AH/21 November 1309 AD, whereas as-Suyūṭī *Ḥusn al-Maḥāḍarah*, vol. I, p.524, lists 13 Jumada II 709; Taftazānī, *Ibn 'Aṭā' Allāh*, p.35.

47. As-Subkī, *Ṭabaqāt ash-Shāfiᶜiyyah*, vol. V, p.176; as-Suyūṭī, *Ḥusn al-Maḥāḍarah*, vol. I, p.524; Ibn Farḥūn, *ad-Dībāj*, vol. I, p.243; al-Yāfiᶜī, *Mir'āt al-Janān*, vol. IV, p.246; an-Nabhānī, *Karāmāt al-Awliyā'*, vol. I, p.525, says 'near the Banū Wafā'; Ibn Ḥajar al-ᶜAsqalānī, *ad-Durar al-Kāminah*, vol. I, p.291; Ibn al-ᶜImād, *Ḥusn al-Maḥāḍarah*, vol. VI, p.20; Ibn Taghribirdī, *an-Nujūm az-Zāhirah*, vol. VIII, p.280, says 'throngs attended his funeral procession'.

48. As for example, the aforementioned miracle at his tomb, p.7.

49. Cf. note 47.

50. Cf. note 40.

51. As-Subkī, *Ṭabaqāt ash-Shāfiᶜiyyah*, vol. V, p.176: Tāj ad-Dīn as-Subkī (d. 771 AH/1369 AD) was a Shāfiᶜī and his father Taqi'd-Din (d. 756 AH/1355 AD) was a Shāfiᶜī *qāḍī* and one of the most famous religious scholars of his day. He was also a student of Ibn ᶜAṭā' Allāh. Cf. next paragraph. Makdisi, 'Ibn ᶜAtā' Allāh', *E.I.*, III, p.723.

52. Ibn Ḥajar al-ᶜAsqalānī, *ad-Durar al-Kāminah*, vol. I, p.292.

53. As-Subkī, *Ṭabaqāt ash-Shāfiᶜiyyah*, vol. V, p.176; as-Suyūṭī, *Ḥusn al-Maḥāḍarah*, vol. I, p.524; Ibn Ḥajar al-ᶜAsqalānī, *ad-Durar al-Kāminah*, vol. I, p.292, adds that he himself studied under Sārah bint as-Subkī who related remarks from her father regarding Shaykh Ibn ᶜAṭa' Allāh; Taftazānī, *Ibn ᶜAṭā' Allāh*, p.26.

54. Ibn ᶜAṭā' Allāh, *Laṭā'if*, pp.175, 224–57 *et passim*. See above, p.3.

55. *Ibid.*, p.316.

56. His full name is Sharaf

ad-Dīn Abū Sulaymān Dā'ūd b. ᶜUmar b. Ibrāhīm al-Iskandarī ash-Shādhilī. He was known to his followers as Da'ūd al-Bākhilī, and other variations include Ibn Bākhilā and Dā'ūd b. Mākhilā. Ahmad al-ᶜAlawī, *Kitāb Qawl al-Maqbūl* (al-Jazīrah: Maṭbaᶜat an-Nahḍah, n.d.), p.41; Danner, 'Ibn ᶜAṭā' Allāh', pp.228–91, 329; al-Yafiᶜī, *Mir'āt al-Janān*, vol. IV, p.144; Taftazānī, *Ibn ᶜAṭā' Allāh*, pp. 27–8, calls him Ibn ᶜAṭā' Allāh's *khalīfah*; al-Ḥasan b. ᶜAbd al-ᶜAzīz, *Irshād ar-Rāghibīn*, pp.42ff. in Muḥammad Ẓāfir al-Madanī's *al-Anwār al-Qudsiyyah* (Istanbul: n.p., 1302 AH/1884 AD); Martin Lings, *A Sufi Saint of the Twentieth Century: Shaikh Aḥmad al-ᶜAlawī* (2nd ed; Berkeley: University of California Press, 1973), p.233; Shaᶜrānī, *Ṭabaqāt al-Kubrā*, section 1, p.163ff., refers to him as Dā'ūd b. Mākhilā. See Appendix, pp.250–51 for a Shādhilī *silsilah* from which the ᶜAlawī branch claims its spiritual lineage.

57. Al-Yāfiᶜī, *Mir'āt al-Janān*, vol. III, p.329; Danner, 'Ibn ᶜAṭā' Allāh', pp.285–88, 328, gives his full name as Shihāb ad-Dīn Abu'l-ᶜAbbās Aḥmad b. Maylaq ash-Shādhilī; Taftazānī, *Ibn ᶜAṭā' Allāh*, p.28.

58. Ibn ᶜAṭā' Allāh, *Laṭā' if*, p.37; ash-Shaᶜrānī, *Ṭabaqāt al-Kubrā*, section 2, p.12.

59. *Ibid.*, p.37; ash-Shaᶜrānī, *Ṭabaqāt al-Kubrā*, section 2, p.12.

60. Ibn ᶜAṭā' Allāh, *Laṭā'if*, pp.19–20.

61. See Appendix for al-Ghazālī, p.233.

62. Ibn ᶜAṭā' Allāh, *Laṭā'if*, p.180: He was highly extolled by both shaykhs. See Appendix for at-Tirmidhī, p.243.

63. See Appendix for al-Qāḍī ᶜIyāḍ, p.240.

64. Ibn ᶜAṭā' Allāh, *Laṭā'if*, pp.179–180: 'Shaykh Abu'l-Ḥasan used to say that the *Iḥyā'* bestowed upon you knowledge and the *Qūt* bestowed upon you light.'

65. Danner, 'Ibn ᶜAṭā' Allāh', p.103.

66. *Ibid.*, p.104. For a discussion and translation of the *Aḥzāb*, see Maddawi *az-Zirr* and ᶜAbdullah Nur ad-Dīn Durkee, trans. *The School of the Shādhdhuliyyah: Vol. I, Orisons*. (Alexandria, Egypt, 1411/1991), pp. 67ff.

67. *Ibid.*, p.319.

68. Other editions of the *Laṭā'if* give the full title as *Kitāb Laṭā'if al-Minan fī Manāqib Abi'l-ᶜAbbās al-Mursī wa Shaykhih Abi'l-Ḥasan*.

69. Ibn ᶜAṭā' Allāh, *Laṭāif*, p.316, refers to his counseling of the Sultan al-Malik al-Manṣūr Lājīn followed by the phrase *raḥimahu'llāh*, which indicates that he was already dead as of that writing. The sultan died in 697 AH/1298 AD, so the *Laṭā'if* was therefore composed sometime thereafter. Danner, 'Ibn ᶜAṭā' Allāh', p.277, suggest that the

Laṭā'if might have been written between 1307 and 1308 after his confrontation with Ibn Taymiyyah. Furthermore, Ibn ᶜAṭā' Allāh mentions both his *Kitāb al-Ḥikam* in the *Laṭā'if* (p.290) and his *Kitāb at-Tanwīr* (p.277), indicating that the *Laṭā'if* was written after these two books.

70. Ibn ᶜAtā' Allāh, *Traité sur le nom Allāh*, trans. by Maurice Gloton (Paris: Les Deux Océans, 1981), p.17.

71. Ibn ᶜAṭā' Allāh, *Laṭa'if*, pp.36–7.

72. Taftazānī, *Ibn ᶜAṭā' Allāh*, p.104; al-Yāfiᶜī, *Mir'āt al-Janān*, vol. IV, p.246; Ibn al-ᶜImād, *Shadharāt adh-Dhahab*, vol. VI, p.20.

73. Ibn ᶜAṭā' Allāh, *Laṭā'if*, p.366; Danner, 'Ibn ᶜAṭā' Allāh', p.320.

74. Taftazānī, p.105.

75. *Ibid.*, p.105; Danner, 'Ibn ᶜAṭā' Allāh', p.320.

76. Those biographers mentioning Ibn ᶜAṭā' Allāh's works include Ibn Farḥūn, *ad-Dibāj*, vol. I, p.242; an-Nabhānī, *Karāmāt al-Awliyā'*, vol. I, p.525; as-Suyūṭī, *Ḥusn al-Maḥāḍarah*, vol. I, p.524; Ibn al-ᶜImād, *Shadharāt adh-Dhahab*, vol. VI, p.20; as-Subkī, *Ṭabaqāt ash-Shāfiᶜiyyah*, vol. V, p.176; ash-Shaᶜrānī, *Ṭabaqāt al-Kubrā*, section 2, p.19.

77. Taftazānī, *Ibn ᶜAṭā' Allāh*, pp.79–80, cites Ḥajjī Khalīfah in his *Kashf aẓ-Ẓunūn*, vol. III, p.82, who quotes Shaykh Abu'l-ᶜAbbās al-Mursī, as saying upon being presented with a copy of the *Ḥikam*, 'My son, you have achieved the aim of the *Iḥyā'* in this book and more'. Danner, 'Ibn ᶜAṭā' Allāh', pp.277, 300–1; Ibn ᶜAṭā' Allāh, *Traité sur le nom Allāh*, trans. by Gloton, p.13.

78. Ibn ᶜAṭā' Allāh, *Laṭā'if*, p.290; *Idem.*, *Kitāb at-Tanwīr fī Isqāṭ at-Tadbīr* (Cairo: Maṭbaᶜat Muḥammad ᶜAlī Subayḥ, 1390 AH/1970 AD), p.92; *Idem.*, *Tāj al-ᶜArūs al-Ḥāwī li-Tahdhīb an-Nufūs* on the margin of *Kitāb at-Tanwīr* (Cairo: Matbaᶜat al-Ḥamīdiyyah al-Miṣriyyah, 1321 AH), p.66. Both Danner, 'Ibn ᶜAṭā' Allāh', p.331, and Taftazānī, *Ibn ᶜAṭā' Allāh*, p.79, cite Ibn ᶜAṭā' Allāh's *ᶜUnwān at-Tawfīq* as containing passages from the *Ḥikam* as well.

79. Danner, 'Ibn ᶜAṭā' Allāh', pp.300–1.

80. In his *Book of Wisdom*, Danner divides the *Ḥikam* into twenty-five chapters of 262 aphorisms, four treatises, and thirty-four intimate discourses. Paul Nwyia in his *Ibn ᶜAṭā' Allāh (m.709/1309) et la naissance de la confrerie Šadilite* (Beyrouth: Dār el-Machreq, 1972), pp. 84–229, numbers the aphorisms differently and divides the work into thirty chapters of 240 maxims, four extracts of letters, and thirty-five colloquies.

81. Danner, 'Ibn ᶜAṭā' Allāh', p.302.

82. See Taftazānī, *Ibn ᶜAṭā' Allāh*, pp.89–96, for a list of over twenty-five commentaries on the *Ḥikam* from the eighth/fourteenth century to the early fourteenth/twentieth century, including ones in Turkish and Malaysian. Taftazānī, pp. 1–2, 84, considers the *Ḥikam* to be Ibn ᶜAṭā' Allāh's most important and most outstanding work and all his other works merely a commentary or explanation of it.

83. See Taftazānī, *Ibn ᶜAṭā' Allāh*, p.92, for Aḥmad Zarrūq's lofty praise of ar-Rundī's *Sharḥ*. Miguel Asin Palacios, *St. John of the Cross and Islam* (New York: Vantage Press, 1981), pp. x, 28–31, views Ibn ᶜAbbād ar-Rundī as the Muslim forerunner of St. John of the Cross based on ar-Rundī's *Sharḥ* of the *Ḥikam* and its Shādhilī mystical doctrines on renunciation. Zaki Mubārak, *at-Taṣawwuf al-Islāmī fi'l-Adab wa'l-Akhlāq* (Cairo: Dār al-Kitāb al-ᶜArabī, 1373 AH/1954 AD), pp.136–37, states that the two most famous commentaries are by ar-Rundī and ᶜAbd Allāh b. Ḥijāzī ash-Sharqāwī (d. 1227 AH/1812 AD) entitled *al-Minaḥ al-Qudsiyyah 'alā' l-Ḥikam al-ᶜAṭā'iyyah*. However, Zarrūq's commentaries have become increasingly popular over the years. A. J. Arberry, *Sufism: An Account of the Mystics of Islam* (London: George Allen & Unwin Ltd., 1979), p.87.

84. Ahmad b. ᶜAjībah, *Īqāẓ al-Himmam fī Sharḥ al-Ḥikam* (Cairo: ᶜAbd al-Ḥamīd Aḥmad Ḥanafī, n.d.), pp.3–4; Danner 'Ibn ᶜAṭā' Allāh', p.304; Taftazānī, *Ibn ᶜAṭā' Allāh*, p.88; Jean-Louis Michon, *Le Soufi Marocain Aḥmad Ibn ᶜAjība et Son Miᶜrāj* (Paris: Librairie Philosophique J. Vrin, 1973), pp.32–3, 36.

85. Taftazānī, *Ibn ᶜAṭā' Allāh*, p.88; Nwyia, *Ibn ᶜAṭā' Allāh*, p.38, states that the spread and popularity of the *Ḥikam* are precisely due to its conformity to the *Sunnah*. Even Ibn al-ᶜImād, *Shadharāt adh-Dhahab*, vol. VI, p.19, comments that Ibn ᶜAṭā' Allāh combines the teachings of the Sufis with those of the early patriarchs (*salaf*) and the legal sciences.

86. Mubārak, *at-Taṣawwuf al-Islāmī*, p.136; Taftazānī, *Ibn ᶜAṭā' Allāh*, p.89.

87. Asin Palacios, *St. John of the Cross*, p.30.

88. For examples, see note 80.

89. Ibn ᶜAṭā' Allāh, *Kitāb at-Tanwīr*, p.13.

90. *Ibid.*, p.92, is one example.

91. *Ibid.*, pp.93–4, 108.

92. *Ibid.*, p.88. The same formula follows the name of Shaykh Abu'l-ᶜAbbās al-Mursī (p.110).

93. Brockelmann, *Geschichte der Arab.Lit.* vol. II, p.143; Tafta zānī, *Ibn ᶜAṭā' Allāh*, p.101.

94. *Ibid.*, p.143; Taftazānī, *Ibn ᶜAṭā' Allāh*, p.101.

95. Muḥammad b. Ibrāhīm b. ᶜAbbād ar-Rundī, *ar-Rasā'il aṣ-Ṣughrā*, ed. by Paul Nwyia (Beyrouth: Imprimerie Catholique, 1958), p.97.

96. Danner 'Ibn ᶜAṭā' Allāh', p.311; Ibn ᶜAjībah, *Īqāẓ al-Himam*, p.9, comments that both the *Tanwīr* and the *Laṭā'if* are a kind of *sharḥ* of the *Ḥikam*.

97. It is also known as *al-Qawl al-Mujarrad fi'l-Ism al-Mufrad*. See Ibn ᶜAjībah, *Īqāẓ al-Himam*, p.9.

98. Ibn ᶜAṭā' Allāh, *Al-Qasd al-Mujarrad fī Maᶜrifat al-Ism al-Mufrad* (London: British Museum manuscript, cat. no. 14519. b. 85), p.12.

99. Danner, 'Ibn ᶜAṭā' Allāh', pp.305–6.

100. Ibn ᶜAṭā' Allāh, *Al-Qaṣd al-Mujarrad*, p.13, cites their quoting of Q. 19:65: 'Knowest thou one that can be named along with Him?' as one proof given against an etymological source. For an expanded discussion, see Ibn ᶜAṭā' Allāh, *Traité sur le nom Allāh*, trans. by Gloton, pp.34–5.

101. Ibn ᶜAṭā' Allāh, *al-Qasd al-Mujarrad*, p.15; these include being derived from *al-walah*, *al-ilāh*, *al-hajb*, *al-ᶜuluw*, and *al-baqā'*.

102. *Ibid.*, p.23.

103. *Ibid.*, pp.19–20.

104. *Ibid.*, pp.29–33, 40–3ff. Although Shaykh Ibn ᶜAṭā' Allāh divides the Ninety-Nine Names according to Names of Essence, Action, etc., nevertheless, he says that none of them can be ranked as first or last nor are they conditioned by time or limits (p.40).

105. *Ibid.*, p.14.

106. Danner, 'Ibn ᶜAṭā' Allāh', p.333.

107. Ibn ᶜAṭā' Allāh, *Traité sur le nom Allāh*, trans. by Gloton, p.22.

108. Taftazānī, *Ibn ᶜAṭā' Allāh*, p.107.

109. Ibn ᶜAṭā' Allāh, *al-Qaṣd al-Mujarrad*, p.76. Cf. *Laṭā'if*, p.196.

110. *Ibid.*, pp.5–6, 68–9. Cf. *Miftāḥ al-Falāḥ wa Miṣbāḥ al-Arwāḥ* (Cairo: Maṭbaᶜat Muṣṭafā al-Bābī al-Ḥalabī, 1381 AH/1961 AD), pp.13–14.

111. See note 70 on Gloton's annotated translation.

112. It is also known as *Tāj al-ᶜArūs wa Qamᶜ an-Nufūs* in Brockelmann, *Geschichte der Arab.Lit.*, vol. II, p.144.

113. See note 78. Taftazānī, *Ibn ᶜAṭā' Allāh*, p.107, points out that the work is also entitled *an-Nubdhah fi't-Taṣawwuf* in the Dār al-Kutub listings (No. 4136) or *at-Tuḥfah fi't-Taṣawwuf*, the latter Brockelmann, *Geschichte der Arab. Lit.*, vol. II, p.143, mistakenly lists as a separate work. In fact, on p.144, Brockelmann gives another listing for a manuscript entitled *Uns al-ᶜArūs*, which is no doubt the same work. Taftazānī also notes that Brockelmann's listing of a

work called *at-Ṭarīq al-Jaddah ilā Nayl as-Saʿādah* is actually part of the *Tuḥfah fi't-Taṣawwuf*.

For an in-depth study of Ibn ʿAṭā' Allāh's works to date, see Taftazānī, pp.112ff. Besides the books previously cited are the following treatises which he lists, annotates, and gives location of when appropriate. Several of these are also mentioned by Brockelmann.

1) *Risālah* on Qur'ān 6:54; manuscript in Dār al-Kutub al-Miṣriyyah #81.

2) *Qaṣā'id* (poems); Berlin Library #7846.

3) *al-Muraqqa ila'l-Quds al-Abqā* — lost work on *fiqh*; mentioned by as-Suyūṭī (cf. note 125) and by Muḥammad b. Cheneb in his *Etude sur les personnages mentionnés dans L'Idjazza du Cheikh Abdel Qadir El Fasy*, p.341, note 17 and p.358.

4) *Muktaṣar Tahdhīb al-Mudawwanah li'l-Barādiʿī* — on Mālikī *fiqh*; also cited by as-Suyūṭī and Cheneb, but Taftazānī, p.113, says he could not find any copy.

5) *Risālah fi'l-Qawā'id ad-Dīniyyah* — on religious precepts and maxims; manuscript in British Museum #2372.

6) *Sermons*; handwritten text in Paris Library #1299.

7) *Ḥizb an-Najāt*; manuscript in Rabat Library #306.

8) *Risālah Taṣawwuf*; manuscript in Aṣif Library #105, 368, 1.

9) *Tanbīh fi Tarīq al-Qawm*, manuscript in Maktabat az-Zaytūnah in Tunis #1882, 168, III.

10) *Risālah fi's-Sulūk*; copy in Maktabat Rambur #144, 341, 1

11) *Ḥizb an-Nūr wa Tamām as-Surūr*; manuscript in Dār al-Kutub al-Miṣriyyah #214 taṣawwuf, 2150 taṣawwuf, and 1598 taṣawwuf.

12) *Duʿā*; copy in Dār al-Kutub al-Miṣriyyah #1632 taṣawwuf.

13) *Tuḥfat al-Khullān fī Sharḥ Naṣīḥat al-Ikhwān*; copy #1401 taṣawwuf was in Dār al-Kutub al-Miṣriyyah but 'it is as good as lost and until now we have not come across another copy' (p.115).

114. Ibn ʿAṭā' Allāh, *Tāj al-ʿArūs*, p.24.

115. *Ibid.*, p.94

116. Ibn ʿAjībah, *Īqāẓ al-Himam*, p.9,

117. Taftazānī, *Ibn ʿAṭā' Allāh*, p.106.

118. Danner, 'Ibn ʿAṭā' Allāh', p.311; Danner adds that 'Taqi'd-Dīn as-Subkī (d. 756 AH/1355 AD), his disciple, transmitted [it] to others, and [it] has always had a certain currency in Sufic circles.'

119. Ibn ʿAṭā' Allāh, *ʿUnwān at-Tawfīq fī Ādāb at-Tarīq, Sharḥ Qaṣīdah Shaykh ash-Shuyūkh Abī*

Madyan Shuʿayb al-Maghribī (Damascus: Maṭbaʿat al-Iḥsān, n.d.). The *Takhmīs* of Muḥyi' d-Dīn b. al-ʿArabī is also included. Taftazānī, *Ibn ʿAṭā' Allāh*, p.111, states that the *ʿUnwān* is mentioned only by al-Ḥajj al-Kawhin in his *Ṭabaqāt ash-Shādhiliyyah*, p.99.

120. Ibn ʿAṭā' Allāh, *ʿUnwān*, p.25. Cf. Taftazānī, *Ibn ʿAṭā' Allāh*, p.111.

121. Ibn ʿAṭā' Allāh, *ʿUnwān*, pp.20–1.

122. *Ibid.*, pp.19, 25.

123. Danner, 'Ibn ʿAṭā' Allāh', p.323.

124. Brockelmann, *Geschichte der Arab. Lit.*, vol. II, pp.143–44.

125. Cf. as-Suyūṭī, *Ḥusn al-Maḥāḍarah*, vol. I, p.424, who mentions two unknown works, *al-Muraqqā ila'l-Quds al-Abqā* and *Mukhtaṣar Tahdhīb al-Mudawwanah li'Barādiʿī* in addition to the *Tanwīr*, *Laṭā'if*, and *Ḥikam*.

126. Danner, 'Ibn ʿAṭā' Allāh', p.324. Cf. note 113.

127. Ibn Taghribirdī, *an-Nujūm az-Zāhirah*, vol. VIII, p.280, states that Ibn ʿAṭā' Allāh had very fine mystical poetry and gives the beginning lines of one of them; Ibn al-ʿImād, *Shadharāt adh-Dhahab*, vol. VI, p.20, says that Ibn ʿAṭā' Allāh's shaykh al-Mursī often used to ask him to repeat the following verse:

كَـمْ مِن قُلُوبٍ قد أُميتت بالهَوَى
أحْيَـا بـهـا مِـن بعـد مـا أحْيـاهـا

How many the hearts that by love have died/I live by them after He did them revive.

128. Taftazānī, *Ibn ʿAṭā' Allāh*, p.111, states that it is also known by the title *Miftāḥ al-Falāḥ fī Dhikr Allāh al-Karīm al-Fattāḥ*, according to Ḥajjī Khalīfah in *Kashf aẓ-Ẓunun*, vol. II, 1869.

129. Since this passage of not quite two pages in length was not part of the body of the work, it was omitted from the translation.

130. *Miftāḥ al-Falāḥ wa Miṣbāḥ al-Arwāḥ* (Cairo: Maṭbaʿat Muṣṭafā al-Bābī al-Ḥalabī, 1381 AH/1961 AD), p.4. Although *uṣūl* is normally translated as 'principles', its use in the singular made the term 'foundation' seem more appropriate as a heading.

131. Not to be confused with *al-qism ath-thānī*, which is translated as Part Two.

132. Cf. previous discussion, pp.16ff.

133. *Miftāḥ al-Falāḥ*, p.3.

134. *Ibid.*, pp.3–4.

135. *Ibid.*, p.4. *Dhikr* in its totality of meaning signifies not only invoking God's Name repeatedly and the Sufi ceremony of so doing but also any sort of mention of Him or a formula containing His Name or inward concentration on God.

136. *Ibid.*, pp.6–8. The sounds described that one hears while invoking, such as the rippling of

water or the sound of the wind, actually refer to spiritual states descending upon one who is totally absorbed in invoking God through His Name and is oblivious to all else.

137. Cf. *Ibid.*, pp.48ff., where Ibn ʿAṭā' Allāh returns to the procedure for invoking and gives further elaboration.

138. *Ibid.*, pp.31, 32.

139. *Ibid.*, p.44.

140. *Ibid.*, p.47.

141. See Appendix for al-Junayd, p.237.

142. See Appendix for al-Ghazālī, p.233.

143. *Miftāḥ al-Falāḥ*, p.56.

144. *Ibid.*, p.57.

145. *Ibid.*, p.58.

146. *Ibid.*, p.61.

147. *Ibid.*, p.64.

148. *Ibid.*, p.67.

149. See above, pp.16–18.

150. *Miftāḥ al-Falāḥ* p.110.

151. Taftazānī, *Ibn ʿAṭā' Allāh*, p.108.

152. Danner, 'Ibn ʿAṭā' Allāh', p.310. For Ibn ʿAṭā' Allāh's confrontation with Taqi'd-Dīn b. Taymiyyah, see Ibn al-ʿImād, *Shadharāt adh-Dhahab*, vol. VI, p.19.

153. Najm ad-Dīn al-Kubrā, *Fawā'iḥ al-Jamāl wa Fawātiḥ al-Jalāl*, ed. by Fritz Meier (Weisbaden: Franz Steiner Verlag GMBH, 1957), pp.2, 4, 14, 21–25.

154. Danner, 'Ibn ʿAṭā' Allāh', p.308.

155. Taftazānī, *Ibn ʿAṭā' Allāh*, pp.37–8.

156. Asin Palacois, *St. John of the Cross*, pp.ix–x, believes that St. John of the Cross was influenced by Ibn ʿAṭā' Allāh through Ibn ʿAbbād ar-Rundī's commentary on the *Ḥikam*. Taftazānī, *Ibn ʿAṭā' Allāh*, pp.1–2, concurs.

157. For examples of twentieth-century studies, see Danner, *Book of Wisdom* and 'Ibn ʿAṭā' Allāh'; Gloton, *Traité sur le nom Allāh*; Maḥmūd, *Abu'l-Ḥasan ash-Shādhilī*; Michon, *Le Soufi Marocain*; Murbārak, *at-Taṣawwuf al-Islāmī*; Nwyia, *Ibn ʿAṭā' Allāh*; Taftazānī *Ibn ʿAṭā' Allāh*; Asin Palacios, *St. John of the Cross* and 'Sadilies y alumbrados', *Al-Andalus*, IX–XVI (1944–1951); Luce Lopez Barault, *San Juan de la Cruz y el-Islam* (Recinto de Rio Piedras: El Colegio de Mexico, A.C., 1985).

158. For an in-depth study, see Lings, *A Sufi Saint of the Twentieth Century*.

Notes to the *Miftāḥ al-Falāḥ*

PART ONE

INTRODUCTION

1. Qur'ān 12:108.
2. Qur'ān 1:2.
3. Qur'ān 37:35
4. This is the *takbīr* which is used in the call to prayer.

5. A formula derived from the *Sunnah* of the Prophet.

6. Qur'ān 2:286.

7. This is another formula based on the *Sunnah*.

8. Qur'ān 24:35. The first sentence is taken verbatim from Najm ad-Dīn al-Kubra's *Fawā'iḥ al-Jamāl wa Fawātiḥ al Jalāl*, p.4, and the rest of the paragraph is a paraphrase of the same. Cf. above, note 153.

9. In other words, as on the Day of Judgment.

10. Qur'ān 37:99.

11. Tirmidhī, 45:87 (nos. 3576 and 3577, with slight differences). References to *ḥadīths* will be made in accordance with the system adopted by A. J. Wensinck in his *Handbook of Early Muhammadan Tradition*. Thus, the collections of *ḥadīths*, such as the *Ṣaḥīḥ* of Muḥammad ibn Ismāʿil al-Bukhārī, the *Ṣaḥīḥ* of Muslim ibn al-Ḥajjāj al-Qushayrī, the *Sunan* of Muḥammad ibn ʿIsa at-Tirmidhī, the *Sunan* of Abū Dā'ūd as-Sijistānī, the *Muwaṭṭa'* of Mālik ibn Anas, the *ʿAmal al-Yawm wa 'l-Laylah* of Abū Bakr Ibn as-Sunnī, *al-Jāmiʿ aṣ-Ṣaghir* of Jalāl ad-Dīn as-Suyūṭī, and the *Ḥilyat al-Awliyā'* of Abū Nu ʿaym al-Isfahānī will be referred to respectively as Bukhārī, Muslim, Tirmidhī, Abū Dā'ūd, Mālik, Ibn as-Sunnī, Suyūṭī, and Abū Nu ʿaym. Each name will be followed, first, by the number of the book (*kitāb*), then that of the chapter (*bāb*), and finally the number of the *ḥadīth* itself within the edited work; but in Ibn as-Sunnī's collection, his name will be followed only by the number of the *ḥadīth* as no other division exists in his work. Full bibliographical data on the editions of the *ḥadīth*-collections used will be given, of course, in the bibliography. Lastly, only those *hadīths* that have been actually verified are cited in the footnotes.

12. Qur'ān 13.28.

13. Qur'ān 24:35.

14. Qur'ān 75:1–2.

15. Qur'ān 40:15.

16. Qur'ān 89:27–30.

17. Qur'ān 33:41–2.

18. Qur'ān 3:191.

19. Qur'ān 33:35.

20. Qur'ān 2:152.

21. Qur'ān 13:28.

22. Qur'ān 3:41.

23. Qur'ān 76:25.

24. Muslim, 48:11 (no. 2701).

25. Tirmidhī, 45:7 (no. 3438, with slight differences).

26. Muslim, 48:11 (no. 2700).

27. Muslim, 6:36 (nos. 240 and 241, with slight differences).

28. Qur'ān 2:248.

29. Muslim 48:1 (no. 2676).

30. Tirmidhī, 45:12 (no. 3666). The word *al-mustahtarun* is derived from the passive voice of Form X of the verb, *ustuhtira*, 'to be devoted, infatuated with something'. Form VIII of the passive voice of the verb, *uhtira*, which is inexplicably

used later in the text, means the same as Form X. Both verbs also carry the sense of being negligent and thoughtless.

31. Bukhārī, 80:65 (no. 6024).
32. Tirmidhī, 45:87 (no. 3577).
33. Tirmidhī, 45:10 (no. 3660).
34. Suyūṭī, II, 18.
35. Suyūṭī, II, 19.
36. Mālik, 15:7 (no. 24).
37. Tirmidhī, 45:5 (no. 3436).
38. Muslim, 6:29 (no. 211).
39. Bukhārī, 80:68 (no. 6023).
40. Bukhārī, 97:15 (no. 6956).
41. Tirmidhī, 45:100 (no. 3597).
42. Tirmidhī, 45:119 (no. 3632).
43. Tirmidhī, 45:4 (no. 3435).
44. Tirmidhī, 45:9 (no. 3444).

Chapter [One]

1. Tirmidhī, 45:36 (no. 3488).
2. Tirmidhī, 45:36 (no. 3489).
3. Ibn as-Sunnī (nos. 181 and 182, with slight differences).
4. Tirmidhī, 45:12 (no. 3673, with slight differences).
5. Qur'ān 2:74.
6. Qur'ān 43:36–7.
7. Abū Dā'ūd, 35:31 (no. 4856).
8. Tirmidhī, 45:8 (no. 3440).
9. Abū Dā'ūd, 35:31 (no. 4855).
10. Ibn as-Sunnī, no. 3.
11. Qur'ān 39:45.
12. Qur'ān 99:7-8.
13. Tirmidhī, 44:19 (no. 5161, with slight differences).
14. In the beginning sentence to this section, the author mentions the rules 'associated with' the invocation as being third in sequence, not second, as they are here.
15. Qur'ān 25:43.
16. Qur'ān 17:22.
17. Qur'ān 36:60.

Chapter [Two]

1. Qur'ān 11:114.
2. See pp.46 and 215, notes 1–5 for references to these formulas.
3. Qur'ān 2:152.
4. Qur'ān 49:13.

Chapter [Four]

1. Qur'ān 2:26.
2. Qur'ān 2:27.
3. Qur'ān 94:4; the verse addresses the Prophet.
4. The preceding material probably relates to the 'first invocation'; otherwise, no mention was made of a first one, although the author will mention a number of other invocations in due course.
5. Qur'ān 47:19.
6. Mālik, 15:8 (no. 32).
7. Plural of *ghayr*, in the sense of 'other-than-God'.
8. Mālik, 15:8 (no. 32).
9. Qur'ān 6:91.
10. Qur'ān 6:91.
11. Qur'ān 6:91.
12. *Hū* in pausal form.
13. During the act of bowing (*rukū*[c]), the worshipper repeats a certain short formula three times, which is an invocation in the sense that it is both short and repetitive,

while the act of bowing itself adds a self-effacing element to the whole.

Chapter [Five]

1. Qur'ān 3:18.
2. The invocation of *Lā ilāha illa' llāh* is what is meant by this.
3. Because these two last-named deeds detract from one's concentration on God and remove all trust in Him from the soul.

Chapter [Six]

1. Because mankind is created in the image of God.
2. Qur'ān 2:268.

Chapter [Seven]

1. That is, one whose interior beliefs contradict his outward behaviour.
2. Although the author previously stated that there were two coverings, he now goes on to mention a third, which is actually the kernel or essence itself.
3. Qur'ān 25:43.
4. Qur'ān 13:15.

Chapter [Eight]

1. Qur'ān 17:44.
2. Qur'ān 29:69.
3. Qur'ān 7:55.
4. Qur'ān 79:40.
5. Qur'ān 39:54.
6. Qur'ān 8:46.
7. Qur'ān 16:114.
8. Qur'ān 68:48.
9. The source for this *ḥadīth* which continues on to the end of the next paragraph is Muslim 6:37 (no. 243).
10. Both the Verse of the Throne (2:255) and *Sūrat Āl ʿImrān* (3:2) contain the formula *Allāh Lā ilāha illā Huwa'l-Ḥayyu'l Qayyūm* (Allāh, there is no divinity but He, the Living, the Self-Subsistent).
11. *Al-Ḥayy* (the Living) and *al-Qayyūm* (the Self-Subsistent).
12. Mālik, 15:8 (no. 32).
13. Mālik, 15:8 (no. 32).
14. Both absence and presence are in relation to God, i.e., absence from God and presence with God.
15. Qur'ān 9:114.
16. Qur'ān 58:22.
17. Abū Nuʿaym 1, 4 (with slight differences).
18. Because his outward state manifests the Divine Name 'the Outward'.
19. Qur'ān 6:149.
20. Since everything is predestined, vying with the world is illusion.
21. Qur'ān 2:247.

Chapter [Nine]

1. *Mubāḥ* (indifferent action) in Islamic law refers to a deed which is permissable but brings neither reward nor punishment.
2. In the past, the patched frock (*muraqqaʿah* or *khirqah*) was

sometimes given to a discipline by the shaykh at the beginning of the path. Here it means spiritual death of the ego.

3. That is, while they were ritually pure, since a Muslim must have performed his ablution before praying.

PART TWO

1. Qur'ān 2:163.
2. In Arabic, *Lā ilāha illa' llāh* is the pausal form of *illa'llāhu*, the final word being really *Allāhu* when pronounced fully and without regard to the preceeding word *illā*.
3. These twin stars of Ursa Minor were used for desert travel.
4. Qur'ān 21:22.
5. The sense of this statement is that *istithnā'* is derived from one of the original meanings of *thanā*, a Form I simple verb.
6. Qur'ān 43:87.
7. In Arabic, the word *ilāha* is in the accusative case following the *lā* that negates the species absolutely.
8. This refers to the formula said before reading the Qur'ān: *a'ūdhu bi'llāhi min ash-shayṭān ar-rajīm* (I seek refuge in God from the accursed devil).
9. Qur'ān 51:50.
10. Qur'ān 6:91.
11. Qur'ān 21:22.
12. Muslim, 1:8 (no. 21).
13. The first condition is declaring *Lā ilāha illa' llāh*.
14. Qur'ān 2:163.
15. Qur'ān 112:1.
16. Qur'ān 16:51.
17. Qur'ān 57:3.
18. Qur'ān 6:59.
19. Qur'ān 28:88.
20. Qur'ān 6:17.
21. Qur'ān 6:76.
22. Qur'ān 6:1.
23. Qur'ān 21:22.
24. Qur'ān 17:42. The beginning of the verse reads: 'Say: If there were other gods along with Him, as they say . . .'.
25. Qur'ān 23:91. The beginning of the verse reads: 'God hath not chosen any son, nor is there any god along with Him; else would each god have assuredly championed that which he created . . .'.
26. Qur'ān 4:172.
27. Qur'ān 16:17.
28. Qur'ān 21:22.
29. Qur'ān 23:91. See above, footnote 25.
30. Qur'ān 17:42. See above, footnote 24.
31. Qur'ān 21:22.
32. Qur'ān 47:19.
33. Qur'ān 112:1.
34. Muslim 1:8 (no. 21).
35. Qur'ān 2:221.
36. Qur'ān 55:46.
37. Possibly at-Tirmidhī.
38. Tirmidhī, 8:7 (no. 983).
39. Qur'ān 10:90.
40. An epithet for Abraham.
41. Qur'ān 10:90.
42. Qur'ān 21:87.

43. Qur'ān 68:48.
44. Qur'ān 37:143–144.
45. Qur'ān 21:87.
46. Qur'ān 10:90.
47. Qur'ān 10:90.
48. Qur'ān 3:18.
49. Qur'ān 12:26. This is in reference to Potiphar's wife who attempted to seduce Joseph and when he stood fast and tried to get away, she falsely accused him. One of her own people, the aforementioned witness, said in verses 26–7, 'If his shirt is torn from the front then she speaketh truth and he is of the liars. And if his shirt is torn from behind, then she hath lied and he is of the truthful.'
50. Qur'ān 35:10.
51. Qur'ān 35:34.
52. Qur'ān 39:74.
53. Qur'ān 10:11.
54. Tirmidhī, 45:9 (no. 3443).
55. Meaning ʿUmar and his son Ibn ʿUmar.
56. That is, on the Day of Judgment.
57. Qur'ān 35:34. The *ḥadīth* containing the Qur'ānic verse is in Suyūṭī, *al-Jāmiʿ aṣ-Ṣaghīr*, II, 136.
58. Muslim, 1:8 (no. 21).
59. In Arabic:

لا إلـه إلاّ اللّـه

60. Munkar and Nakīr who examine the dead as to their faith.
61. Qur'ān 2:30. The entire verse reads: 'And when thy Lord said unto the angels: Lo! I am about to place a viceroy in the earth, they said: Wilt Thou place therein one who will do harm therein and will shed blood, while we, we hymn Thy praise and sanctify Thee? He said: Surely I know that which ye know not.'
62. According to Islamic law.
63. Qur'ān 2:30.
64. That is, when God addressed the souls before their descent into this world to be born.
65. Qur'ān 7:172.
66. That is, the devil.
67. Qur'ān 2:163.
68. Qur'ān 2:163.
69. Qur'ān 17:70.
70. Qur'ān 9:28.
71. Qur'ān 24:26.
72. Qur'ān 19:90.
73. *Iḥsān* connotes performing good deeds or doing what is morally and ethically correct.
74. Qur'ān 55:60.
75. Qur'ān 2:40.
76. Qur'ān 19:93.
77. Qur'ān 55:60.
78. Qur'ān 10:27.
79. Qur'ān 41:33.
80. Qur'ān 39:18.
81. Qur'ān 16:90.
82. Qur'ān 17:7.
83. Qur'ān 10:27.
84. The complete verse, not cited here, is: 'For those who do good is the best reward, and even more'.
85. Qur'ān 13:14.
86. Qur'ān 109:6. The Prophet Muḥammad is the speaker.
87. Qur'ān 30:4.

88. Qur'ān 40:16.
89. Qur'ān 53:42.
90. Qur'ān 41:33.
91. Qur'ān 16:90.
92. Qur'ān 16:90.
93. Qur'ān 17:7.
94. Qur'ān 4:129.
95. Qur'ān 22:24.
96. That is to say, the definite article in *aṭ-ṭayyib* (the good), which comprises all that is good in the way of speech.
97. Qur'ān 14:24.
98. That is, in the Near East.
99. Qur'ān 35:10.
100. Qur'ān 14:27.
101. Qur'ān 48:26.
102. That is, Abraham.
103. Qur'ān 43:28.
104. Qur'ān 43:26–7.
105. Qur'ān 41:30.
106. Qur'ān 9:40.
107. Qur'ān 53:17, referring to Muḥammad's Ascension (*Miʿrāj*) to the presence of God.
108. Qur'ān 9:33.
109. Qur'ān 16:60.
110. Qur'ān 13:35 and 47:15.
111. Qur'ān 19:87.
112. Qur'ān 19:90–91.
113. Qur'ān 43:86.
114. Qur'ān 2:256.
115. Qur'ān 39:33.
116. Qur'ān 3:64. Muslims are addressing Jews and Christians in this verse.
117. That is, *Allāh* is derived from *al-ilāh*. For a similar discussion, cf. above, pp.16–18.
118. Perfect and imperfect verbs respectively, meaning 'he became bereft of his reason or intellect' due to grief or love.
119. Technically it is a glottal stop which can carry the vowels *a*, *i*, or *u*.
120. Passive particle of *walaha*.
121. This seems to be more in keeping with *lāha*, *yalīhu*, *layhan*, which means 'to be hidden', 'to be high', and 'to rise'.
122. Qur'ān 7:127.
123. Qur'ān 43:45. At-Tilimsānī is saying that *ilāhah* of the previous verse is nearer in meaning to the *ālihah* of this verse.
124. That is, the Ninety-Nine 'Most Beautiful Names' (*al-Asmā' al-Ḥusnā*) of God in the Qur'ān.
125. Qur'ān 19:65.
126. Qur'ān 56:74.
127. That is, this world and the next and their respective periods.
128. Because the breathing and the invocation go together.
129. Qur'ān 13:15.
130. In the name *Allāh*.
131. The word *Allāh*, in Arabic, contains an *alif*, three *lāms*, and a *hā'*; but the second of these *lāms* has the sign for doubling the consonant over it (*shaddah*), so that, in reality, there are only two *lāms* actually written.
132. Mt. ʿArafāt outside Makkah is one of the stations of the annual pilgrimage. Standing on Mt. ʿArafāt symbolizes standing on the Day of Judgment.
133. Namely, the *hā'* and the *wāw*.

134. In the word *hawā'* (air).

Conclusion

1. Ibn as-Sunnī, no. 339.
2. Ibn as-Sunnī, no. 340.
3. Ibn as-Sunnī, no. 341.
4. Ibn as-Sunnī, no. 343.
5. Ibn as-Sunnī, no. 344.
6. Qur'ān 21:87. The *ḥadīth* is in Ibn as-Sunnī, no. 345.
7. Qur'ān 2:255, which reads '*Allah!* There is no divinity save Him, the Living, the Eternal. Neither slumber nor sleep overtaketh Him. Unto Him belongeth whatsoever is in the heavens and whatsoever is in the earth. Who is he that intercedeth with Him save by His leave? He knoweth that which is in front of them and that which is behind them, while they encompass nothing of His knowledge save what He will. His throne includeth the heavens and the earth, and He is never weary of preserving them, and He is the Sublime, the Magnificent.'
8. Chapter 2 (the Cow).
9. Ibn as-Sunnī, no. 346.
10. Ibn as-Sunnī, no. 347.
11. Referring to Anas b. Mālik.
12. Ibn as-Sunnī, no. 348. Abān, the transmitter of this *ḥadīth* from Anas ibn Mālik, is the Aḥmar addressed by Anas ibn Mālik.
13. Qur'ān 112:1–4.
14. Ibn as-Sunnī, no. 349.
15. Qur'ān 2:156.
16. Referring to the beginning of verse 156 which reads: 'Those who say when a misfortune striketh them . . .'.
17. Ibn as-Sunnī, no. 355.
18. Ibn as-Sunnī, no. 356.
19. Ibn as-Sunnī, no. 357.
20. Ibn as-Sunnī, no. 358.
21. Qur'ān 3:18.
22. Ibn as-Sunnī, no. 437.
23. Ibn as-Sunnī, no. 359.
24. Qur'ān 4:110. The rest reads 'then seeketh pardon of God, will find God Forgiving, Merciful'. The *ḥadīth* is from Ibn as-Sunnī, no. 361.
25. Ibn as-Sunnī, no. 366.
26. Ibn as-Sunnī, no. 363.
27. Ibn as-Sunnī, no. 367.
28. Ibn as-Sunnī, no. 368.
29. Ibn as-Sunnī, no. 371 (with slight differences).
30. Ibn as-Sunnī, no. 373.
31. Ibn as-Sunnī, no. 375.
32. Ibn as-Sunnī, no. 376.
33. Qur'ān 112.
34. Qur'ān 113.
35. Qur'ān 114.
36. Ibn as-Sunnī, no. 377.
37. This refers to the salutations said immediately after the prayer when seated, following the example of the imām.
38. Qur'ān 112.
39. Ibn as-Sunnī, no. 378.
40. Ibn as-Sunnī, no. 379.
41. Ibn as-Sunnī, no. 381.
42. Ibn as-Sunnī, no. 383.

CHAPTER [TEN]

1. Ibn as-Sunnī, no. 578.
2. Ibn as-Sunnī, no. 580.
3. Ibn as-Sunnī, no. 583.
4. Ibn as-Sunnī, no. 583.
5. Muslim, 39:25 (no. 2203).
6. Qur'ān 57:3.
7. Qur'ān 33:41–2.
8. Qur'ān 40:55.
9. Qur'ān 20:130.
10. Bukhārī, 80:1 (no. 5965).
11. Muslim, 48:10 (no. 2692).
12. Muslim, 48:18 (no. 2723).
13. Bukhārī, 80:15 (no. 5942).
14. Tirmidhī, 45:13 (no. 3448).
15. Tirmidhī, 45:81 (no. 3567, with slight differences).
16. Bukhārī, 80:65 (no. 6019).
17. Bukhārī, 80:65 (no. 6019).
18. Muslim, 38:2 (no. 2137).
19. Qur'ān 112.
20. Qur'ān 113 and 114.
21. Tirmidhī, 45:21 (no. 3462).
22. Bukhārī, 80:7 (no. 5933).
23. Qur'ān 112.
24. Qur'ān 113.
25. Qur'ān 114.
26. Tirmidhī, 45:21 (no. 3462).
27. Qur'ān 2:255. For the entire verse, see p.250, note 7.
28. Bukhārī, 59:10 (no. 3063).
29. Qur'ān 2:285–286.
30. Muslim, 6:43 (no. 256).
31. Ibn as-Sunnī, no. 770.
32. The number thirty-four is unusual, thirty-three being the normal figure; but it has been left at thirty-four, because all texts agree on that number.
33. Ibn as-Sunnī, no. 744.
34. Tirmidhī, 45:18 (no,. 3458).
35. Tirmidhī, 45:17 (no. 3457).
36. Bukhārī, 80:5 (no. 5930).
37. Ibn as-Sunnī, no. 43.
38. Ibn as-Sunnī, no. 46.
39. Ibn as-Sunnī, no. 48.
40. That is, ʿAbbās and the son of ʿAbbās.
41. Ibn as-Sunnī, no. 50.
42. Ibn as-Sunnī, no. 54.
43. Qur'ān 53:37.
44. Qur'ān 30:17–19. The *ḥadīth* is in Ibn as-Sunnī, no. 77.
45. Qur'ān 30:17–19.
46. Ibn as-Sunnī, no. 78.
47. Qur'ān 59.
48. Ibn as-Sunnī, no. 79.
49. Ibn as-Sunnī, no. 82.
50. One of the Prophet's names is *Ṣāḥib ash-Shafāʿah*, 'The Intercessor.'
51. It is a question of asking blessings upon the Spirit of the Prophet for he is also known as *Rūḥ al-Quds*, 'the Holy Spirit'.
52. The Prophet is also called *Miftāḥ ar-Raḥmah*, 'the Key of Mercifulness', that is, the key to God's mercifulness.
53. Ibn as-Sunnī, no. 84.
54. Ibn as-Sunnī, no. 85.
55. Ibn as-Sunnī, no. 85.
56. Ibn as-Sunnī, no. 100.
57. A *rakʿah* (unit) is a prayer cycle that includes standing, bowing, and prostration.
58. The speaker is the father of Mubashir b. Abi'l-Malīḥ, a *ḥadith* transmitter.

59. Ibn as-Sunnī, no. 101.
60. Ibn as-Sunnī, no. 108.
61. Ibn as-Sunnī, no. 118.
62. Qur'ān 2:255.
63. Qur'ān 3:18.
64. Qur'ān 3:26. The rest reads: 'Thou givest sovereignty unto whom Thou wilt, and Thou withdrawest sovereignty from whom Thou wilt. Thou exaltest whom Thou wilt and Thou abasest whom Thou wilt. In Thy hand is the good. Lo! Thou art able to do all things.'
65. Qur'ān 3:27. The beginning of the verse reads: 'Thou causest the night to pass into the day and Thou causeth the day to pass into the night. And Thou bringeth forth the living from the dead and Thou bringeth forth the dead from the living.'
66. Ibn as-Sunnī, no. 123 (with slight differences).
67. Ibn as-Sunnī, no. 124.
68. Ibn as-Sunnī, no. 127.
69. Ibn as-Sunnī, no. 131.
70. Ibn as-Sunnī, no. 131.
71. Ibn as-Sunnī, no. 132.
72. Ibn as-Sunnī, no. 138.
73. Ibn as-Sunnī, no. 139.
74. Qur'ān 112:1–4.
75. Ibn as-Sunnī, no. 142.
76. Ibn as-Sunnī, no. 143.
77. Ibn as-Sunnī, no. 144.
78. Ibn as-Sunnī, no. 181.
79. Ibn as-Sunnī, no. 182.
80. Ibn as-Sunnī, no. 211.
81. Ibn as-Sunnī, no. 212.
82. Ibn as-Sunnī, no. 230 (with slight differences).
83. Ibn as-Sunnī, no. 337.
84. Ibn as-Sunnī, no. 338.
85. Ibn as-Sunnī, no. 335.
86. The speaker is Anas ibn Mālik.
87. Ibn as-Sunnī, no. 336.
88. Ibn as-Sunnī, no. 492.
89. Ibn as-Sunnī, no. 493.
90. Ibn as-Sunnī, nos. 494 and 499 (with slight differences).
91. Qur'ān 11:41.
92. Qur'ān 6:91. The *ḥadīth* is in Ibn as-Sunnī, no. 501.
93. The speaker is Mūsā b. Wardān, one of the traditionists who transmitted this *ḥadīth* from Abū Hurayrah.
94. Ibn as-Sunnī, no. 506.
95. Ibn as-Sunnī, no. 508.
96. Ibn as-Sunnī, no. 509.
97. Qur'ān 3:83.
98. Ibn as-Sunnī, no. 511.
99. The speaker is the traditionist Abū Barīdah al-Aslamī.
100. Ibn as-Sunnī, no. 516.
101. Ibn as-Sunnī, no. 524.
102. Ibn as-Sunnī, nos. 525 and 529.
103. Ibn as-Sunnī, no. 533.
104. Ibn as-Sunnī, no. 534.
105. Ibn as-Sunnī, no. 535.
106. Ibn as-Sunnī, no. 536.
107. Ibn as-Sunnī, no. 541.
108. Ibn as-Sunnī, no. 542.
109. Ibn as-Sunnī, no. 544.
110. Ibn as-Sunnī, no. 545.
111. Ibn as-Sunnī, no. 548.
112. Ibn as-Sunnī, no. 549.

113. The speaker is ʿUthmān ibn Abi'l-ʿĀṣ, the Companion; the *ḥadīth* is in Ibn as-Sunnī, no. 550.

114. Ibn as-Sunnī, no. 551.

115. Ibn as-Sunnī, no. 552.

116. Qur'ān 112:3–4.

117. Ibn as-Sunnī, no. 558.

118. Ibn as-Sunnī, no. 571.

119. Ibn as-Sunnī, no. 563.

120. Ibn as-Sunnī, no. 588.

121. Ibn as-Sunnī, no. 592.

122. The *istikhārah* is a special prayer said before going to bed with the hope that God will reveal the answer in a dream.

123. Ibn as-Sunnī, no. 603.

124. Ibn as-Sunnī, no. 602.

125. That is, the Seal (the last) of the Prophets.

126. Qur'ān 3:173.

APPENDIX I

Key persons mentioned in the text

(The following names are alphabetised according to the first name as given in the text.)

ABĀN B. ABĪ ᶜAYYĀSH was a Follower (of the Companions of the Prophet Muḥammad) and younger contemporary of Anas b. Mālik from whom he related *ḥadīths*. He lived in the latter half of the first/seventh century.

ᶜABD ALLĀH IBN BISHR [or BUSR] AS-ṢAḤĀBĪ was a Companion of the Prophet and a transmitter of *hadīths* (*muḥaddith*). He was the last of the Companions in Damascus to die, in 88 AH/707 AD.

ᶜABD ALLĀH B. JAᶜFAR B. ABĪ ṬĀLIB was the nephew of ᶜAlī, the Prophet's son-in-law and cousin. He tried unsuccessfully to dissuade his cousin al-Ḥusayn b. ᶜAlī from going to Kūfa to be proclaimed caliph. He died c.80 or 85 AH/699-704 AD.

ᶜABD AL-MALIK B. MARWĀN B. AL-ḤAKAM, born in 26 AH/646-47 AD, was the fifth caliph of the Umayyad line and reigned from 65-86 AH/685-705 AD. He maintained a strong central administration, issued gold coinage, substituted Arabic for Greek and Persian in the bureaucracy, and was occupied with the Byzantines and rebellions in Iraq and Mesopotamia. In religious matters he had the ᶜUthmānic text of the Qur'ān re-issued and built the Dome of the Rock. He died in 86 AH/705 AD.

ᶜABD AR-RAḤĪM AL-QINĀ'Ī [or AL-QUNNĀ'Ī] was a pious Sufi shaykh and descendant of ᶜAlī b. Abī Ṭālib. From North Africa, he moved to Mecca then settled permanently in Quna in southern Egypt, where he died in 592 AH/1196 AD at the age of 77. Miracles were attributed to him.

ABRAHAM, or IBRĀHĪM in Arabic, is considered a prophet in Islam. According to the Qur'ān, he came with a revealed text (*Suḥuf Ibrāhīm*) and was called a *ḥanīf* (monotheist). He is mentioned in 25 *sūrahs* and is said to have attacked the idol worship of his father, almost sacrificed his firstborn son Ismāᶜīl (Isaac to Jews and Christians), and restored the Kaᶜbah with Ismāᶜīl. Abraham is regarded as the spiritual ancestor of both Jews and Christians through Isaac and of Muslims through Ismāᶜīl.

ABŪ BAKR AṢ-ṢIDDĪQ ᶜAbd Allāh b. ᶜUthmān b. ᶜĀmir b. ᶜAmr b. Kaᶜb b. Saᶜd b. Taym was the first caliph chosen after Muḥammad's death. His daughter ᶜĀ'isha married the Prophet. During his caliphate, he defeated the apostates in the Riddah wars and dealt with Arab expansion into Syria and Iraq. He was three years younger than the Prophet, being born after 570 AD and died a natural death in 13 AH/634 AD at about the age of 63. He was known for his truthfulness and pious sincerity.

ABU'L-ᶜĀLIYAH Rufay' b. Mihrān ar-Riyāḥī was a liberated slave of the Banū Riyāḥ who transmitted *ḥadīths* and the Qur'an. He belonged to the first generation of *Tābiᶜūn* (Followers of the Companions of the Prophet), residing in Basra (Iraq), where he died in 90 or 96 AH/708-9 or 714-15 AD.

ABU'D-DARDĀ' al-Anṣārī al-Khazrajī was a younger contemporary of Muḥammad. He transmitted *ḥadīths*, was an authority on the Qur'an, and one of the few who collected revelations during the Prophet's lifetime. Sufis consider him a *zāhid* (ascetic) belonging to the *Ahl aṣ-Ṣuffah* (contemplatives). He was sent to Damascus as a judge, but he also taught the Qur'an. He died there in c. 32 AH/652-53 AD.

ABŪ DĀ'ŪD AS-SIJISTĀNĪ, Sulaymān b. al-Ashᶜath was a disciple of Ibn Ḥanbal, the founder of the Ḥanbalī school of jurisprudence, and a traditionist whose reputation for knowledge and piety made him one of the established authorities. He wrote *Kitāb as-Sunan*, one of the six major canonical books, which contains 4800 *ḥadīths*, and he was the first to include critical notes.

Abū Hurayrah was a close Companion of the Prophet and one of the most prolific transmitters of *ḥadiths* due to his extraordinary memory. About 3500 *ḥadīths* are attributed to him. He was named prefect of Bahrain under the caliph ʿUmar and died in 57 or 58 AH/676-78 AD at the age of 78.

Abū Mūsā ʿAbd Allāh b. Qays b. Salīm al-Ashʿarī was a Companion, transmitter of *ḥadīths*, and military leader. The Prophet sent him to Yemen with Muʿādh b. Jabal to teach the Qur'ān and spread Islam. The caliph ʿUmar appointed him governor of Basra (Iraq) where he participated in the Arab conquest of Mesopotamia. Later he was made governor of Kūfa (Iraq) at the behest of its citizens and died there in c. 42 AH/662 AD.

Abū Muslim al-Agharr al-Madanī al-Kūfī was a Follower who related *ḥadīths* from Abū Hurayrah and Abū Saʿīd al-Khudrī. No dates are known but since he was their contemporary, though probably younger, he would have lived in the late first and early second centuries AH/late seventh and early eighth centuries AD.

Abū Nuʿaym al-Iṣfahānī, Aḥmad b. ʿAbd Allah b. Aḥmad b. Isḥāq b. Mūsā b. Mihrān ash-Shāfiʿī was an expert *ḥāfiẓ* (one who has memorized the Qur'ān) and traditionist and an authority on Islamic jurisprudence and Sufism. Born in Iṣfahān (Iran) in c. 336 AH/948 AD, to a family whose grandfather was a well-known ascetic and whose father was a scholar who had him taught by the best teachers, he continued his education by travelling to Iraq, the Ḥijāz, and Khurasān (Iran) to study. He wrote *Ḥilyat al-Awliyā' wa Ṭabaqāt as-Asfiyā'*, which was completed in 422 AH/1031 AD. It includes a discussion of Sufism, various etymologies of the origin of the word, and an account of the lives and sayings of the Muslim saints and their miracles. He also wrote a history of Iṣfahān. He died in 430 AH/1038-39 AD.

ABŪ SAʿĪD AL-KHARRĀZ, whose full name is Abū Saʿīd Aḥmad b. ʿĪsā al-Kharrāz, was an early third/ninth century mystic from Baghdad who associated with several Sufi shaykhs including as-Sarī as-Saqaṭī and Dhu'n-Nūn as-Miṣrī. He is the author of *Kitāb as-Sirr* and like his contemporary al-Junayd advocated a 'sober' type of mysticism in conformity with the *Sharīʿah*. He believed that *fanāʿ*, which he defined as 'the annihilation of the consciousness of manhood', and *baqāʿ*, 'subsistence in the contemplation of the Godhead', were the highest stages a mystic could reach. He died in 286 AH/899 AD.

ABŪ SAʿĪD AL-KHUDRĪ, whose full name is Abū Saʿīd Saʿd b. Mālik b. Sinān b. Thaʿlab al-Khudrī, was one of the Companions of the Prophet and a member of the *Anṣār*, supporters of Muḥammad from Medina. He accompanied the Prophet on twelve expeditions and died in Medina in 74 AH/693-94 AD.

ABŪ UMĀMAH AL-BĀHILĪ was a Companion of the Prophet and a transmitter of *ḥadīths* and items of *fiqh* (Islamic law) to the Muslim community. He lived in the first/seventh century.

ĀDAM is the name of the first man whom God created, as in the Old Testament. He is also considered to be the first prophet in Islam.

AḤMAD B. ḤANBAL, the 'imām of Baghdad', was not only a famous theologian, *faqīh*, and *muḥaddith*, but also the founder of one of the four Sunnī schools of jurisprudence which was named after him. His most well-known work is his *Musnad*, a collection of *ḥadīths* arranged according to the transmitter rather than subject matter. His dates are 164-241 AH/780-856 AD.

ʿĀ'ISHAH bint Abī Bakr was the third wife of the Prophet (after Khadījah bint al-Khuwaylid and Sawdah bint Zamʿah) and his favourite. She was born c.614 in Makkah. Because of her special position, she was able to relate many traditions of the Prophet. She was also known for her knowledge of poetry and eloquence as well as Arab history. At the Battle of the Camel in 35 AH/656 AD, she along with Talḥa and az-Zubayr led the opposition against ʿAlī. The latter two opponents were killed and she withdrew from political life and was ultimately reconciled with ʿAlī. She died in 58 AH/678 AD.

ʿALĪ B. ABĪ ṬĀLIB was the cousin and son-in-law of the Prophet. He was among the first to embrace Islam and later married Fāṭimah, one of Muḥammad's daughters, and by her had (al-)Ḥasan and (al-)Ḥusayn. ʿAlī accompanied the Prophet and took part in all of his expeditions. As the fourth caliph, he was pious and like his two predecessors, he was assassinated in 39 AH/659–60 AD in his sixth year of rule at the age of 62 or 63.

ʿALĪ B. MŪSĀ AR-RIḌĀ, whose full name is Abu'l-Ḥasan ʿAlī ar-Riḍā b. Mūsā al-Kāẓim b. Jaʿfar aṣ-Ṣādiq b. Muḥammad al-Bākir b. ʿAli Zayn al-ʿĀbidīn, was the eighth of the twelve Shiʿite imāms. The caliph al-Ma'mūn gave his daughter Umm Habīb to him in marriage and wanted to make him his successor but the ʿAbbāsids rejected him as an outsider. He was born in Medina in 151 or 153 AH/768 or 770 AD and died in 202 or 203 AH/817-19 AD.

ʿALQAMAH B. ʿABD ALLĀH b. Sunan al-Mazanī al-Baṣrī was a *muḥaddith* who related traditions handed down from his father and Ibn ʿUmar among others and was cited by Qatādah and other transmitters. He died in the caliphate of ʿUmar b. ʿAbd al-ʿAzīz, c. 100 AH/720 AD.

ʿAMR B. QAYS AL-MALĀ'Ī, known as Abū ʿAbd Allāh al-Kūfī, was a pious *muḥaddith* who related traditions from many authorities. He died in 146 AH/763-64 AD.

ANAS B. MĀLIK, also known as Abū Ḥamzah, was a Companion of the Prophet and his servant. He was one of the most prolific transmitters of *ḥadīths*, given his unique position, and many of them are found in the *Musnad* of Aḥmad b. Ḥanbal. After the Prophet's death, he took part in military campaigns and was quite old when he died in Baṣra in c.91-3 AH/709-12 AD, between 97 and 107 years of age.

ᶜAṬĀ'. Perhaps it is Abū Muḥammad ᶜAṭā' b. Abī Rabāḥ Aslam (or Sālim) b. Ṣafwān who was an esteemed jurisconsult, Follower, traditionist, and devout ascetic who derived his knowledge of law and *ḥadīth* from Jābir b. ᶜAbd Allāh al-Anṣārī (a Companion who died in 78 AH/697-98 AD at the age of 94), ᶜAbd Allāh b. ᶜAbbās, ᶜAbd Allāh b. az-Zubayr, and other Companions. Many cited him as an authority on *ḥadīth* including Qatādah and Mālik b. Dinār. Abū Ḥanīfah (79-149 AH/698-767 AD), the founder of the Ḥanafī school of jurisprudence, attended his lectures. He also held the office of *muftī* and was considered the most learned man in his day regarding the rites of the Pilgrimage, according to Qatādah. He was born in Yemen and died in 114 or 115AH/ 732-34 AD.

AL-AZHARĪ, Abū Manṣūr Muḥammad b. Aḥmad was an Arab lexicographer born in 282 AH/895 AD in Herat (Afghanistan) and died there in 370 AH/980-81 AD. He studied grammar with Niftawayh and wrote many lexicographical works including *Tahdhīb al-Lughah*, a dictionary in ten volumes.

AL-BARĀ' B. ᶜĀZIB b. al-Ḥārith al-Awsī al-Anṣārī was a Companion of the Prophet who also related *ḥadīths*. He took part in military campaigns with the Prophet and later in the wars of conquest. After retiring to Kūfa (Iraq), he became blind near the end of his life and died c. 72 AH/691-92 AD.

AL-BUKHĀRĪ, Muḥammad b. Ismāᶜīl Abū ᶜAbd Allāh al-Juᶜfī was a famous *muḥaddith* who studied traditions with the most outstanding teachers of Makkah and Medina, Egypt, Iraq, and central Asia. His *Jāmiᶜ aṣ-Ṣaḥīḥ* (or *Ṣaḥīḥ al-Bukhārī*, as it is often called), a collection of *ḥadīths* arranged according to chapters of jurisprudence, established him as one of the six accepted canonical authorities. He was born in 194 AH/809-10 AD in Bukhara (Uzbekistan), and died there in 256 AH/870 AD.

AD-DAQQĀQ, Abu'l-ᶜAlī al-Ḥasan b. ᶜAli was a great Sufi shaykh who became the teacher and father-in-law of another famous Sufi master Abu'l-Qāsim ᶜAbd al-Karīm al-Qushayrī. He held regular gatherings (*majālis*) where he taught his disciples. His death date is 421 AH/1021 AD.

ĀZAR is the commonly accepted name of Abraham's father, based on Q.6:75. Since he was known as Terah, it is assumed that either Āzar is a second name, as was Israel for Jacob, or a title. In any case, the name is recognized as foreign and listed among the *muᶜarrabāt* of the Qur'ān.

DAVID, or Dā'ūd in Arabic, is considered a prophet in Islam who received the psalms from God and had the gift of song. He was wise like his son Solomon. According to Islamic tradition, David fought Goliath (Jālūt), married the daughter of Saul (Ṭālūt), sharing power with his father-in-law who became jealous and sought to kill him. Consequently David fled to a cave where a spider spun a web over the entrance to protect him. Moreover, the story of his love for Bathsheba, the wife of Uriah, his repentance, and the building of the temple in Jerusalem are also accepted.

DHU'N-NŪN AL-MIṢRĪ Abu'l Fayḍ Thawbān b. Ibrāhīm al-Miṣrī was a great Sufi mystic who was the first to teach about the nature of the gnostic path and the mystic states and stations. He held the view of the uncreatedness of the Qur'ān. His teachings on Sufi doctrine are found in the writings of others. He was born in Upper Egypt c. 180 AH/796 AD, and he died in Giza in 246 AH/860-61 AD.

FAKHR AD-DĪN AR-RĀZĪ, whose full name is Abū ᶜAbd Allāh Muḥammad b. ᶜUmar b. al-Ḥusayn b. al-Ḥasan b. ᶜAlī at-Taymī al-Bakrī aṭ-Ṭabarastānī, was also known as Ibn al-Khaṭīb. He was a famous and pious Shāfiᶜ scholar and *faqīh*, philosopher and metaphysician and wrote many works in each of his areas of expertise including scholastic theology (*kalām*) and commentaries on the Qur'ān, on grammar and jurisprudence. His dates are c. 555-606 AH/1150-1210 AD.

AL-FARRĀ', the sobriquet of Abū Zakariyā' Yaḥya b. Ziyād ad-Daylamī, was one of the most famous grammarians of Kūfa (Iraq). He was the disciple of al-Kisā'ī and renowned for his encyclopaedic knowledge not only of grammar but also the history of the Arabs (*ayyām al-ʿArab*), astrology, medicine, *ḥadīth*, and *fiqh*. He was born in 144 AH/761-62 AD, and died on his way to Makkah in 207 AH/822-23 AD.

FĀṬIMAH was one of the four daughters born to the Prophet Muḥammad and his first wife Khadījah (the others are Ruqayyah, Umm Kulthūm, and Zaynab). She was a very pious and devoted daughter who married ʿAlī b. Abī Ṭālib and bore Ḥasan and Ḥusayn and two daughters also named Umm Kulthūm and Zaynab. She died six months after her father in 11 AH/632 AD at about the age of thirty. Fāṭimah is considered to be the highest of the women in Paradise after the Virgin Mary.

GABRIEL, Jabrā'īl or Jibrīl in Arabic, is one of the four archangels of God and the messenger through whom the revelation was sent to the Prophet Muḥammad. He is identified with the Spirit and guided Muḥammad on his Ascension (*Miʿrāj*). He appeared to him and his followers as a man with black hair and flowing white robes.

AL-GHAZĀLĪ, Abū Ḥāmid Muḥammad b. Muḥammad aṭ-Ṭūsī (450-505 AH/1058-1111 AD) was a brilliant theologian, jurist (*faqīh*), philosopher, and mystic of Islam, who is called the 'Proof of Islam' (*Ḥujjat al-Islām*) because of his writings which reconciled exoteric and esoteric Islam, henceforth making the two inseparable. In later life he became a spiritual master. The scope of his writings embraced among others *Iḥyā' ʿUlūm ad-Dīn* (The Revival of Religious Sciences), his *magnum opus* in four volumes; *al-Munqidh min al-Ḍalāl* (The Redeemer from Error), his autobiography which discusses his spiritual struggle; *Tahāfut al-Falāsifah* (The Collapse of the Philosophers), a critique of philosophers; and *Minhāj al-ʿĀbidīn* (The Way of the Worshippers), his last work.

AL-ḤAJJĀJ B. YŪSUF b. al-Ḥakam b. ʿĀqil ath-Thaqafī, Abū Muḥammad (41-95 AH/661-714 AD) was the most famous governor of the Umayyads. Though extremely harsh, he was a capable administrator who quelled revolts for the Caliph ʿAbd al-Mālik, expanded the empire under the Caliph Walīd, maintained the discipline of the Arab troops, and stabilized the economy.

AL-ḤAKĪM (see Muḥammad at-Tirmidhī).

ḤAMMĀD. Perhaps it is Ḥammād b. Salama, known as Abū Salama who was an expert and authority on traditions and was known for his piety and learning. He died in 168 AH/784-85 AD.

ḤĀRITHAH. Perhaps it is Ḥārithah b. Wahb al-Khuzāʿī, a brother of ʿUbayd Allāh b. ʿUmar on his mother's side and a Companion of the Prophet from whom he related *ḥadīths*. He lived in the early first/seventh century and accompanied those who went to Kūfa (Iraq) to settle.

AL-ḤASAN b. ʿAlī b. Abī Ṭālib (c. 3-49 AH/624-25 to 669-70 AD) was the first son of ʿAlī and Fāṭimah, the Prophet's daughter. He laid claim to the caliphate for a time until he relinquished it to Muʿāwiyah b. Abī Sufyān in order to avoid bloodshed. For the Shīʿīs, he is considered the second *imām* after ʿAlī; his brother al-Ḥusayn (c.5-61 AH/626-80 AD), the third.

IBLĪS is the proper name of the devil, also known as ash-Shayṭān. By some Muslims he is considered to be a *jinn* created of fire who disobeyed God by refusing to bow down to Adam. However, Sufis say that he was originally an archangel named al-Ḥārith who, thinking himself higher than Adam, refused to bow down to him in disobedience to God. Consequently, he was cast out accursed and succeeded in tempting Adam and Eve in the Garden of Eden.

IBN ʿABBĀS, whose full name is Abu'l-ʿAbbās ʿAbd Allāh b. al-ʿAbbās, was the first cousin of the Prophet (the son of his paternal uncle), and a famous traditionist. He was called the 'doctor of the community' (*Ḥibr al-Ummah*) and was well known for Qur'ānic exegesis, the biography of the Prophet, poetry and *fiqh*. He was born three years before the Hijra in 619 AD and died in 68 AH/687-88 AD.

IBN AL-AʿRĀBĪ (not to be confused with Ibn al-ʿArabī), whose full name is Abū ʿAbd Allāh Muḥammad b. Ziyād b. al-Aʿrābī was a philologian of the Kūfan school and a student of al-Kisā'ī among others. He was an expert in grammar, lexicography, Arab genealogies, and poetry and had many pupils. Born in Kūfa in 150 AH/767 AD, he died in 231 AH/846 AD.

IBN DURAYD, Abū Bakr Muḥammad b. al-Ḥasan was a learned philologist, genealogist, lexicographer and poet who wrote a great deal of poetry and philological works. Born in Basra in 223 AH/837-38 AD, he belonged to the south Arabian tribal group of ᶜAzd and died in Baghdad in 321 AH/933 AD.

IBN MASᶜŪD, whose full name is ᶜAbd Allāh b. Ghāfil b. Ḥabīb b. Masᶜūd al-Hudhaylī, was one of the earliest Muslims and Companions of the Prophet, following him to Medina. A Qur'ān reciter, he received the verses directly from the Prophet. His *hadīths* are frequently cited by at-Tirmidhi. He was a bedouin of humble origin and died in c. 32 AH/652-53 AD.

IBN MUKARRAM, whose full name is Abū Faḍl Muḥammad b. Mukarram b. ᶜAlī b. Aḥmad al-Anṣārī al-Ifrīqī al-Miṣrī Jamāl ad-Dīn, was the *qāḍī* (judge) of Tripoli (North Africa) and one of the *kuttāb* (scribes) under the sultan Qalā'ūn (r. 678-89 AH/1279-90 AD). He is also the author of several works including the famous *Lisān al-ᶜArab*, a dictionary based on five earlier ones and arranged according to the third radical of the verb. He was born in 630 AH/1233 AD and died in 711 AH/1311-12 AD.

IBN AS-SUNNĪ, whose full name is al-Ḥāfiẓ al-Imām Abū Bakr Aḥmad b. Muḥammad b. Isḥāq b. Ibrāhīm b. Asbāṭ ad-Dinawārī, was a *mawlā* (client) of Jaᶜfar b. Abī Ṭālib (the brother of ᶜAlī) and a pious *muḥaddith* who compiled and transmitted *ḥadīths* from an-Nasā'ī, one of the authors of the six canonical collections, and summarized his *Sunan* in a book called *al-Mujtabā*. He also wrote *ᶜAmal al-Yawm wa'l-Laylah*. He died while writing *ḥadiths* in 364 AH/974-75 AD at about eighty years of age.

IBN ᶜUMAR, whose full name is ᶜAbd Allāh b. ᶜUmar b. al-Khaṭṭāb, was the son of the second caliph and the most often quoted *muḥaddith* because of his high morals and piety. Known also for his gentleness, humility and noble character, he was offered the caliphate three times but refused the position and also declined the office of *qāḍī*, fearing he might misinterpret the *Sharīʿah*. He remained neutral during the struggle between ʿAlī and Muʿāwiyah. Born before the Hijra (622 AD), he was only fifteen when he fought at the Battle of Uhud in 2 AH/623-24 AD. He also participated in other battles. He died in 73 AH/693 AD when he was over eighty years old. His life became a model of virtue for later generations.

IBRĀHĪM AL-KHAWĀṢṢ, whose full name is Abū Isḥāq Ibrāhīm b. Aḥmad b. Ismāʿīl al-Khawāṣṣ, was a great Sufi shaykh of the third/ninth century on a level with Shaykhs al-Junayd and an-Nūrī. He died in 291 AH/903-4 AD in Rayy (Iran).

IDRĪS is one of the prophets of Islam who is mentioned in the Qur'ān as a man of truth and sincerity, coming between Adam and Noah. He is considered to be an immortal who received revelations and was taken bodily into Paradise, where the Prophet later met him during his Ascension (*Miʿrāj*). He is usually identified with Enoch.

ʿĪSĀ B. MARYAM is the name for Jesus in the Qur'ān, where he is referred to in twelve *sūrahs*. His other various titles are *al-Masīḥ* (the Messiah), *nabī* (prophet), *rasūl* (messenger) *ibn Maryam* (son of Mary), *min al-muqarrabīn* (of those brought near [to God]), *wajīh* (eminent in this world and the next), *mubārak* (blessed), *ʿAbd Allāh* (slave of God), *kalimat Allāh* (the Word of God), and *qawl al-ḥaqq* (the Word of Truth). His birth to the Virgin Mary was announced by Gabriel and is considered a creative decree by God like that of Adam. He performed many miracles such as speaking from the cradle (19:30), raising the dead (3:49), and bringing down a prepared table (5:112-15). Islam views Jesus as a prophet, not the Son of God (4:171), who was not crucified by the Jews but only appeared so (4:157), and was taken up by God unto Himself (4:158). He is called the Messiah who will return again to be a witness on the Day of Judgment (4:159) against unbelieving Jews and Christians. According to Tradition, during his *Miʿrāj* the Prophet met Jesus who is to return, kill the Antichrist, and bring on a reign of peace for forty years before dying a natural death. The Sufis consider Jesus the Seal of Sanctity while Muḥammad is considered the Seal of Prophecy.

ISRĀFĪL is one of the four archangels of God. It is he who blows the trumpet on the Day of Judgment to awaken the dead.

JESUS (see ʿĪsā b. Maryam)

JONAH or Yūnus (b. Mattai) in Arabic is one of the prophets in Islam who was sent to the people of Nineveh, and when his people did not heed his words, he denounced them and fled, not waiting to see that they had repented. He took a ship but was cast off as a bad omen (37:139-41). The Qur'ān also refers to him as Dhu'n-Nūn or 'Man of the Fish' (21:87) because he was swallowed up. After repenting and praising God, he was forgiven and thrown up on an island and eventually sent as a guide to over 100,000 people (assumed to be Nineveh again). He lived in the time of the Assyrian Empire, estimated by some authorities to be c. 800 BC.

JOSEPH or Yūsuf (b. Yaʿqūb) in Arabic is a prophet in Islam who was known for his extreme steadfastness, patience and devotion to God and his incomparable beauty. The twelfth chapter of the Qur'ān is named *Sūrah Yūsuf* and deals with his life and separation from his father, his virtuous conduct in the face of difficult trials, tribulations and temptations, and how he was rewarded and elevated in rank and reunited with his brothers and beloved father.

AL-JUNAYD, whose full name is Abu'l-Qāsim b. Muḥammad b. Al-Junayd al-Khazzāz al-Qawārīrī an-Nihāwandī, was a famous Sufi shaykh and the nephew and disciple of Shaykh as-Sarī as-Saqaṭī. Born in Baghdad, he studied Islamic law and associated with Ḥārith al-Muhāsibī, who like him advocated a 'sober' and rigorous kind of Sufism. He is said to have influenced al-Ḥallāj. Parts of his *Rasā'il* are cited in as-Sarrāj's *Kitāb al-Lumaʿ*. He died in 298AH/910 AD.

AL-JURAYRĪ, Abū Muḥammad who died in 311 AH/923-24 AD,

was, according to as-Sulamī, one of the chief disciples of al-Junayd as well as a disciple of Sahl b. ʿAbd Allāh at-Tustarī and one of the most learned of Sufi shaykhs to preside after al-Junayd 'due to the perfection of his state and the soundness of his knowledge.' He also related *ḥadīths*.

KHAWWĀT B. JUBAYR b. Nuʿmān b. Umayyah b. al-Burak was one of the Companions of the Prophet who related *ḥadiths*. He fought and was wounded at the Battle of Uhud in 2 AH/623-24 AD, and died at the age of 74 in Medina in 40 AH/660-61 AD.

AL-KISĀ'I, Abu'l-Ḥasan ʿAlī b. Ḥamza b. ʿAbd Allāh b. Bahmān b. Fayrūz (d. 737–805) was a well-known Arab philologist and Qur'ān reader. Born in Iraq c.119 AH/737 AD, he studied Arabic with al-Khalīl b. Aḥmad and then was advised to go live among the tribes of Najd, the Ḥijāz and Tihāma to perfect his Arabic. He taught Qur'ānic diction and became the teacher of Hārūn ar-Rashīd's sons al-Amīn and al-Ma'mūn. He composed the *Risālah fī Laḥn al-ʿAmmah* (Treatise on the Mistakes of the Vulgar Language), perhaps the oldest work on the subject. His death date is usually given as 189 AH/805 AD However, other dates have been suggested such as 179–183, 185, 193, and 197 AH.

MĀLIK IBN ANAS, whose full name is Abu ʿAbd Allāh Mālik b. Anas b. Mālik b. Abī ʿĀmir b. ʿAmr b. al-Hārith b. Ghaymān b. Khuthayl b. ʿAmr b. al-Hārith al-Asbaḥī, was called the 'imām of Medina'. A noted Muslim jurist and *ḥadīth* transmitter, he was the author of *al-Muwaṭṭa'*, the earliest work on Islamic jurisprudence, which codified and systemized the legal traditions of Medina. This Medinan school became known as the *Mālikī madhhab*, one of the four main schools of Islamic jurisprudence. Malik died in 179 AH/795 AD at about the age of 85.

MĀLIK B. DINĀR, Abū Yaḥyā was a *mawlā* (client) of the Banū Sāma b. Lu'ay, a subgroup of the Banū Quraysh. He was noted for his learning and intense piety and spent his time teaching and writing out copies of the Qur'an. He died in his native Basra in 131 AH/748-49 AD.

AL-MA'MŪN b. Hārūn ar-Rashīd, born in 170 A.H./786 AD, was the son of the ᶜAbbāsid caliph and a Persian slave. He ultimately defeated his brother al-Amīn in a fierce struggle to become caliph in 198 AH/813 AD. He officially supported Muᶜtazilism, (the view which held that the Qur'ān was created) and encouraged learning by building a library and astronomical observatory in Baghdad and a medical school in Jundī Shāpur (Iran). He also patronized poetry, philosophy, the exact sciences, and Arabic translations from Greek works. Because of his Persian sympathies, he was not popular with the Arabs. There were many political uprisings and wars with the Byzantines. He died fighting the latter in 218 AD/833 AD, but not before appointing his brother al-Muᶜtaṣim as his successor.

MARY, or MARYAM in Arabic, is the mother of Jesus (ᶜĪsā). She is mentioned in the Qur'an in several *sūrahs*, including one entire *sūrah* named after her. According to the Qur'ān, Mary was a pious virgin to whom the archangel Gabriel announced the tidings of a son. She is revered in Islam and among women occupies the highest level of Paradise. Some Medieval sources state that both Mary and Jesus were born without the touch or sting of Satan, which makes newborn children cry.

MOSES, OR MŪSĀ in Arabic, is a prophet in Islam as in Judaism and Christianity. He was sent to Pharaoh as a warning and the Israelites as a guide.

MUᶜĀDH B. JABAL was one of the Companions of the Prophet of whom Muḥammad said that he was 'the most knowledgeable in my community of what is permitted and what is forbidden'. He was among those Companions who compiled the Qur'ān in the time of the Prophet and transmitted *ḥadīths*. He died in the caliphate of ᶜUmar b. al-Khaṭṭāb (r.13–23 AH/634–44 AD).

MUᶜĀWIYAH B. ABĪ SUFYĀN was one of the Companions of the Prophet who served him as secretary, later becoming governor of Syria and after the assassination of ᶜAlī, the first Umayyad caliph. He distinguished himself as a capable and energetic military leader and brilliant administrator who expanded the caliphate, ended anarchy, created a disciplined army with regular pay, organized the finances of the empire, and won over his rivals with political finesse and politeness. His men were devoted to him and he ruled for forty years. Born c.600 AD in Makkah before the Hijra, he died in Damascus in 60 AH/680 AD, in his eighties. He succeeded in getting his son Yazīd named as caliph after him.

MUḤAMMAD B. AL-ḤAJJĀJ B. YŪSUF was the son of the famous Umayyad governor al-Ḥajjāj b. Yūsuf. He aided his father in maintaining order in the provinces and died in 91 AH/710 AD on the same day as his paternal uncle Muḥammad b. Yūsuf, which was a double loss to his father.

MUḤAMMAD AL-ḤAKĪM AT-TIRMIDHĪ, whose full name is Abū ᶜAbd Allāh Muḥammad b. ᶜAlī b. Ḥusayn at-Tirmidhī, also known as al-Ḥakīm (the wise), was a mystic, *muḥaddith*, Sunni theologian, and Ḥanafī *faqīh*. In his writings such as *Nawādir al-Uṣūl* and *Khatm al-Wilāyah*, he discusses such mystical ideas as the *Nūr Muḥammadī*, the *Ḥaqīqah Ādamiyyah*, the symbolism and value of the twenty-eight letters of the Arabic alphabet, angelology, and the criteria for determining sanctity. From quotations and references he was the first to compile biographies on the history of Sufism. Louis Massignon, the famous French orientalist calls him the 'true precursor of Ibn al-ᶜArabī who three centuries later studied him closely and admired him'. He died in 285 AH/898 AD.

MUḤAMMAD B. MŪSĀ B. NUᶜMĀN, whose full name is Shaykh Shams ad-Dīn Muḥammad b. Mūsā b. an-Nuᶜmān Abū ᶜAbd Allāh al-Marākishī al-Fāsī at-Tilimsānī aṣ-Ṣūfī al-Mālikī, was a deeply pious ascetic who was very knowledgeable in Mālikī *fiqh* (jurisprudence). He was born in 607 AH/1210–11 AD and went to Alexandria as a youth where he eventually had a following. He died in 683 AH/1284–85 AD and is buried in Cairo.

MUSLIM b. al-Ḥajjāj Abu'l-Ḥusayn al-Qushayrī an-Nīsābūrī was an Arab traditionist who became famous for his compilation of *ḥadīths* entitled *Ṣaḥīḥ Muslim*, which forms one of the six canonical works on Tradition. He travelled extensively to collect *ḥadīths* in Arabia, Syria, Iraq and Egypt and arranged them according to subject matter, including an introduction and a conclusion with a *tafsir* (commentary). He wrote other books on *fiqh* and traditionists but none is extant. Born in 202 or 206 AH/817 or 821 AD in Nīsābūr (Persia), he died in 261/875 and is buried in a nearby suburb of his native town.

AN-NASĀ'Ī, Abū ʿAbd ar-Raḥmān Aḥmad b. Shuʿayb b. ʿAlī b. Baḥr b. Sinān is another of the well-known *ḥadīth* collectors whose work became one of the six standard canonical books on the Traditions of the Prophet. His compilation is distinguished by the fact that it includes forms of bequests and donations and endowments which the other collections lack. He travelled widely to gather his information and is said to have written two other works: *Kitāb Khaṣā'iṣ Amīr al-Mu'minīn ʿAlī b. Abī Ṭālib* and *Kitāb ad-Duʿafā'*. He died a martyr's death in 303 AH/915-16 AD and is buried in Makkah.

AN-NAWAWĪ (or an-Nawāwī), Muḥyi'd-Dīn Abū Zakariyā Yaḥyā b. Sharaf b. Nūrī b. Ḥasan b. Ḥusayn b. Muḥammad b. Jumʿa b. Ḥizām al-Ḥizāmī ad-Dimashqī was one of the leading authorities famed for his knowledge of *ḥadīth* and Shāfiʿī jurisprudence. In addition to his *ḥadīth qudsī* (sacred traditions), he wrote a significant commentary on Muslim's *Ṣaḥīḥ*. Born in Nawa, south of Damascus in 631 AH/1233–34 AD, he died in 676 AH/1277–78 AD.

PHARAOH, or Firʿawn in Arabic, is a proper name in the Qur'ān referring to the king of Egypt in the time of Moses as well as in the time of Joseph c.400 years earlier. Pharaoh is described as a tyrant who oppressed the Israelites and crucified his own magicians when they acknowledged the supremacy of the God of Moses. As in the Old Testament account, Pharaoh and his host were drowned while Moses and his people passed safely to the other side of the sea. The Qur'ān states that Pharaoh repented (10:91-2) as he was drowning, but it is generally believed that it was not accepted.

Al-Qāḍī ʿIyāḍ, whose full name is Abu'l-Faḍl ʿIyāḍ b. Mūsā b. ʿIyāḍ al-Yaḥsubī as-Sābtī al-Mālikī was a Malīkī judge (*qāḍī*) and jurist, traditionist, historian, scholar and poet. Born in Ceuta (Morocco) in 476 AH/1083 AD where he was educated, he moved on to Cordova to devote himself to the study of *ḥadīth*. Later he served as a respected *qāḍī* first in his hometown, then in Cordova for a short time before resuming his previous position in Ceuta. He wrote an apologetic history of the Prophet called *Kitāb ash-Shifā' bi-Taʿrīf Ḥuqūq al-Muṣṭafā*; a dictionary of rare terms found in Mālik b. Anas's *Muwaṭṭa'* and al-Bukhārī's *Ṣaḥīḥ* and Muslim's *Ṣaḥīḥ* called *Mashāriq al-Anwār ʿalā Ṣiḥāḥ al-Āthār*; and a biographical dictionary of Mālikī scholars entitled *Kitāb Tartīb al-Madārik wa Taqrīb al-Masālik li-Maʿrifat Aʿlām Madhhab Mālik*. He died in Marrakash in 544 AH/1149–50 AD.

Qatādah. Perhaps it is Abu'l-Khaṭṭāb Qatādah b. Diʿāma b. ʿAzīz b. ʿUmar b. Rabīʿa b. ʿAmr b. al-Ḥārith b. Sadūs as-Sadūsī who was one of the Followers (*Tābiʿūn*) of the Companions. Blind from his birth in Basra in 60 AH/679–80 AD, he became very learned in history and poetry and was also the expert of his day on the genealogies of the Arab tribes. He was the first to coin the word *Muʿtazila* for the group around ʿAmr b. ʿUbayd who had separated from Ḥasan al-Baṣrī and his circle. He died in 117 or 118 AH/735–36 AD.

Razīn, whose full name is Abu'l-Ḥasan Razīn b. Muʿāwiyah b. ʿAmmār al-ʿAbdarī was the Mālikī *imām* in Makkah and an expert on *ḥadīth* and history. In his *Kitāb Razīn* he collected and classified all the *ḥadīths* found in the *Ṣaḥīḥ* of al-Bukhārī and the *Ṣaḥīḥ* of Muslim, the *Muwaṭṭa'* of Mālik b. Anas, the *Sunan* of at-Tirmidhī, and the *Sunan* of Abū Dā'ūd. He also wrote a history of Makkah which is an abridged work based on al-Azraqī's. He was born in Saragossa, Spain and died there in c.525 AH/1130 AD.

Sahl at-Tustarī, whose full name is Abū Muḥammad Sahl b. ʿAbd Allāh b. Yūnus, was a mystic and Sunnī theologian born in 203 AH/818–19 AD in Tustar (Iran). He taught that the spirit (*rūḥ*) is superior to the soul (*nafs*) and survives after death and that there are four levels of meaning to the Qur'ān. His teachings on the obligatory character of repentance (*tawbah farḍ*) led to his exile in Baṣra where he died in 283 AH/896 AD. Although he wrote no works, his pupil Muḥammad b. Sālim (d. 297/909) collected his sayings, which ultimately gave rise to the Sālimiyyah theological school.

ASH-SHIBLĪ, Abū Bakr Dulaf b. Jaḥdar was a Sunnī mystic, born in Baghdad in 247 AH/861 AD. Originally he worked as a government official until the age of forty, when he was drawn to asceticism by Khayr Nassāj, a friend of al-Junayd. He publicly denied his friend al-Ḥallāj though he secretly admired him. Eventually his strange behaviour and eccentricities landed him in an asylum where he discoursed on mysticism to distinguished guests. His sayings are preserved in collections on ecstatic expressions (*shaṭḥiyāt*), though he left no books. In dogma he followed al-Junayd, a more sober type than al-Ḥallāj, and the Mālikī *madhhab*. In the chain of transmission, he comes between al-Junayd and Naṣrābādhī, his disciple. He died in Baghdad in 334 AH/945–46 AD.

SHUᶜBAH, whose full name is Abū Biṣtam Shuᶜbah b. al-Ḥajjāj b. al-Ward, was an expert in *ḥadīths*, having studied them from a great number of followers (*Tābiᶜun*), as well as a poet and a man of great learning, piety, asceticism, and kindness. Ash-Shāfiᶜī said that the *ḥadīths* extant in Iraq would have been lost, if not for him. He is said to have known about two thousand of them and was also a master of Arabic. He died in 160 AH/776–77 AD at the age of seventy-five.

SOLOMON, or Sulaymān ibn Dā'ūd, is considered a prophet in Islam who had dominion over the jinn and nature. He knew the languages of birds and animals and had powers of magic and divination. Solomon was also known for his wisdom. He corresponded with Bilqīs, the Queen of Sheba, and summoned her to Islam (submission to the One God) which she accepted.

AṬ-ṬABARĀNĪ, Abu'l-Qāsim Sulaymān b. Aḥmad b. Ayyūb. b. Mutayr al-Lakhmī was a traditionist and the chief *ḥāfiẓ* of his day. He left Syria and spent thirty-three years studying in Iraq, the Ḥijāz, Yemen, Egypt and Mesopotamia. He is said to have had a great memory and learned *ḥadīth* from about one thousand people. He wrote *al-Muʿjam al-Kabīr*, a work on *ḥadīth* and traditionists, and *al-Muʿjam aṣ-Ṣaghīr*, an abridged version. He was born in Ṭabariyah (Tiberias) in Palestine and settled in Iṣfahān where he died in 360 AH/971 AD at the age of about one hundred.

ṬALQ B. ḤABĪB al-ʿAnazī al-Baṣrī was a Follower (*Tābiʿ*) who related *ḥadīths* from ʿAbd Allāh b. ʿAbbās, Ibn az-Zubayr, Ibn ʿAmr b. al-ʿĀṣ, and others. He was a Murjiʿite who felt that when a Muslim committed a mortal sin, he was still a Muslim whose faith only God could judge. He died in the reign of al-Ḥajjāj b. Yūsuf (c.75–95 AH/694–714 AD).

AT-TILIMSĀNĪ, ʿAfīf ad-Dīn Sulaymān b. ʿ Ali b. ʿAbd Allāh b. ʿAlī b. Yāsīn was a Sufi who wrote poetry on Sufi love. For a time he was also a government official in Syria. Of his works only his *Dīwān*, a collection of mystical poems, and his *Risālah fī ʿIlm al-ʿAruḍ* have survived. He claimed to have reached *ʿirfān* (gnosis) on his deathbed and apparently was an admirer and follower of Ibn al-ʿArabī. He was born in 616 AH/1219 AD and died in Damascus in 690 AH/1291 AD.

AT-TIRMIDHĪ, Abū ʿĪsā Muḥammad b. ʿĪsā b. Sawra b. Shaddād is the author of one of the six canonical collections of *ḥadīths*. He travelled extensively in Khurasān (Iran), Iraq, and the Ḥijāz (Saudi Arabia) to collect *ḥadīths*, learning from such teachers as Aḥmad b. Muḥammad b. Ḥanbal, al-Bukhārī, and Abū Dā'ūd as-Sijistānī. His *Ṣaḥīḥ* contains fewer traditions than those of al-Bukhārī and Muslim but also fewer repetitions, and is distinguished by critical remarks regarding the *isnād*, the chain of transmission, and the points of difference among the four *madhhabs* (schools of jurisprudence). His other works are not extant. Born in 208–9 AH/

824 AD, his death date is variously given as 279 AH/892-93 AD or 275/888-89 or 270/833-84.

ᶜUMAR B. AL-KHAṬṬĀB was the second caliph after Abū Bakr and one of the best leaders of the early period of Islam. Born about thirty years before the Hijra, he became caliph in 13 AH/634 AD and instituted a register or *dīwān* of those eligible for military pensions, established regulations concerning non-Muslims, founded military centres which evolved into great cities, and created the office of *qāḍī* (judge). The title of *khalīfah* (caliph) was changed to *amīr al-mu'minīn* (commander of the faithful) during his rule. He was greatly respected and feared because of his moral integrity. A Persian slave named Abū Lu'lu'a, who had appealed to him in vain about a heavy tax, mortally wounded him. He died in 23 AH/644 AD.

ᶜUTHMĀN B. ABI'L-ᶜĀṢ, whose full name is Abū ᶜAbd Allāh ᶜUthmān b. Abi'l-ᶜĀṣ ath-Thaqafī aṭ-Ṭā'ifī was a Companion and a transmitter of *ḥadīths* about the Prophet and his mother Āminah. He stated that he saw her when she delivered Muḥammad. The Prophet put him in charge of the *ṭawāf* (circumambulation of the Kaᶜba), and he prevented his tribe, the Banū Thaqīf, from participating in the wars of Apostasy. He died in c.51 or 55 AH/671 or 75 AD in Basra.

ᶜUTHMĀN B. ᶜAFFĀN was the third caliph after Abū Bakr and ᶜUmar and the first convert of high social rank–a rich merchant from the great Meccan family of the Banū Umayyah. He was handsome, good natured and pious and married to Muḥammad's daughter Ruqayyah. After her death, he married her sister Umm Kulthūm. As Caliph (r.23–35 AH/644–56 AD), he was faulted for putting his relatives in key positions and for destroying the various readings of the Qur'ān, no doubt in order to have one uniform version. He was badly advised. The first half of his reign was said to have been a period of good government and the last half of confusion with rebellions in Iraq and elsewhere. He was besieged in his home and killed in 35 AH/656 AD, and his wife wounded, by a group of disgruntled Egyptians who were led to believe that he intended punishing them.

YŪNUS B. ʿUBAYD, Abū ʿAbd Allāh was a pious *ḥadīth* transmitter who belonged to the generation of the Followers of the Companions of the Prophet. He was from Kūfa and a *mawlā* (client) of ʿAbd al-Qays. He died in 139 or 140 AH/756–58 AD.

ZAYD B. ARQAM was one of the Companions and a member of the *Anṣār* of Medina from the Banū Ḥārith b. al-Khazraj and a *ḥadīth* transmitter. He lived in Kūfa and died there in 68 AH/687–88 AD.

AZ-ZUBAYR B. AL-ʿAWWĀM, whose full name is Abū ʿAbd Allāh az-Zubayr b. al-ʿAwwām b. Khuwaylid b. Asad b. ʿAbd al-ʿUzza b. Quṣayy b. Kilāb al-Ḥawārī, was a cousin of the Prophet and a nephew of Khadījah (bint Khuwaylid). He was one of the earliest converts to Islam (the fifth one according to tradition) and one of the ten Companions promised Paradise by Muḥammad. He married Asmā', the daughter of Abū Bakr, and took part in two *hijras* to Abyssinia and all the great battles. Known for his courage and gallantry, he was esteemed by the Prophet and died at the Battle of the Camel in 35 AH/ 655–56 AD at the age of 60 to 67.

APPENDIX II

Glossary of terms

Allāh: the Arabic word for God.

Alterities (*aghyār*; pl. of *ghayr*): what is other-than-God; illusion.

ʿĀrif (pl. *ʿārifūn*): gnostic; one who 'knows' God directly.

Al-Asmāʾ al-Ḥusnā: the Ninety-Nine Most Beautiful Names of God which refer to His Attributes.

Asrār: see *sirr*.

Associationism: See *Shirk*.

Baqāʾ: the spiritual station of abiding in God's presence after *fanāʾ*.

Baṣīrah: spiritual perception or discernment.

Basṭ: spiritual expansion of the soul having psychological fruits expressed as joy, happiness, and exaltation.

Bāṭin: inner, esoteric, hidden.

Dhāt: the essence of something as opposed to its attributes.

Dhawq: literally, taste, but synonymous with intuition.

Dhikr: remembrance, remembering, invocation, invoking.

Dhikru'llāh: the remembrance or invocation of God, invoking His Name repeatedly, or the ritual of so doing.

Fanā': the spiritual station of annihilation in God of all perception of oneself.

Faqīr: (pl. *fuqarā'*): an initiate in a Sufi order, a seeker who cultivates spiritual poverty; detachment from all inner worldliness, representing wealth or richness of mind in a negative and dissipative sense, permitting the Spirit to be unveiled.

Ghaflah: forgetfulness or ignorance of God.

Ḥadīth (pl. *aḥādīth*): the sayings and deeds of the Prophet Muḥammad, which constitute the basis of his *Sunnah* (Norm).

Ḥāl (pl. *aḥwāl*): a spiritual state which may be temporary, as opposed to *maqām*.

Ḥaqīqah: esoteric Truth; inner reality of something; reality.

Ḥaqq: the Truth, the Real.

Iḥsān: virtuous conduct; being virtuous; one of the three principles of religion, the other two being *īmām* and *islām*.

Īmān: faith or belief in God; faith in God, His angels, His books, His messengers, the Day of Judgment, in the predestination of good and evil and the resurection of the dead; one of the three principles of religion, the other two being *islām* and *iḥsān*.

ʿIrfān: see *Maʿrifah*.

Islām: literally, submission; submission to the Divine Will through the five pillars of religion, *viz.*, the Testimony of Faith, the five daily prayers, fasting during the month of Ramaḍān, legal alms, and the pilgrimage to Makkah; one of the three principles of religion, the other two being *īmān* and *iḥsān*.

Ism (pl. *asmā'*): see *al-Asmā' al-Ḥusnā*.

Jabarūt: the transcendent spirtual world beyond the psychical domain of the *Malakūt*; it contains angelic and archangelic realities.

Khalq: the entire Creation in its spiritual, psychical, and physical aspects.

Malakūt: the domain of the World Soul, wherein one finds individual souls and subtle psychical realities.

Maqām (pl. *maqāmāt*): spiritual station which is a permanent or abiding state, as opposed to *ḥāl*.

Maʿrifah: gnosis; direct intuitive knowledge of God.

Muḥaddith: a traditionist; one who transmits the *aḥādīth* of the Prophet Muḥammad.

Mulk: the physical world, coming below the *Jabarūt* and the *Malakūt*.

Murīd: an initiated novice on the Sufi Path.

Mushrik: an idolator or associator; one who associates or attributes partners to God.

Muwaḥḥid: a unitarian; one who affirms God's Oneness and Unity.

Nafas: breath; the life-force or vital spirit.

Nafs: the ego or self which is worldly and self-centred; the soul.

Nūr (pl. *anwār*): light in the physical, psychological, or spiritual sense.

Qabḍ: spiritual contraction of the soul having psychological fruits expressed as sadness, melancholy, and depression.

Qalb: the subtle heart which is the centre of spiritual discernment and intuitions; the physical heart.

Rubūbiyyah: the quality of Divine Lordship; the opposite of *ʿubūdiyyah*.

Rūḥ: the Transcendent Spirit in man as opposed to the soul; the immortal soul.

Shahādah: the Testimony of Faith that there is no deity but God and that Muḥammad is His Messenger.

Sharīʿah: the Religious Law of Islam based on the Qur'ān and the *Sunnah* which covers all areas of public and private life.

Shaykh: a spiritual master in Sufism who can guide others to the way of realization.

Shirk: associationism or polytheism; attributing partners to God or placing them on an equal footing.

Ṣifah (pl. *ṣifāt*): an attribute of God.

Sirr (pl. *asrār*): literally mystery or secret; the innermost centre of consciousness or being in man; the Self, the innermost Spirit.

Sunnah: the Norm or conduct of the Prophet Muḥammad, based on Qur'ānic prescriptions and *aḥādīth*.

Tadbīr: self-direction or willful planning as opposed to accepting God's direction and providential decrees.

Ṭarīqah: the spiritual path or way; a Sufi brotherhood or order.

Taṣawwuf: Islamic mysticism or Sufism which is inseparable from Islam.

Tawḥīd: the Oneness or Unity of God which admits of no partners.

ʿUbūdiyyah: the spiritual station of true servanthood, contrasted with *rubūbiyyah*.

Ẓāhir: outer, exoteric, outward.

APPENDIX III

The *Silsilah* of the Shādhilī Order*

A. From the Prophet Muḥammad to Shaykh Ibn ᶜAṭā' Allāh

1. Muḥammad b. ᶜAbd Allāh
2. ᶜAlī b. Abī Ṭālib
3. Al-Ḥasan b. ᶜAlī
4. Abū Muḥammad Jābir
5. Saᶜīd al-Ghaznawī
6. Fatḥ as-Suᶜūd
7. Saᶜd
8. Abū Muḥammad Saᶜīd
9. Aḥmad al-Marwānī
10. Ibrāhīm al-Baṣrī
11. Zayn ad-Dīn al-Qazwīnī
12. Muḥammad Shams ad-Dīn
13. Muḥammad Tāj ad-Dīn
14. Nūr ad-Dīn Abu 'l-Ḥasan ᶜAlī
15. Fakhr ad-Dīn

* This *silsilah* or chain of authority is taken from Aḥmad b. Muṣṭafā al-ᶜAlawī, *Kitāb al-Qawl al-Maqbūl* (Tunis: Maṭbaᶜat an-Nahḍah, n.d.), pp. 40-42.

16. Tuqay ad-Dīn al-Fuqayyir
17. ʿAbd ar-Raḥmān al-ʿAṭṭār az-Zayyāt
18. ʿAbd as-Salām b. Mashīsh
19. Abu 'l-Ḥasan ash-Shādhilī
20. Abu 'l-ʿAbbās al-Mursī
21. Aḥmad Ibn ʿAṭā' Allāh

B. From Shaykh Aḥmad Ibn ʿAṭā' Allāh to Shaykh Aḥmad b. Muṣṭafā al-ʿAlawī*

21. Aḥmad Ibn ʿAṭā' Allāh
22. Dā'ūd al-Bākhilī
23. Muḥammad Wafā
24. ʿAlī b. Wafā
25. Yaḥyā 'l-Qādirī
26. Aḥmad b. ʿUqba al-Ḥaḍramī
27. Aḥmad Zarrūq
28. Ibrāhīm al-Faḥḥām
29. ʿAlī aṣ-Ṣanhājī ad-Dawwār
30. ʿAbd ar-Raḥmān al-Majdhūb
31. Yūsuf al-Fāsī
32. ʿAbd ar-Raḥmān al-Fāsī
33. Muḥammad b. ʿAbd Allāh
34. Qāsim al-Khaṣṣāṣī
35. Aḥmad b. ʿAbd Allāh
36. Al-ʿArabī b. Aḥmad b. ʿAbd Allāh

* For a detailed description of the Shādhilī order with its various sub-branches, see Martin Lings, *A Sufi Saint of the Twentieth Century*, pp. 232-33.

37. ᶜAlī al-Jamal
38. Al-ᶜArabī b. Aḥmad ad-Darqāwī
39. Muḥammad b. ᶜAbd al-Qādir and Abū Yaᶜza al-Muhājī
40. Muḥammad b. Qaddūr al-Wakīlī
41. Muḥammad b. Ḥabīb al-Būzīdī
42. Aḥmad b. Muṣṭafā ' al-ᶜAlawī

BIBLIOGRAPHY

ʿAbd al-Bāqī, Muḥammad Fu'ād. *Taysīr al-Manfaʿah bi-Kitabay Miftāḥ Kunūz as-Sunnah*. Cairo: Maṭbaʿat al-Manār, 1353 AH/ 1935 AD.

— —*Al-Muʿjam al-Mufahras li Alfāẓ al-Qur'ān al-Karīm*. Beirut: Dār lḥyā' al-Turāth al ʿArabī, n.d.

Abū Dā'ūd as-Sijistānī. *Sunan Abī Dā'ūd*. 4 vols. Ed. by Muḥammad Muḥyi' d-Dīn ʿAbd al-Ḥamīd. n.p: Dār Iḥyā' as-Sunnah an-Nabawiyyah, n.d.

'Abū Hurayrah'. *Shorter Encyclopaedia of Islam*, 1953.

Abū Nuʿaym al-Iṣfahānī. *Ḥilyat al-Awilyā'*. 10 vols. Beirut: Dār al-Kutub al-ʿArabī, 1967-68.

— —*Kitāb Dhikr Akhbār Iṣfahān*. 2 vols. Leiden: E. J. Brill, 1931–34.

Al-ʿAlawī, Aḥmad b. Muṣṭafā. *Kitāb al-Qawl al-Maqbūl*. Tunis: Maṭbaʿat an-Nahḍah, n.d.

ʿAli, A. Yūsuf, trans. *The Holy Qur'ān*. Brentwood, MD: Amara Corp., 1983.

— —*The Meaning of the Glorious Qur'ān*. Cairo: Dār al-Kitāb, n.d.

Arberry, A. J. *Discourses of Rumi*. New York: Samuel Weiser, Inc., 1972.

— —*Sufism: An Account of the Mystics of Islam*. London: George Allen & Unwin Ltd., 1979.

Asin Palacios, Miguel. 'Šadilies y alumbrados'. *Al-Andalus*, IX–XVI (1944-51).

— — *Saint John of the Cross and Islam*. New York: Vantage Press, 1981.

ʿAttār, Farīd al-Dīn. *Muslim Saints and Mystics*. Trans. by A. J. Arberry. London: Routledge & Kegan Paul, Ltd., 1976.

Ateş, Aḥmad. 'Ibn al-ʿArabī'. *Encyclopaedia of Islam*, III, 1971.

Brockelmann, Carl. *Geschichte der Arabischen Litteratur*, 2 vols. Leiden: E. J. Brill, 1949.

— — *Geschichte der Arabischen Litteratur*. 3 Supplements. Leiden: E. J. Brill, 1938.

— — 'al-Kisāʾī'. *First Encyclopaedia of Islam*: 1913–36, vol. IV, 1987.

al-Bukhārī, Muḥammad Ismāʿīl. *Ṣaḥīḥ al-Bukhārī*. Commentary by al-Kirmānī. 25 vols. Cairo: al-Maṭbaʿah al-Bahiyyah al-Miṣriyyah, 1352–81 AH/1933–62 AD.

The Cambridge History of Islam. Edited by P. M. Holt, Ann K. Lambton, and Bernard Lewis. London: Cambridge University Press, 1978.

Cattenoz, Henri-Georges. *Tables de Concordance des Ères Chrétienne et Hegirienne*. 3rd ed. Rabat: Editions Techniques Nord-Africaines, n.d.

Chittick, William C. *The Sufi Path of Love: The Spiritual Teachings of Rumi*. Albany: State University of New York Press, 1983.

Danner, Victor. 'Ibn ʿAṭāʾ Allāh: A Ṣūfi of Mamlūk Egypt'. Unpublished Ph.D. dissertation, Harvard University, 1970.

— — *Ibn ʿAṭāʾillāh: The Book of Wisdom*. New York: Paulist Press, 1978.

Adh-Dhahabī, Muḥammad b. Aḥmad, *Tadhkirat al-Ḥuffāẓ*. Edited by ʿAlī Muḥammad ʿUmar. Cairo: Maktabat Wahbah, 1973.

Ernst, Carl W. *Words of Ecstasy in Sufism*. Albany: State University of New York Press, 1985.

Freeman-Grenville, G.S.P. *The Muslim and Christian Calendars*. London: Oxford University Press, 1963.

Gardet, L. 'Dhikr.' *Encyclopaedia of Islam*, vol. II, 1965.

Al-Ghazālī, Abū Ḥāmid Muḥammad. *Ihyāʾ ʿUlūm ad-Dīn*. Cairo: Maṭbaʿat al-Istiqāmah, n.d.

— —*Inner Dimensions of Islamic Worship*. Translated by Muhtar Holland. London: The Islamic Foundation, 1983.

Al-Ḥallāj, al-Ḥusayn b. Manṣūr. *Kitāb al-Ṭawāsīn*. Edited by Louis Massignon. Paris: Librairie Paul Geuthner, 1913.

The History of aṭ-Ṭabarī: The ʿAbbasid Revolution. Translated by John Alden Williams. Albany: State University of New York Press, 1985.

Hitti, Philip K. *History of the Arabs*. 10th ed. London: The Macmillan Press, Ltd., 1973.

Hughes, Thomas Patrick. *A Dictionary of Islam*. London: W. H. Allen & Co., 1935.

Al-Hujwīrī, ʿAlī b. ʿUthmān al-Jullābī. *Kashf al-Maḥjūb: The Oldest Persian Treatise on Sufism*. Translated by Reynold A. Nicholson. London: Luzac & Co., Ltd., 1976.

Ibn ʿAbbād ar-Rundī, Muḥammad b. Ibrāhīm. *Ar-Rasā'il aṣ-Ṣughrā*. Edited by Paul Nwyia, S. J. Beyrouth: Imprimerie Catholique, 1957.

Ibn Abī-Yaʿlā, Abu' l-Ḥusayn Muḥammad. *Ṭabaqāt al-Ḥanābilah*. Cairo: Maṭbaʿat as-Sunnat al-Muḥammadiyah, 1952.

Ibn ʿAjībah, Aḥmad b. Muḥammad. *Īqāẓ al-Himam fī Sharḥ al-Ḥikam*. Cairo: ʿAbd al-Ḥamīd Aḥmad Ḥanafi, n.d.

Ibn al-ʿArabī, Muḥyi' d-Dīn. *Journey to the Lord of Power: A Sufi Manual on Retreat*. Translated by Rabia Terri Harris. New York: Inner Traditions International Ltd., 1981.

— —*Sufis of Andalusia: (The Rūḥ al-Quds* and *ad-Durrat al-Fākhirah* of Ibn al-ʿArabī.) Translated by R.W.J. Austin. Los Angeles: University of California Press, 1971.

Ibn al-ʿArīf, *Maḥāsin al-Majālis: The Attractions of Mystical Sessions*. Translated by William Elliot and Adnan K. Abdulla. Amersham, England: Avebury Publishing Co., Ltd., 1980.

Ibn al-Athīr, ʿIzz ad-Dīn. *Usd al-Ghābah fī Maʿrifat aṣ-Ṣaḥābah*. Cairo: Maktabat Wahbah, 1965.

Ibn al-ʿImād al-Ḥanbalī. *Shadharāt al-Dhahab fī Akhbār Man Dhahab*. vols. 5-6. Beirut: al-Maktab at-Tijārī, n.d.

Ibn al-Mulaqqin, ʿUmar b. ʿAlī. *Ṭabaqāt al-Awliyā'*. Edited by Nūr ad-Din Sharībah. Cairo: Maktabat al-Khanajī, 1973.

Ibn as-Sunnī, Aḥmad b. Muḥammad. *ʿAmal al-Yawm wa'l-Laylah*. Edited by ʿAbd al-Qādir Aḥmad ʿAṭā'. Cairo: Maktabat al-Kulliyyāt al-Azhariyyah, 1389 AH/1969 AD.

Ibn ʿAṭā' Allāh al-Iskandarī, Aḥmad b. Muḥammad. *Kitāb al-Ḥikam* in *Īqāz al-Himam fī Sharḥ al-Ḥikam* by Aḥmad b. Muḥammad b. ʿAjībah. Cairo: ʿAbd al-Ḥamīd Aḥmad Ḥanafī, n.d.

— — *Laṭā'if al-Minan*. Edited by ʿAbd al-Ḥalīm Maḥmūd. Cairo: Ḥassān Publishers, 1974.

— — *Miftāḥ al-Falāḥ wa Miṣbāḥ al-Arwāḥ* Ms. Dār al-Kutub al-Miṣriyyah, Cairo, No. 44262.

— — *Miftāḥ al-Falāḥ wa Miṣbāḥ al-Arwāḥ*. Ms. Dār al-Kutub al-Miṣriyyah, Cairo, No. 52746.

— — *Miftāḥ al-Falāḥ wa Miṣbāḥ al-Arwāḥ*. Cairo: Maṭbaʿat Muṣṭafā al-Bābī al-Ḥalabī, 1381 AH/1961 AD.

— — *Al-Qaṣd al-Mujarrad fī Maʿrifat al-Ism al-Mufrad*. Cairo: Maṭbaʿah Muḥammad ʿAlī Ṣubayḥ, n.d.

— — *Tāj al-ʿArūs al-Ḥāwī li-Tahdhīb an-Nufūs* on margin of *at-Tanwīr fī Isqāṭ at-Tadbīr*. Cairo: Maṭbaʿah al-Ḥamīdiyyah al-Miṣriyyah, 1321 AH.

— — *At-Tanwīr fī Isqāṭ at-Tadbīr*. Cairo: Maṭbaʿah Muḥammad ʿAlī Ṣubayḥ, 1390 AH/1970 AD.

— — *Traité sur le nom Allāh*. Translated by Maurice Gloton. Paris: Les Deux Oceans, 1981.

— — *ʿUnwān at-Tawfīq fī Ādāb aṭ-Ṭarīq: Sharḥ Qaṣīdah Shaykh ash-Shuyūkh Abī Madyan Shuʿayb al-Maghribī*. Damascus: Maṭbaʿat al-Iḥsān, n.d.

Ibn Farḥūn, Ibrāhīm b. ʿAlī. *Ad-Dībāj al-Mudhhab fī Maʿrifat Aʿyān ʿUlamā' al-Madhhab*. Edited by Muḥammad al-Aḥmadī Abu'n-Nūr. Cairo: Dār at-Turāth, 1972.

Ibn Ḥajar al-ʿAsqalānī, Aḥmad b. ʿAlī. *Ad-Durar al-Kāminah*. Edited by Muḥammad Sayyid Jād al-Ḥaqq. Cairo: Dār al-Kutub al-Ḥadīthah, 1385 AH/1966 AD.

— — *Tahdhīb at-Tahdhīb*. Beirut: Dār Ṣādir, 1968.

Ibn ʿIyāḍ, al-Qāḍī Abu'l-Faḍl. *Mashāriq al-Anwār ʿalā Ṣiḥāḥ al-Āthār*. 2 vols. n.p: al-Maktabah al-ʿAtīqah, 1333 AH.

Ibn Kathīr, Ismāʿīl b. ʿUmar. *al-Bidāyah wa'n-Nihāyah*. Cairo: Maṭbaʿat as-Saʿādah, n.d.

Ibn Khallikān, Shams ad-Dīn. *Al-Wafayāt al-Aʿyān*. Edited by Baron McGlucker de Slane. 4 vols. New York: Johnson Reprint Corp., 1842–71.

Ibn Saʿd, Muḥammad. *Aṭ-Ṭabaqāt al-Kubrā*. Beirut, Dār Bayrūt, 1380 AH/1960 AD.

Ibn Saʿīd, ʿAlī b. Mūsā al-Maghribī. *An-Nujūm aẓ-Ẓāhirah fī Ḥulā Ḥadrat al-Qāhirah*. Cairo: Maṭbaʿat Dār al-Kutub, 1970.

Ibn Taghribirdī, Abu'l-Maḥāsin Yūsuf. *An-Nujūm az-Zāhirah fī Mulūk Miṣr wa'l-Qāhirah*. Cairo: Matbaʿat Dār al-Kutub al-Miṣriyyah, 1348 AH/1949 AD.

Jāmī, Nūr ad-Dīn ʿAbd ar-Raḥmān. *Lawā'iḥ: A Treatise on Sufism*. Translated by E. H. Whinfield and Mirza Muhammad Kazvini. London: Theosophical Publishing House, Ltd., 1978.

Jeffrey, A. 'Abu' l-Dardā' al-Anṣārī al-Khazrajī'. *Encyclopaedia of Islam*, I, 1960.

— — 'Āzar'. *Encyclopaedia of Islam*, I, 1960.

Al-Kalābādī, Abū Bakr. *The Doctrine of the Sufis* (*Kitāb at-Taʿarruf li-Madhhab Ahl at-Taṣawwuf*). Translated by A. J. Arberry. Cambridge: Cambridge University Press, 1978.

Lammens, H. 'Muʿāwiyah'. *Encyclopaedia of Islam*, III, 1936.

Lane, E. W. *Arabic-English Lexicon*, 2 vols. Cambridge: The Islamic Texts Society, 1984.

Lings, Martin. *A Sufi Saint of the Twentieth Century: Shaikh Aḥmad al-ʿAlawī*. 3rd ed. Cambridge: The Islamic Texts Society, 1993.

— — *Muḥammad: His Life Based on the Earliest Sources*. Cambridge: The Islamic Texts Society, 1993.

Lopez Barault, Luce. *San Juan de la Cruz y el Islam*. Recinto de Rio Piedras: El Colegio de Mexico, A.C., 1985.

Maḥmūd, ʿAbd al-Ḥalīm. *Abu'l Ḥasan ash-Shādhilī.* Cairo: Dār al-Kātib al-ʿArabī, 1967.

Makdisi, George. 'Ibn ʿAṭā' Allāh'. *Encyclopaedia of Islam*, III, 1972.

Mālik ibn Anas. *Al-Muwaṭṭa'*. 2 vols. Edited by Muḥammad Fu'ād ʿAbd al-Bāqī. Cairo: Dār Iḥyā' al-Kutub al-ʿArabiyyah, 1380 AH/1951 AD.

Ma'lūf, Fr. Louis, ed. *Al-Munjid fi'l-Lughah wa'l-Adab wa'l- ʿUlūm.* 19th ed. Beirut: al-Maṭbaʿah al-Kāthūlīkiyyah, 1966.

Massignon, L. 'At-Tirmidhī, Abū ʿAbd Allāh Muḥammad'. *Encyclopaedia of Islam*, IV, 1934.

Mawlay al-ʿArabī ad-Darqāwī. *The Darqāwī Way: Letters from the Shaykh to the Fuqarā'*. Translated by ʿĀ'isha ʿAbd ar-Raḥmān at-Tarjumāna. Cambridge: Cambridge University Press, 1981.

Michon, Jean-Louis. *Le Soufi Marocain Aḥmad Ibn ʿAjība et Son Miʿrāj.* Paris: Librairie Philosophique J. Vrin, 1973.

Mubarāk, Zakī. *At-Taṣawwuf al-Islāmī fi'l-Adab wa'l-Akhlāq*. Cairo: Dār al-Kitāb al-ʿArabī, 1373 AH/1954 AD.

Al-Muḥibbī, Muḥammad Amīn b. Faḍl Allāh. *Khulāṣat al-Āthār*. Beirut: Maktabat Khayyāṭ, n.d.

Muslim b. Ḥajjāj. *Ṣaḥīḥ*. Edited by Muḥammad Fu'ād ʿAbd al-Bāqī. 1st ed. Cairo: Dār Iḥyā' al-Kutub al-ʿArabiyyah, 1374–75 AH/1955–56 AD.

An-Nabhānī, Yūsuf b. Ismāʿīl. *Jāmiʿ Karāmāt al-Awliyā'*. 2 vols. Edited by Ibrāhīm ʿAtuwat ʿAwḍ. Cairo: Muṣṭafā al-Bābī al-Ḥalabī, 1381 AH/1962 AD.

Najm ad-Dīn al-Kubrā. *Fawā'iḥ al-Jamāl wa Fawātiḥ al-Jalāl.* Edited by Fritz Meier. Wiesbaden: Franz Steiner Verlag GMBH, 1957.

Nicholson, Reynold A. *A Literary History of the Arabs*. Cambridge: Cambridge University Press, 1977.

Nwyia, Paul. *Ibn ʿAṭā' Allāh* (m. 709 AH/1309 AD) *et la naissance de la confrerie šadilite*. Beyrouth: Dar el-Machreq, 1972.

Ozak, Shaykh Muzaffer. *The Unveiling of Love: Sufism and the*

Remembrance of God. Translated by Muhtar Holland. New York: Inner Traditions International, 1981.

Pareja Casañas, Felix M. *Islamologie*. Beyrouth: Imprimerie Catholique, 1957–63.

Paret, R. 'Ibrāhīm'. *Encyclopaedia of Islam*, III, 1971.

Pickthall, Mohammed Marmaduke, trans. *The Meaning of the Glorious Koran*. New York: The New American Library, n.d.

'Al-Qāḍī 'Iyāḍ b. Mūsā'. *Encyclopaedia of Islam*, II, 1927.

Al-Qushayrī, Abu'l-Qāsim ʿAbd al-Karīm b. Hawāzin. *Ar-Risālah al-Qushayriyyah*. Edited by ʿAbd al-Ḥalīm Maḥmūd and Maḥmūd ash-Sharīf. Cairo: Dār al-Kutub al-Ḥadīthah, 1966.

Raḥmān, F. 'Dhawḳ'. *Encyclopaedia of Islam*, II. 1965.

Rāzī, Najm ad-Dīn. *The Path of God's Bondsmen from Origin to Return*. Translated by Hamid Algar. Delmar, New York: Caravan Books, 1982.

Aṣ-Ṣafadī, Ṣalāḥ ad-Dīn Khalīl b. Aybak. *Kitāb al-Wāfī bi'l-Wafayāt*. Wiesbaden: Franz Steiner Verlag, GMBH, 1979.

Schacht, J. 'Mālik b. Anas'. *First Encyclopaedia of Islam: 1913–36* V, 1987.

Schimmel, Annemarie. *Mystical Dimensions of Islam*. Chapel Hill: The University of North Carolina Press, 1975.

Sezgin, Fuat. *Geschichte der Arabishen Schrifttums*. 9 vols. Leiden: E. J. Brill, 1967-84.

Ash-Shaʿrānī, ʿAbd al-Wahhāb Aḥmad. *Aṭ-Ṭabaqāt al-Kubrā*. Edited by ʿAbd al-Qādir Aḥmad ʿAṭā'. Cairo: Maktabat al-Qāhirah, 1970.

Ash-Shīrāzī, Abū Isḥāq Ibrāhīm b. ʿAlī. *Ṭabaqāt al-Fuqahā'*. Edited by Iḥsān ʿAbbās. Beirut: Dār al-Rā'id al-ʿArabi, 1970.

Sirāj ad-Dīn, Abū Bakr. *The Book of Certainty*. Cambridge: The Islamic Texts Society, 1992.

As-Subkī, Tāj ad-Dīn ʿAbd al-Wahhāb b. ʿAlī. *Ṭabaqāt ash-Shāfiʿiyyah al-Kubrā*. 1st ed. Cairo: al-Maṭbaʿah al-Ḥusayniyyah al-Miṣriyyah, n.d.

Al-Sulamī, Muḥammad b. al-Ḥusayn. *Kitāb Ṭabaqāt aṣ-Ṣūfiyyah*. Edited by Johanns Pedersen. Leiden: E. J. Brill, 1960.

——*The Book of Sufi Chivalry: Lessons to a Son of the Moment—Futuwwah*. Translated by Sheikh Tosun Bayrak al-Jerrahi al-Halveti. New York: Inner Traditions International, 1983.

As-Suyūṭī, Jalāl ad-Dīn ʿAbd ar-Raḥmān. *Ḥusn al-Maḥāḍarah fī Tarīkh Miṣr wa 'l-Qāhirah*. Edited by Muḥammad Abu'l Faḍl Ibrāhīm. n.p: ʿĪsā al-Bābī al-Halabī and Co., n.d.

——*Al-Jāmiʿ as-Ṣaghīr fī Aḥādīth al-Bashīr an-Nadhīr*. 4th ed. Cairo: Dār al-Kutub al-ʿIlmiyyah, 1373 AH/1954 AD.

At-Taftazānī, Abu'l-Wafā' al-Ghunaymī. *Ibn ʿAṭā' Allāh al-Sakandarī wa Taṣawwufuh*. 2nd ed. Cairo: Maktabat al-Anjalū al-Miṣriyyah, 1969.

Tashkubrizadeh, Aḥmad b. Muṣṭafā. *Ṭabaqat al-Fuqahā'*. Edited by al-Ḥajj Aḥmad Nilah. Mosul, Iraq: az-Zahra al-Ḥadīthah, n.d.

At-Tirmidhī, Muḥammad Abū ʿAbd Allāh b. ʿAlī b. Ḥasan al-Ḥakīm. *Kitab Khatm al-Awliyā'*. Edited by ʿUthmān Ismāʿīl Yaḥyā. Beirut: al-Maṭbaʿah al-Kāthūlīkiyyah, 1965.

At-Tirmidhī, Muḥammad Abū ʿĪsā. *Sunan at-Tirmidhī*. 5 vols. Cairo: al-Maktabah as-Salafiyyah, 1384–87 AH/1964–67 AD.

Vaglieri, L. Veccia. "ʿAlī b. Abī Ṭālib'. *Encyclopaedia of Islam*, I, 1960.

Watt, W. Montgomery. 'Abū Bakr'. *Encyclopaedia of Islam*, I, 1960.

——'Al-Ghazālī'. *Encyclopaedia of Islam*, II, 1965.

Wensinck, A. J. *A Handbook of Early Muhammadan Tradition*. Leiden: E. J. Brill, 1960.

——'At-Tirmidhī, Abū ʿĪsā Muḥammad'. *Encyclopaedia of Islam*, IV, 1934.

Wustenfield, F. *Die Geschichtschreiber der Araber und ihre Werke*. New York: Burt Franklin, n.d.

Al-Yāfiʿī ʿAbd Allāh b. Asʿad. *Mir'āt al-Janān wa ʿIbrat al-Yaqzān*. 2nd ed. Beirut: Mu'assasat al-Aʿlamī, 1970.

SUGGESTED READINGS

Addas, Claude. *Quest for the Red Sulphur, the life of Ibn ʿArabī.* Cambridge: The Islamic Texts Society, 1993.

ʿAttār, Farīd ad-Dīn. *Muslim Saints and Mystics.* Trans. by A. J. Arberry. London: Routledge & Kegan Paul, Ltd., 1976.

Chittick, William C. *The Sufi Path of Love: The Spiritual Teachings of Rumi.* Albany: State Unviersity of New York Press, 1983.

Chodkiewicz, Michel. *Seal of the Saints, prophethood and sainthood in the doctrine of Ibn ʿArabī.* Cambridge: The Islamic Texts Society, 1993.

Danner, Victor. *Ibn ʿAṭā' illāh: The Book of Wisdom.* New York: Paulist Press, 1978.

— — *The Islamic Tradition: An Introduction.* New York: Amity House, 1988.

Eaton, Charles LeGai. *Islam and the Destiny of Man.* Cambridge: The Islamic Texts Society, 1994.

Ernst, Carl W. *Words of Ecstasy in Sufism.* Albany: State University of New York Press, 1985.

Al-Ghazālī, [Abū Ḥāmid Muḥammad]. *Inner Dimensions of Islamic Worship.* Trans. by Muhtar Holland. London: The Islamic Foundation, 1983.

— — *The Ninety-nine Beautiful Names of God.* Trans. by D. Burrell and N. Daher. Cambridge: The Islamic Texts Society, 1995.

Eaton, Charles LeGai. *Islam and the Destiny of Man.* Cambridge: The Islamic Texts Society, 1994.

al-Hujwīrī, ʿAlī b. ʿUthmān al-Jullābī. *Kashf al-Maḥjūb: The Oldest Persian Treatise on Sufism*. Trans. by Reynold A. Nicholson. London: Luzac & Co., Ltd., 1976.

Ibn al-ʿArabī, Muhyiddin. *Journey to the Lord of Power: A Sufi Manual on Retreat*. Trans. by Rabia Terri Harris. New York: Inner Traditions International, Ltd., 1981.

Ibn al-ʿArīf. *Maḥasin al-Majālis: The Attractions of Mystical Sessions*. Trans. by William Elliot and Alvan K. Abdulla. Amersham, England: Avebury Publishing Co., Ltd., 1980.

Ibn ʿAṭā' Allāh. *Traité sur le nom Allāh*. Trans. by Maurice Gloton. Paris: Les Deux Oceáns, 1981.

Jāmī, Nūr ad-Dīn ʿAbd ar-Raḥmān. *Lawā'iḥ: A Treatise on Sufism*. Trans. by E. H. Whinfield and Mirzra Muhammad Kazvini. London: Theosophical Publishing House, Ltd., 1978.

Al-Jīlānī, ʿAbd al-Qādir. *The Secret of Secrets*, interpreted by Shaykh Tosun Bayrak. Cambridge: The Islamic Texts Society, 1992.

Al-Jīlī, ʿAbd al-Karīm. *Universal Man: Extracts Translated with Commentary by Titus Burckhardt*. English trans. by Angela Culme-Seymour. Sherborne, England: Beshara Publications, 1983.

Al-Kalābādhī, Abū Bakr. *The Doctrine of the Sufis* (*Kitāb at-Taʿarruf li-Madhhab Ahl at-Taṣawwuf*). Trans. by A. J. Arberry. Cambridge: Cambridge University Press, 1978.

Lings, Martin. *A Sufi Saint of the Twentieth Century: Shaikh Ahmad al-Alawi*. 3rd ed. Cambridge: The Islamic Texts Society, 1993.

– – *Muhammad: His Life Based on the Earliest Sources*. Cambridge: The Islamic Texts Society, 1992.

– – *What is Sufism?* Cambridge: The Islamic Texts Society, 1993.

Mawlay al-Arabi ad-Darqawi. *The Darqawi Way: Letters from the Shaykh to the Fuqara*. Trans. by ʿĀ'isha ʿAbd ar-Rahmān at-Tarjumāna. Cambridge: Cambridge University Press, 1981.

Nasr, Seyyed Hossein. *Sufi Essays*. New York: Schocken Books, 1977.

——*Ideals and Realities of Islam*. Boston: Beacon Press, 1975.

Nwyia, Paul. *Ibn ʿAṭāʾ Allāh et la naissance de la confrerie šadilite*. Beirut: Dar el-Machreq, 1972.

Ozak, Shaykh Muzaffer. *The Unveiling of Love: Sufism and the Remembrance of God*. Trans. by Muhtar Holland. New York: Inner Traditions International, Ltd., 1981.

Rāzī, Najm ad-Dīn. *The Path of God's Bondsmen from Origin to Return*. Trans. by Hamid Algar. Delmar, N.Y: Caravan Books, 1982.

Schimmel, Annemarie. *And Muhammad Is His Messenger: The Veneration of the Prophet in Islamic Piety*. Chapel Hill: The University of North Carolina Press, 1985.

——*Mystical Dimensions of Islam*. Chapel Hill: The University of North Carolina Press, 1975.

Schuon, Frithjof. *Understanding Islam*. Trans. by D. M. Matheson. Baltimore, Maryland: Penguin Books, Inc., 1972.

Sirāj ad-Din, Abū-Bakr. *The Book of Certainty*. Cambridge: The Islamic Texts Society, 1992.

Al-Sulami, Muḥammad b. al-Ḥusayn. *The Book of Sufi Chivalry: Lessons to a Son of the Moment–Futuwwah*. Trans. by Sheikh Tosun Bayrak al-Jerrahi al-Halveti. New York: Inner Traditions International, 1983.

INDEX OF NAMES

al-Barā' b. ʿĀzib, 186, 231
al-Bukhārī, 57, 59–61, 183, 185, 231
al-Būzīdī, Muḥammad b. Ḥabīb, 14, 253
Daniel, 178
ad-Daqqāq, Abu'l-ʿAlī, 148, 231–2
David, 181, 232
adh-Dhahabī, 9
Dhu'n-Nūn al-Miṣrī, 66, 232
ad-Dimyāṭī, Sharaf ad-Dīn, 3
al-Farrā', 55, 232–3
Fāṭimah, 185, 233
Gabriel, 54, 152, 161, 190, 233
al-Ghazālī, Abū Ḥāmid, 11, 30–1, 37, 47, 109, 113, 115–16, 233
al-Ḥajjāj b. Yūsuf, 153, 176–7, 233–4
al-Ḥāmid al-Aswad, 65
Ḥammād, 197, 234
Ḥārithah b. Wahb al-Khuzāʿī, 150, 234
al-Ḥasan b. ʿAlī, 64, 234, 251
al-Hāshimī, Muḥammad, 39
Iblīs, 157, 234
Ibn ʿAbbād ar-Rundī, 14, 16
Ibn ʿAbbās, 61, 154, 156, 161, 166, 168, 182, 234
Ibn ʿAjībah, 14, 20
Ibn al-Aʿrābī, 56, 234–5
Ibn al-ʿArabī, Muḥyi'd-Dīn, 8, 20, 37
Ibn al-Maylaq, Shihāb ad-Dīn, 10
Ibn as-Sunnī, 63, 187, 235
Ibn ʿAṭā'Allāh, ʿAbd al-Karīm, 2
Ibn ʿAṭa'Allāh, Muḥammad, 2, 5
Ibn Durayd, 235
Ibn Ḥajar al-ʿAsqalānī, 9
Ibn Masʿūd, 58, 235
Ibn Mukarram, 189, 235
Ibn Taymiyyah, Taqi'd-Dīn, 8–9
Ibn ʿUmar, 154, 235–6
Ibrāhīm al-Khawāṣṣ, 65, 236
Idrīs, 150, 236
Imām al-Ḥaramayn al-Juwaynī, 11
ʿĪsā b. Maryam, 49, 236–7
al-Iṣfahānī, Shams ad-Dīn, 3
Isrāfīl, 190, 237
Isrā'īl, Banu, 71, 152
Jamāl ad-Dīn b. Abu'l-ʿAbbās al-Mursī, 5
al-Jilānī, ʿAbd al-Qādir, 20
Jesus, son of Mary (see ʿĪsā b. Maryam; also Messiah)
Jonah, 152, 176, 237
Joseph, 152, 237
al-Junayd al-Baghdādī, 29, 101, 121, 169, 237
al-Jurayrī, Abū Muḥammad, 48, 237–8
Kamāl ad-Dīn b. al-Ḥamām, 7–8
Khawwāt b. Jubayr, 198, 238
al-Kisā'ī, 55, 238
Makīn ad-Dīn al-Asmar, 3, 10, 19
Mālik b. Anas, 58–9, 238
Mālik b. Dinār, 64, 238
al-Ma'mūn, 154, 239
al-Marjānī, Abū Muḥammad, 16
al-Mārūnī, Muḥyi'd-Dīn, 3
Mary, 49, 239
Mawlay al-ʿArabī, 14
Messiah, 147
Michael, 190
Moses, 150, 198, 239
Muʿādh b. Jabal, 63, 149, 239
Muʿāwiyah, 54, 239–40
Muḥammad b. al-Ḥajjāj b. Yūsuf, 177, 240
Muḥammad b. Mūsā b. Nuʿmān, 189, 240

INDEX OF TERMS